SNOWBOARDING
The Ultimate Guide

Holly Thorpe

GREENWOOD GUIDES TO EXTREME SPORTS
Holly Thorpe and Douglas Booth, Series Editors

GREENWOOD

AN IMPRINT OF ABC-CLIO, LLC
Santa Barbara, California • Denver, Colorado • Oxford, England

Library of Congress Cataloging-in-Publication Data

Thorpe, Holly.
  Snowboarding : the ultimate guide / Holly Thorpe.
    p. cm. — (Greenwood guides to extreme sports)
  Includes bibliographical references and index.
    ISBN 978–0–313–37622–1 (hardcopy : alk. paper) — ISBN 978–0–313–37623–8 (ebook) 1. Snowboarding. I. Title.
  GV857.S57T45   2012
  796.939—dc23   2011042824

ISBN: 978–0–313–37622–1
EISBN: 978–0–313–37623–8

16 15 14 13 12   1 2 3 4 5

This book is also available on the World Wide Web as an eBook.
Visit www.abc-clio.com for details.

Greenwood
An Imprint of ABC-CLIO, LLC

ABC-CLIO, LLC
130 Cremona Drive, P.O. Box 1911
Santa Barbara, California 93116-1911

This book is printed on acid-free paper ∞

Manufactured in the United States of America

To Kris, Geoff and Anna—for always supporting my love of the mountains
&
To Jose, Brook, Jack, and George—may we slide sideways together for many years to come

contents

series foreword

of interest to students and enthusiasts alike, extreme sports are recharging and redefining athletics around the world. While baseball, soccer, and other conventional sports typically involve teams, coaches, and an extensive set of rules, extreme sports more often place the individual in competition against nature, other persons, and themselves. Extreme sports have fewer rules, and coaches are less prominent. These activities are often considered to be more dangerous than conventional sports, and that element of risk adds to their appeal. They are at the cutting edge of sports and are evolving in exciting ways.

While extreme sports are fascinating in their own right, they are also a window on popular culture and contemporary social issues. Extreme sports appeal most to the young, who have the energy and daring to take part in them, and who find in them an alternative culture with its own values and vocabulary. At the same time, some extreme sports, such as surfing, have long histories and are important to traditional cultures around the world. The extreme versions of these sports sometimes employ enhanced technology or take place under excessively challenging conditions. Thus, they build on tradition yet depart from it. Extreme sports are increasingly significant to the media, and corporations recognize the marketing value of sponsoring them. Extreme sports have increasingly become linked with products, their star athletes become celebrities, and their fans are exposed to a range of media messages. Local governments might try to regulate skateboarding and other extreme activities, sometimes out of safety concerns and sometimes out of moral ones. Yet other communities provide funding for skateboard parks, indoor rock climbing facilities, and other venues for extreme sports enthusiasts. Thus, extreme sports become part of civil discourse.

Designed for students and general readers, this series of reference books maps the world of extreme sports. Each volume looks at a particular sport and includes information about the sport's history, equipment and techniques, and important players. Volumes are written by professors or other authorities and are informative, entertaining, and engaging. Students using these books learn about sports that interest them and discover more about cultures, history, social issues, and trends. In doing so, they become better prepared to engage in critical assessments of extreme sports in particular and of society in general.

preface

my passion for snowboarding began during my first year at university in the south island of New Zealand. Growing up in a small beach town, the mountains were foreign terrain for me. But, having spent many years on the periphery of the surfing and skateboarding cultures, snowboarding captured my imagination like no other sport before it. Snowboarding quickly became an all-consuming lifestyle; I hitchhiked to the mountains after class, slept on friends' couches in crowded ski resort flats, and saved scrupulously to follow the winter overseas. Between 1998 and 2004, I spent more than 500 days snowboarding on approximately 30 mountains in Canada, New Zealand, and the United States. During this time I engaged the culture, sport and industry at many levels; beginning as a novice, quickly becoming a weekend-warrior, and then later as an instructor and competitive athlete. In pursuit of new terrain and fresh challenges, I (sometimes unwittingly) ventured into extreme territories—I broke ribs, dislocated fingers, and suffered numerous concussions while training for freestyle snowboarding competitions in terrain parks and half-pipes, and practicing new maneuvers on jumps built in the backcountry. However, I would not describe any of my past snowboarding experiences as "extreme." Moreover, while I still enjoy the thrills of carving down snowy slopes with speed, I no longer seek out the biggest jumps or the most technical rails in the terrain park. As I spend more time in the university context and less time on the mountains, I find myself becoming increasingly cautious. Despite my changing roles within the sport and culture, I continue to have a deep respect and awe for those who are redefining what is possible on a snowboard.

A number of sociological questions emerged during my snowboarding excursions: How is snowboarding unique from more traditional institutionalized sports, and other action sports? What are some of the broader social, cultural, and political factors that have contributed to the rapid growth of snowboarding? In 2005, I commenced a three-year research project with the aim of answering some of these questions. At the end of this project, I still had a number of outstanding questions, and thus conducted another three years postdoctoral research on the global snowboarding culture. Between 2005 and 2010, I conducted fieldwork in an array of snowboarding communities and ski resorts in Canada, France, Italy, New Zealand, Switzerland, and the United States. I interviewed more than 80 snowboarders from around the world, ranging from novice and recreational snowboarders to Olympic athletes and judges. I also conducted interviews with various individuals involved in the snowboarding industry, including snowboarding magazine editors, journalists, photographers, filmmakers, snowboard company owners, snowboard shop employees and owners, and snowboard instructors and coaches. In conjunction with my multisited fieldwork and interviews, I also gathered evidence from cultural sources, such as magazines, films, newspapers, television, and Web sites, to help deepen my understanding of the complexities of snowboarding culture. Although I have never truly entered the extreme realm, I believe my snowboarding experiences and research into the sociology, history, and culture of the sport, equip me to write this book. What follows then, is a guide to extreme snowboarding framed by personal experiences and honed by scholarly analysis.

Written as an introductory reference work for high school students and general readers rather than for scholars, *Snowboarding: The Ultimate Guide* comprises seven chapters. In Chapter 1, I explain the concept of "extreme" as it applies to the cultural and physical environments of snowboarding. I examine the history of snowboarding in Chapter 2 describing how snowboarding has developed from a marginal activity for a few alternative youth to an Olympic sport with millions of enthusiasts around the world in the past four decades. In Chapter 3, I delve into three scientific aspects of extreme snowboarding: (1) the physics of freestyle snowboarding, (2) avalanche science, as well as (3) some of the socio-psychological aspects of extreme snowboarding. Following this scientific excursion, I describe the cultural and physical geography of four key snowboarding locations and two events of cultural significance (Chapter 4) and the attributes and feats of legendary snowboarders (Chapter 5). Big mountain and freestyle snowboarding are highly skilled pursuits and in Chapter 6, I examine some of the key technical aspects, notably around equipment, training and rescues, before concluding in Chapter 7 with a look into the future. The book closes with a glossary and bibliography.

A number of people provided invaluable sources, advice and help in compiling this book: Douglas Booth, José Borrero, George Butler, Richard Pringle, Ste'en Webster, and Belinda Wheaton. Thanks also to the many snowboarders who have so willingly shared their experiences and reflections during interviews and conversations, and to those photographers and snowboarding companies who kindly offered such wonderful images.

Holly Thorpe (University of Waikato), Raglan, New Zealand, 2011

timeline

1964

Sherman Poppen invents the Snurfer.

1970

East coast surfer Dimitrije Milovich starts developing early snowboard prototypes by combining surfboard design and ski technologies.

1975

Milovich establishes Winterstick Production in Utah, and receives national exposure with a two-page photo spread in the March issue of *Newsweek*.

1978

Jake Burton Carpenter establishes Burton Boards; Tom Sims establishes Sims Snowboards.

1979–1980

The activity of snowboarding receives coverage in *Skateboarder* and *Action Now* magazines.

1982

First American National Snowsurfing Championships held at Suicide Six Ski Area, Vermont; some competitors use Snurfers, others employ rudimentary snowboard designs.

In collaboration with the North American Snowboard Association, Japan hosts their first national snowboarding competition, the All Japan Snowboard Championship.

1983

Stratton Mountain, Vermont becomes first major U.S. ski field to allow snowboarders.

Jake Burton Carpenter organizes the first National Snowboarding Championships at Snow Valley, Vermont; Tom Sims hosts the inaugural World Snowboarding Championships at Soda Springs Ski Bowl, Lake Tahoe.

1985

Less than 7 percent (39 of approximately 600) of U.S. ski resorts allow snowboarding.

The first snowboarding magazine, *Absolutely Radical*, appears (renamed *International Snowboarder Magazine* six months later).

The first Mt. Baker legendary Banked Slalom Event is held at Mt. Baker Ski Area, Washington.

1986

A number of regional snowboarding events and competitions are held in Europe, such as the Swiss Championships in St. Moritz.

Stratton Mountain, Vermont becomes the first U.S. resort to offer organized snowboard instruction.

1987

Two World Championships held simultaneously, one in Livigno, Italy and St. Mortiz, Switzerland, the other in Breckenridge, Colorado.

Snowboarding is featured in a national TV commercial for Wrigley's chewing gum.

North American Snowboard Association (NASBA) established with the goal of working with the Snowboard European Association (SEA) to create a unified World Cup tour.

1987–1988

The first World Cup is held during the winter season with two events in Europe and two in the United States. The circuit also introduces major corporate sponsorship (O'Neill, Suzuki, and Swatch) into the competitive arena.

1990

The International Snowboard Association recognizes 36 "professional snowboarders" worldwide.

Vail Ski Resort develops one of the first "snowboard parks," other resorts quickly follow suit.

1993

The International Ski Federation (FIS) votes to recognize snowboarding at their June meeting and discuss possible Olympic inclusion.

1994

Ride Snowboards goes public on the NASDAQ stock exchange.

1996

Dave Barlia completes the first successful snowboard B.A.S.E. jump off a 1,500-foot cliff in Switzerland.

1997

Snowboarding features in the first ESPN Winter X Games at Snow Summit Mountain Resort, Big Bear Lake, California.

1998

Snowboarding debuts as an official medal sport at the Nagano Olympics with men's and women's giant slalom and half-pipe events. Canadian giant slalom gold medal winner Ross Rebagliati tests positive for marijuana; the incident grabs headlines around the world.

Snowboarding is among the most popular sports at the first Winter X Games at Big Bear Lake, California; the event is televised to 198 countries and territories in 21 different languages.

1999

Nike begins marketing snowboards, boots, and bindings.

2002

American's Ross Powers (gold), Danny Kass (silver), and J.J. Thomas (bronze) sweep the men's Olympic half-pipe in Salt Lake City, and Kelly Clark wins the gold in the women's Olympic half-pipe.

2003

Snowboard legend Craig Kelly is killed in an avalanche in British Columbia, Canada.

2004

Tara Dakides is hospitalized following a fall during a live stunt on *The Late Show with David Letterman*; the accident is covered by national and international news programs, and features in newspapers across the United States.

Travis Rice (U.S.) and Romain DeMarchi (Switzerland) become the first snowboarders to successful jump the infamous Chad's Gap in the back-country canyons in Salt Lake City, Utah.

2005
Norwegian snowboarder Mads Jonsson sets a world record when he performs a 360 degree rotation over a distance of 187 feet on a specially designed jump in Hemesedal, Norway.

2006
Snowboarders compete in three events (half-pipe, snowboard-cross, and giant slalom) at the Winter Olympics in Torino, Italy.

2007
A snowboarder paralyzed from a fall in a terrain park at a ski resort in Washington State is awarded $14 million compensation, marking the largest jury award levied against a U.S. ski resort; the verdict prompts many ski resorts in North America to reassess terrain park construction and management.

2008
Norwegian Terje Haakonsen sets a new world record at the Arctic Challenge (Norway) performing a 360 degree rotation 32 feet above the specially designed quarter-pipe.

2010
Global snowboarding industry estimated to be worth $2.2B/annum.

Shaun White wins his second Olympic half-pipe gold medal at the Winter Olympics in Vancouver; Australian snowboarder Torah Bright wins the women's half-pipe event; the snowboarding events are among the most popular and widely watched of the Games.

2011
Torstein Horgmo completes the first "triple cork" maneuver in the men's Big Air finals at the Winter X Games; Kelly Clark completes the first 1080 degree rotation in the women's Super-Pipe finals.

Slopestyle is officially added as a medal event for men and women at the 2014 Winter Olympics in Sochi, Russia.

1. explanations

it is a cold Friday night in January, yet a huge crowd gathered at the 2011 X Games men's Big Air Finals in Aspen, Colorado, roars in anticipation. Standing atop of the enormous scaffolding is Torstein Horgmo—a young Norwegian professional snowboarder—preparing to make X Games history. Earlier in the evening, Horgmo had experienced a serious crash while attempting the first "triple cork"—a 1440 degree rotation performed off-axis—to be performed in competition. Determined, he ignores his newly broken ribs and expected concussion, and returns to the top of the jump to try again. After an "almost" successful second attempt, he is now preparing for his third and final jump. With the commentators booming, cameras flashing, and the crowd chanting him on, Horgmo bends down to tighten his bindings, and focus his attention. He then leans forward, dropping into the ramp and quickly gaining momentum. The nervous spectators become hushed, and the lights dim. He then proceeds to explode off the top of the jump, performing a dizzying rotation over the large gap and through the clear Colorado night skies. As his board makes a controlled touchdown, his arms shoot for the sky, his head drops back in relief and exuberance, and the crowd erupts. With a microphone under his chin and cameras zoomed in to catch every expression, Horgmo explains with a huge smile across his face: "It's probably the stupidest thing I've done in my whole life" (cited in Larsen, 2011, para. 3). His performance was quickly acclaimed "among the top X Games tricks ever performed" (cited in Thomas, 2011, para. 1), and his status as one of the sport's most "exemplary" athletes was confirmed (DC Snowboarding, 2011, para. 2).

Horgmo's gold-medal winning performance captured the imagination of audiences around the world; outside the United States, the event was delivered live to 382 million homes in 154 countries and territories via ESPN's multimedia platforms, including television, Internet, and cellphones. Indeed, footage of Horgmo's feat became the most viewed

ESPN YouTube video ever, with more than 5.6 million viewings (Winter X, 2011). While many snowboarders around the world celebrated Horgmo's success and appreciated this efforts to "push the progression of snowboarding" (DC Snowboarding, 2011, para. 2), for many viewers unfamiliar with the sport's historical developments and cultural complexities, Horgmo's performance reinforced stereotypes of snowboarders as radical, risk-taking youth.

Snowboarding has been labeled a daredevil, alternative, and "extreme" pursuit since its inception in the 1970s (Thorpe, 2007a, 2011). But today, with more than 70 million snowboarders worldwide, and participants ranging from novice to expert, and from five to seventy-five years of age, the notion of snowboarding as extreme seems obtuse (Hansom & Sutherland, 2010; Wark, 2009). Certainly, there is an element of danger involved, but in most cases risk is a subjective calculation that individuals make in the context of their ability. For example, a sign at a Swiss resort that reads, "Runs are extremely dangerous. 60 degree slope. One fall could result in loss of life," might petrify some and exhilarate others.

Statistics on the rates and severity of injuries incurred while snowboarding offer contradictory evidence. According to a national study on recreational injury in the United States, more people are injured snowboarding than any other outdoor activity (Lewis, 2008). One study shows snowboarding as the third most dangerous sport behind boxing and tackle football (Comprehensive Study, 2003), and another suggests that snowboarders are more than twice as likely as skiers to sustain serious fractures, become concussed and lose consciousness, dislocate joints, and have their teeth knocked out (O'Neill & McGlone, 1999). Medical research shows that advanced snowboarders who travel at high speeds and try dangerous maneuvers, such as jumps and other aerial tricks, are at risk of serious injuries, including trauma to the neck, head, and abdomen. Jumping is the cause of 77 percent of snowboarding injuries in contrast to just 20 percent of skiers, and the rate of spinal injuries among snowboarders is four times that of skiers (Tarazi, Dvorak & Wing, 1999). Several reported case studies reveal 80 percent of injured snowboarders are male, with a median age of 20 years (Chow, Corbett & Farstad, 1996; Weir, 2001).

Despite the seriousness of injuries among advanced snowboarders, beginner snowboarders are the most frequently injured; the majority of the latter, however, tend to be minor injuries, such as wrist, ankle, and knee sprains and fractures (Dunn, 2001; Facts About, 2009; Ferrera, McKenna & Gilman, 1999; Moore, 2000; Yamakawa, Murase, Sakai, Iwama,

Katada, Niikawa, Sumi, Nishimura & Sakai, 2001). With falling identified as the lead cause of these injuries, it is perhaps not surprising that almost one-quarter of all snowboarding injuries occur during a person's first time, and approximately one-half occur during the first winter season. While colliding with a tree is the most common cause of severe injury among snowboarders, fortunately such occurrences are rare. Interestingly, the National Ski Areas Association has reported that, in terms of the average number of deaths on the slopes, snowboarding is actually significantly safer than bicycling or swimming (Facts About, 2006). Traumatic brain injury accounts for 88 percent of snowboarding fatalities; most snowboarding fatalities are men (85%) from their late teens to late 30s (70%) (Facts About, 2006).

While snowboarding has the potential to be a dangerous activity for advanced participants, it is not an overly risky pursuit for the majority of participants. So, what is so extreme about snowboarding? The term *extreme* has relevance in four distinct ways (see Thorpe, 2007a). First, snowboarding's countercultural origins contributed to the stereotyping of participants as "radical" and "risk-taking" youths and subsequent extreme labeling of the activity. Second, the hedonistic practices widely celebrated within the après snow culture reinforce public perceptions of snowboarders as rebellious and sensation-seeking youth. Third, when television and corporate sponsors recognized the huge potential in snowboarding to tap into the highly lucrative (yet elusive) youth market, great efforts were made to portray snowboarders as extreme in their thrill-seeking approach to the activity and lifestyle, which has had consequences for the safety of professional snowboarders. Here I refer particularly to the trend toward building ever larger jumps, and hosting events designed primarily as exciting spectator events which emphasize the risks involved in freestyle snowboarding. Fourth, big mountain snowboarding, in which individuals are exposed to the raw power of the natural environment (i.e., freezing temperatures, almost vertical slopes, cliffs and crevasses, ice and rocks, avalanches) is certainly extreme.

"bad boys" (and girls) on boards

The distinctive tastes and styles embodied by many young snowboarders during the 1980s and early 1990s contributed to the general public's negative stereotyping of snowboarders. Early professional male snowboarders, such as Damian Sanders and Shaun Palmer, epitomized the hedonistic identities celebrated by young, committed snowboarders during this period. According to snowboarding historian, Suzanna Howe (1998), Damian, the younger brother of Avalanche founder Chris Sanders, was "perhaps the most visible poster boy of snowboarding's 'radical,' 'extreme' image. He embodied this with everything from clothing to riding style, Spiky hair and Day-Glo head bands; every flashy mutation of the board garb was 'extreme' . . . over-extended postures, gritted teeth, and clenched fists, were signs of aggression and in vogue [among boarders]" (p. 70). In response to a rider poll in an early *Transworld Snowboarding* magazine in which he was voted as the "most extreme snowboarder," Sanders admits performing for his peers, "the wilder I was the better they [boarders] like it" (cited in Howe, 1998, p. 73).

Another early professional snowboarder, Shaun Palmer, further epito-mized the rebellious image of snowboarding. As Howe (1998) recalls, he was foul-mouthed and "would drink and do drugs all night, and win half-pipe contests in the morning" (Howe, 1998, p. 78). Palmer was essentially snowboarding's "first real bad boy," he was "cocky, rude, and couldn't lose a contest between 1988 and 1990" (Howe, 1998, p. 70). Palmer's irreverent lifestyle, athletic prowess, and constant bravado, combined to create a cul-tural icon that appealed to many young males. While the hypermasculine image endorsed by early male snowboarders such as Palmer intimidated some women (and men), others negotiated space within the culture and embraced the "alternative" identity offered by snowboarding. Early U.S. snowboarder Tina Basich (2003), for example, describes her group of female snowboarding friends as "the misfits of the misfits—the anti-cheerleaders. We didn't fit in [at high school]. Snowboarding was a savior to us" (p. xi).

When the mass media began reporting on snowboarding in the late 1980s and early 1990s, it tended to sensationalize the sport by focusing on "color-ful" characters such as Sanders and Palmer. The exaggerated mass-mediated image of snowboarding during this period was such that in 1988, *Time* magazine declared snowboarding "the worst new sport." While negative mass media influenced the general public's dislike of snow-boarding and its distrust of participants, it had the opposite effect on "alter-native" youth who were attracted to the sport. In the words of early professional snowboarder Todd Richards (2003), "we were outcasts, viewed negatively—or at least warily—by public opinion. But this only fuelled the fire of the snowboarding youth movement" (p. 67).

Whereas the mass media tended to condemn snowboarders' reckless and hedonistic behavior, the niche snowboarding media (e.g., magazines, films) endorsed the risk-taking, hedonistic, drunken, and disorderly exploits of early professional snowboarders, such as Palmer. For example, *Blunt* magazine, established in 1993 by snowboarders Ken Block and Damon Way, had more cultural authenticity among core snowboarders than any other magazine because it was seen as accurately representing the snowboarding lifestyle (see Thorpe, 2007b). Richards (2003) describes the *Blunt* formula as "alcohol, party, party, party, oh, and snowboarding," and adds, "it was really popular among snowboarders and really unpopular among ski resorts, parents, and snowboarding companies because of its blatant disregard for authority" (p. 162).

The *Whiskey* videos produced by core Canadian boarders Sean Kearns and Sean Johnson in the mid- to late 1990s further epitomized the hedonistic and belligerent snowboarding lifestyle. They featured young male snowboarders, many of whom were also skateboarders, consuming excessive amounts of alcohol, vomiting, performing violent acts against themselves and others (e.g., smashing empty beer bottles over their own heads or over their friends' heads, often repeatedly), and engaging in destructive behavior (e.g., smashing windows). Women appeared only as soft-pornographic appendages. The low-budget *Whiskey* videos were among the first to document this aspect of the snowboarding lifestyle. "In those days, *Whiskey* was the dope shit," recalled Sean Kearns, "fuckin' smash, break and crash—that was it" (cited in LeFebvre, 2005, para. 9). In the first *Whiskey* video, a conversation between snowboarder Kris Markovick (who is seen vomiting violently) and the unknown camera operator reveals the criteria for inclusion into this hypermasculine group:

Kris:	"Someone told me the only way to get into the *Whiskey* videos was to throw up."
Camera operator:	"It's either that or you smash a bottle over your head. You chose the easier way" [vomiting from excessive alcohol consumption].
Not wanting to appear "weak" Kris replies:	"I'll do the bottle later." (*Whiskey The Movie*, 1994)

The young men in these videos show a complete disregard for their own and their friends' safety and health.

Despite the increasing professionalism in snowboarding, some contemporary athletes are very aware of the economic value of the sports countercultural image. In an interview with *Snowboarder* magazine, for example, professional snowboarder Romain DeMarchi admitted to being "a hard-core partier" and being arrested four times, before explaining that that this "bad boy image" has advantages in the highly competitive snowboarding industry: "People say, 'Ah, Romain's the wild guy, he's going to go out and rage his ass off and be a f—ker and a dickhead!' But you know, who cares if these things are said? People label me as crazy, and it's good for me. It sells, so the sponsors use it and the magazines use it" (Bridges 2004, cited in Thorpe, 2007a, p. 291).

Physical prowess, risk-taking, and a "hard-core" image (e.g., irreverent and hedonistic lifestyle, antiauthoritarian, hyperheterosexuality, pranks, and high jinks) were all important aspects of the "core" snowboarding identity embodied by many early boarders, and endorsed by the niche media. Many young committed participants embraced a reckless, short-term approach to the body. For example, professional snowboarder Scotty Wittlake sarcastically described his relationship to his body: "My body's a temple, so only the finest fast foods enter it. And with a mug like this, you need beauty sleep, so I try to get at least six hours a week. When it comes to exercise . . . I try to do as many 40-ounce curls as I can" (How Do, 2003, p. 16).

The glorification of injuries was also prevalent in the early snowboarding culture and is a continuing trend in many niche media. Some snowboarding magazines, films, and Web sites endorse the physical prowess and risk-taking embodied by professional boarders. Interviews in magazines often include "worst injury" questions with replies reported in detail. In interviews with professional athletes, snowboarding journalists often insist on revealing the gory minutiae, prompting riders for the particulars of their injuries. For example, *Transworld Snowboarding* journalist Chris Coyle narrated the injury of professional rider Scotty Wittlake as follows:

> A brutal knee to face contact completely shattered his cheekbone. Apparently, Scotty's eye was so distended that doctors had to come up with a temporary fix to hold it in until the swelling went down. His eyelid became so swollen it turned inside out and oozed pus. (Yellow Snow, 2002, p. 206)

The article bestowed symbolic status on Wittlake, praising his commitment to snowboarding: "Just a few weeks after the surgery, Scotty headed up to Oregon to help Whitey film using his one good eye. Now *that's* punk"

(Yellow Snow, 2002, p. 206). Such mediated accounts are common and construct professional riders as heroes for risking physical injury and tolerating pain.

Many young committed snowboarders also accept injury and risk-taking as part of the snowboarding experience. The following comments, shared with me proudly by a core male snowboarder during an interview, illustrate the reckless relationships many young men have with their bodies:

> In the 2002 X-Games at Whakapapa, I was competing. I came down to the medical bay; I had 4 cracked ribs and a twisted knee and I was the least injured guy there; fractured skulls, massive back injuries, guys with their calves ripped open, you name it. It was crazy. I was just like, "give me my two Panadols [painkillers] and I'll be on my way." *Accidents happen aye.* (Hamish, interview, 2005, cited in Thorpe, 2007a, p. 293)

Many committed female snowboarders have also internalized the cultural value system that celebrates courage and taking risks, and are experiencing their share of injuries (see Thorpe, 2005, 2009, 2011); some embrace short-range views on participation. Professional female snowboarder Annie Boulanger, for example, says she plans to continue snowboarding "until Advil [painkillers] in the morning doesn't do it anymore" (cited in Thorpe, 2004, p. 194). "I've broken stuff in my back and I've broken my ankle, and bad strains and I've blown my knee out. But I have been quite lucky. I've been injury free, really" proclaimed Phillipa (interview, 2005). In sum, snowboarding while injured, resuming full participation shortly after injury, and the media representation of such practices, clearly distinguish pros from poseurs, and reinforce the extreme image of the sport.

ride hard, party hard: the snowboarding lifestyle

The physical act of snowboarding has always been intimately connected to the hedonistic après snow culture (Thorpe, 2011b). Many early snowboarding competitions were organized primarily as social events. According to pioneer Tom Sims, almost everyone attending the early snowboarding races was "drunk and disorderly, and really just there to revel in the rarity of an occasion that made snowboarding seem like a real culture with more than a few members" (cited in Howe, 1998, p. 43). Similarly, Phillipa, an early New Zealand snowboarder, fondly recalls the après snow culture: "Partying after competitions was always a high-light—the video clip and music of the event made the whole day seem larger than life. We always got drunk, it was pretty easy after the mental and physical exertion of the day—and we were always among great friends. Everyone took it to different levels—but the common thread was that of 'riding hard—partying hard'" (interview, 2008).

The contemporary snowboarding culture continues to offer a plethora of opportunities for hedonistic social experiences in various cafes, bars, nightclubs, as well as other social spaces (e.g., snowboarding events, competitions, shared houses, hotels, youth hostels or backpackers):

> Snowboarders' party, that's a fact. When you think about it, it's composed of a counter culture of alternative people who tend to resist social norms. At certain snowboarding events and contests, all these people are grouped together and the wheels fall off. . . . Sometimes things get broken, sometimes you forget to sleep, and sometimes you're forced to sleep in jail. (Eric, professional Canadian snowboarder, interview, 2008)

> For many people, snowboarding is associated with letting your hair down, going away to the mountains, to a foreign country, and trying something new. . . . Boarders often get drunk and naked and then climb trees in places like Whistler. I've seen people running around naked, trying to see how many hot tubs they can get into without getting busted. (Jenny Jones, British Olympic snowboarder, cited in Thomson, 2006, para. 25)

The après snow culture is central to the snowboarding lifestyle of many young core snowboarders; it is also an integral part of the winter ski holiday experience for many less committed snowboarders (e.g., tourists, "weekend warriors"). A recent study of British snow-sport tourists revealed that "45 percent planned to drink every night" during their winter sport holiday (Bradley, 2010). Similarly, an Australian study found 56 percent of the 1,084 young adult snowfield resort visitors surveyed had consumed 11 or more standard alcoholic drinks on the previous night; 65 percent reported having less than four hours sleep; and 77 percent had used psycho-stimulants in the previous 24 hours (cited in Sherke, Finch, Kehoe & Doverty, 2006).

While the après snow culture offers participants many opportunities for hedonistic social interactions and experiences, it also carries risks (e.g., criminal charges, serious injury, and death) which can have serious consequences for snow-sport tourists, core snowboarders, and professional athletes alike. Jeff Anderson—a talented 22-year-old professional U.S. snowboarder—died from head injuries sustained from a fall during a post-competition party in Nagano, Japan. Staying in the same hotel with Anderson and his older brother, the tragic incident prompted fellow competitor Todd Richards (2003) to reflect: "He was out with his buddies, drinking, having a good time. . . . Jeff had been doing what all of us have done at some time in our lives: sliding down the hotel's exterior stair banister on his butt. But lost his balance and fell over backward four stories to the ground below" (p. 278). Describing the grief as "so close and so overwhelming," Richards (2003) was prompted to reflect critically upon the dangers faced by young snowboarders in the après snow culture: "I thought about the things I'd done when I was just screwing around. Now that I have a family . . . I definitely think twice about things . . . Of course, this sense of self-preservation also comes with age. When I was twenty-two, forget about it. I got away with crazy things, but I was lucky" (p. 278).

The boundaries between the on-piste and après snow cultures are often blurred, with many snow-sport participants drinking alcohol or consuming recreational drugs while on the mountain. A recent poll conducted by More Than Travel insurance company found that British winter sports enthusiasts have on average seven units of alcohol in their blood when they arrive on the slopes in the morning (this is the equivalent of being almost twice over the legal drink-drive limit in the UK) (Bradley, 2010). Commenting on this trend, an online snowboarding journalist writes: "Whether its whiskey from a hip flask, smoking green in the gondola, or snorting lines of white powder, snowboarders and skiers have been known to dabble whist on the slopes" (Baldwin, 2006a, para. 1). For one male Canadian snowboard instructor: "Smoking a bowl [of marijuana] before riding puts me in the zone and I like the sensation of cruising when I'm stoned. I feel more confident, spin smoother and it just feels good" (cited in Baldwin, 2006a, para. 9).

Others, however, recognize that snowboarding under the influence of marijuana compromises both safety and the overall psycho-physical experience: "I've tried snowboarding after smoking weed, but I prefer to ride with a clear head. I like to be totally aware of my surroundings and weed makes me feel blinkered. The last time I smoked a joint on a chair lift I ended up sitting in the snow outside a lodge and falling asleep" (Core

Australian male snowboarder, cited in Baldwin, 2006a, para. 13).
Numerous studies show a direct correlation between alcohol and recreational drug consumption and skiing and snowboarding injuries. In 2008, more than 30 Britons died in alpine accidents, half of whom were under 25—many died because they underestimated the risk of drinking at high altitude (Britain Tells, 2009).

While skiers have long celebrated the après snow culture, the influx of young snowboarders into ski-resort destinations has increased the visibility of such practices. The excessive alcohol and drug consumption of snowboarders (and skiers) now has the attention of local councils, national agencies, ski resort organizations, and the mass media, as well as insurance companies. For example, a study by the British Foreign Ministry estimated that at least one third of skiers and snowboarders under the age of 25 had "experienced problems abroad linked to a mixture of altitude, adrenaline, and alcohol" (Bradley, 2010, para. 10). In response to such studies, and an increasing number of accidents (both on and off the mountain) involving skiers and snowboarders under the "strong influence of alcohol," the British Consulate General launched a campaign during the 2009–2010 winter seasons in an array of snow-resort destinations in France, Italy, and Switzerland. According to Sir Peter Westmacott, Britain's Ambassador to France, the campaign was a coordinated attempt by local and UK authorities to discourage the "let's get pissed on the piste" attitude (cited in Davies, 2009, para. 8). With posters displayed in airports and hotels, the aim of the campaign was to educate "young British nationals who perhaps are not fully aware of the effects of low temperatures and how the body reacts to alcohol at altitude" (Bradley, 2010, para. 5). The message on the posters is clear: "Alcohol can affect you more quickly at high altitude and limit your awareness of danger and cold. Your reactions are slower, reckless behavior can lead to crime. Alcohol abuse can simply ruin your holiday." Similar campaigns are being launched internationally. The intoxicated, boisterous, and disorderly practices of (particularly young) snowboarders on the mountain, and in ski resort destinations, have certainly contributed to the extreme labeling of the sport.

"go big or go home": xxl freestyle snowboarding

Freestyle riding is currently among the most popular forms of snowboarding. Freestyle snowboarders practice and perform creative and technical

A snowboarder performs a "method" maneuver in a half-pipe at a ski resort in New Zealand. (Courtesy of Brook Thorpe.)

maneuvers on jumps and other obstacles (e.g., rails) in found and purposely created spaces (e.g., terrain parks, half-pipes). While many of these maneuvers have their roots in skateboarding, the "tricks" developed and refined by snowboarders have influenced many other board sports including surfing, kite-surfing, and wake-boarding. Indeed, the recent trend toward aerial maneuvers in surfing was partly inspired by freestyle snowboarding. Moreover, as will be discussed in more depth in Chapter 2, many skiers are also drawing inspiration from the physical performances, clothing styles, and technologies of freestyle snowboarders.

In response to the growing popularity of freestyle snowboarding during the late 1990s and 2000s, some ski resorts began investing heavily in equipment and personnel needed to design, construct, and maintain highly technical terrain parks and half-pipes. An advertisement for Heavenly Resort in Lake Tahoe, California featured in *Transworld Snowboarding* magazine, for example, boasted "$200 million in improvements" including "three new terrain parks with 29 rails, 20 tables [jumps], 13 fun-boxes and sick designs like the Dual C Boxes and Wall Ride" (Resort Guide, 2005, pp. 48–49). Two other Californian resorts, Mammoth Mountain and Big Bear Mountain, also employ 20 and 35 full-time park staff, respectively, to build and maintain their extensive terrain park facilities. Many ski resorts build terrain parks and half-pipes directly under chairlifts, thus providing passengers with entertainment in the form of boarders (and skiers) jumping, sliding, spinning, flailing, grabbing, landing, and crashing. With a large group typically gathered at the top of the park awaiting their turn, and the steady stream of passengers overhead, many terrain parks and half-pipes have become spaces of extreme exhibitionism.

During the late 1990s and early 2000s, some ski resorts responded to the demands of the highly lucrative snowboarding demographic by building terrain parks with enormous jumps and highly technical obstacles (e.g., rails, wall rides, and quarter-pipes). Observing this trend, Pamela notes:

> Terrain parks are getting so big these days. At Blackcomb the park is enormous! It's so big I wouldn't even want to ride in it. It's a little bit frightening, its dividing people up and its taking the fun element out a little bit. And the people who can do it have less patience for those who can't, that get in your way, and things get more aggressive. (interview, 2005)

Extralarge terrain parks appeal to elite participants with high-level skills and who are seeking new challenges. However, these developments have also increased the likelihood of serious injury, particularly among the growing number of enthusiastic, yet less experienced newcomers to the sport. Recent medical research conducted in Canada, France, and the United States shows that, in comparison to other snowboarding injuries, those suffered in terrain parks are more likely to be severe in nature and require admission to hospital; the rates of joint dislocation, and head, spine, chest, and ACL injuries, are also higher among terrain park users (Ski Injury, 2010; Yamakawa et al., 2001). The U.S.-based study also revealed that 82 percent of terrain park injuries were incurred by men, and 78 percent of those injured were under 25 years old (Ski Injury, 2010). Attempting to minimize terrain-park injuries and avoid expensive liability claims, some resorts have downsized jumps, reduced the difficulty of obstacles, built separate terrain parks for different skill levels, and established procedures for the careful monitoring of access and participation (see Chapter 6).

With terrain parks increasingly becoming spaces of controlled and regulated risk, many committed freestyle snowboarders are heading out of bounds or into the backcountry to build jumps to their own specifications. Groups of professional snowboarders may spend days preparing (i.e., watching the weather, finding a location, sourcing equipment) to build a jump upon which they will attempt to perform their most technical maneuvers and capture the action on film. The quality of the snow (e.g., powder), avalanche risk, the weather (e.g., temperature, wind) and light quality, and group dynamics are all important factors in planning such backcountry jump-building and filming excursions. For some professional snowboarders, footage captured on these jumps is a key factor in their salaries; contracts with snowboarding companies are contingent upon photos and images of the athletes appearing in niche magazines and films. In an increasingly competitive industry, however, professional snowboarders face mounting pressure to perform ever-more spectacular, technical, and dangerous maneuvers. The following comments from professional U.S. snowboarder Marc Frank Montoya are insightful here:

> It's a *lot* harder [today] 'cause there's more competition out there. A lot of new blood coming in . . . just like any other sport, it's like a big ol' production. It's definitely not as much fun as it used to be when you could go to a resort and ride all day. Now you have to work, hike . . . build some big ol' jump . . . make sure the landing's all good. It's too big of an ordeal. I didn't start snowboarding to be pro. I didn't start to watch myself on film but *I have to now because that's what I get paid to do*. I busted my ass this winter . . . filming, filming, filming . . . I got burned out on it. (cited in Yant, 2001, para. 22, emphasis added)

As Montoya suggests, with "more competition" and ever more snowboarding "crews" heading into the backcountry to film, professional snowboarders face mounting pressure to pioneer new spaces, perform more daring maneuvers, and "get the shot" first.

Recent performances on Chad's Gap—a colossal jump with a 120-plus-foot gap between the take-off and landing—located in the backcountry canyons of Salt Lake City, Utah offer a good example of the efforts by professional freestyle snowboarders to charter new terrain. In March 2004, professional U.S. snowboarders, Travis Rice and Romain DeMarchi, became the first snowboarders to successfully jump Chad's Gap. Video footage and photos of Rice performing a 1080-degree rotation while soaring approximately 200 feet were circulated across the global snowboarding culture, such that the Chad's Gap quickly became "the jump that nobody can shut up about" and was put on "every jibbers 'to Do Before I Die' list" (Alder, no date, para. 1).

In the hypercommercial and competitive snowboarding industry, some professional male snowboarders are also eagerly trying to establish records for the longest and highest jump. For example, on May 9, 2005, professional Norwegian snowboarder Mads Jonsson (nicknamed "Big Nads") set a world record when he performed a 360-degree rotation over a distance of 187 feet in Hemsedal, Norway. On his second jump, he broke his hand attempting to land a 720-degree rotation. Jonsson's feat gained extensive mass media attention, as well as coverage in the majority of snowboarding magazines and Web sites, and was compared to Danny Way's world-record skateboarding stunts (e.g., jumping a distance of 79 feet on a skateboard; constructing a megaramp and jumping over the Great Wall of China) and the big-wave surfing of Laird Hamilton. Further records were set at June Mountain, California later that year when U.S. professional snowboarder Josh Dirksen reached a height of 33 feet when jumping off "a hip [type of jump] of enormous proportions" (Dresser, September 2005, p. 135). In 2008, Norwegian snowboarder Terje Haakonsen performed the "largest air in the history of transition riding" when he completed a 360-degree rotation 32 feet above the specially designed quarter-pipe at the Arctic Challenge event in Norway (Terje Breaks, 2008, para. 1). For their record-breaking attempts, professional snowboarders such as Haakonsen, Rice, DeMarchi, and Jonsson receive extensive mainstream and snowboarding-specific media exposure, corporate sponsorship deals and, most importantly, peer esteem.

As the size of jumps continues to grow, so too do the consequences of error. Many snowboarders and cultural commentators are raising concerns about the risks facing professional snowboarders in a context where "now, more than ever, there is a fixation, fascination and fetishization with BIG. Jumps are measured, and bigger is always better" (Andrew, interview, 2006). Olympic snowboarding judge and magazine editor, Ste'en Webster observed that the "consequences of pushing your limits have changed . . .

we never used to do jumps that could kill you . . . people are dying now" (interview, 2005, cited in Thorpe, 2007a, p. 293). Similarly, snowboarding cinematographer Zane has seen the sport

> becoming more and more dangerous because people have to keep pushing the limits to get *more recognition* . . . kids don't *respect* anything if someone's not going 100 feet [size of jump] and doing a 1080 [degree spin]; it is way harder to *get noticed*. I think a lot of these guys [professional snowboarders] are taking these risks with confidence but [it is the kids] who [are] going to suffer [because] they think to be good they have to do the craziest thing ever, and this is starting to catch up . . . more people are dying. (interview, 2005; cited in Thorpe, 2007a, p. 294)

Despite some concerns within the culture, the majority of committed and professional snowboarders have internalized the philosophy that only those demonstrating physical prowess and courage deserve peer recognition (Young et al., 1994). But Marc Frank Montoya is not perturbed: "I get broken ribs, concussions, broken fingers, separated shoulders, but I don't mind—it's worth it" (cited in Rossi, 2002, para. 16).

In the hypercommercial context of Winter Olympics and X Games, new snowboarding disciplines and competition formats are being developed that lend themselves to large numbers of spectators and television coverage (e.g., boarder-cross, slope-style, big-air competitions). Since 1994, the annual Air and Style mega-event held in Innsbruck, Austria has attracted crowds of up to 45,000 who cheer for snowboarders from around the world as they compete for large prize monies. In 2000, the winner of the Big Air event received $250,000 in prize money, and a new Audi A3. Snowboarding events, particularly snowboard-cross, slope-style, and half-pipe, are a central feature of the annual Winter X Games, which attracts crowds of more than 70,000 over the course of the weekend, and is televised to more than 122 countries. Such events are "spectacular to watch," and make for good television primarily because "you're more or less guaranteed to see someone crash" (Reed, 2005, p. 95). Indeed, the snowboard-cross event was identified as the most hazardous sport at the 2010 Vancouver Winter Olympics with nearly 75 percent of female athletes sustaining injuries in the races (Engebretsen et al., 2010).

Today, many professional snowboarders and competitive athletes are embracing the new opportunities for media exposure, corporate sponsorship, and mainstream celebrity, offered by mega events such as the

Snowboard-cross is widely recognized as a high risk event.
(AP Photo/Manu Fernandez.)

X Games and Winter Olympics. Yet, there are inherent dangers for the athlete within this highly mediatized context. Reporting from the Winter X Games, one journalist writes:

> The X Games marks the spot where, sooner or later, an athlete
> is going to die in the name of televising a stupid human trick.
> The painfully uncomfortably question is, when is the needle so
> dangerously pushed into the red zone that these stunt men and
> women become exploited for our vicarious thrills? (cited in
> Winter X, 2009, para. 5)

The 2010 Winter Olympic half-pipe minutes before the men's final competition. (Courtesy of Holly Thorpe.)

Professional snowboarder and X Games competitor Spencer O'Brien also expresses concern that the schedule for the Games "allows no wiggle room for a postponement due to unsafe conditions, even if the health of athletes should be the No. 1 concern" (cited in Winter X, 2009, para. 5). As snowboarding stunts have gained greater visibility in the mass media, some mainstream viewers and sports commentators are asking questions about the risks for athletes. Such issues were particularly evident just before the 2010 Winter Olympic Games.

In the lead-up to the much anticipated 2010 Vancouver Winter Olympics, Red Bull paid more than $500,000 to build Shaun White a private super-pipe in the Colorado backcountry, accessed only by helicopter, and with a specially designed foam-pit built into one wall. With exclusive use of this world-class training facility, White was able to invent, practice, and perfect an array of new highly technical and creative maneuvers. Rumors regarding "Project X" quickly spread around the global snowboarding community, and many of White's competitors were angered by the inequalities in training facilities, and felt betrayed by his highly individualistic and secretive approach to training. White confirmed many of his peers' fears when he unleashed his never done-before "double cork" maneuver at a competition in New Zealand just months before the

Olympic Games. According to Tom Hutchinson, coach of the Canadian national team, "because it's such a fast-evolving thing for these Olympics, people haven't really taken the time to learn it on airbags . . . everyone's in such a panic [to learn the 'double cork']. People are pushing it to levels they're just not comfortable with. I think going into the Olympics, it's going to be whoever survives" (cited in Blount, 2010, para. 14).

Only a few replicated this double cork maneuver, one of whom was U.S. Olympic-team hopeful Kevin Pearce. However, while practicing the maneuver at Park City, Utah on December 31, 2009, Pearce fell and suffered a severe brain injury. In critical condition at the University of Utah Hospital intensive care unit in Salt Lake City, the doctors warned that he had a very long recovery ahead. The incident prompted a frenzied media response with mainstream reporters asking, somewhat paternalistically: "Should snowboarders be allowed to go so big?" Particularly vocal in her argument was *USA Today* columnist, Christine Brennan: "the fact that you get more points the higher you go is asking these young, fearless, athletes to do things that are probably not best for them . . . I think the International Olympic Committee and the U.S. Olympic Committee . . . need to reign this in, so there aren't more injuries like this" (Risky Maneuver, 2010, paras. 10, 22).

Brennan's statements infuriated many snowboarders, such that the "Snowboarders against Christine Brennan" Facebook page hosted more than 7,000 members. "The Angry Snowboarder," posted the following comments on his personal blog: "The mainstream media needs to step back from talking out of their ass with these hack job reporters that don't know shit about snowboarding and put it back in the hands of those of us that eat, sleep, breathe snowboarding" (The Mainstream, 2010, para. 7). Another blogger also proclaimed: "to say that big air isn't the best thing for these elite snowboarders is taking away their agency and self-determination . . . the people doing this, like Kevin Pearce, are professionals . . . they aren't children" (Ober, 2010, para. 11). When asked to comment, British Olympic snowboarder Lesley McKenna, explained that while her peers are professionals, they would likely baulk at any attempts by authorities to limit their performances: "Can you imagine telling 30 of the best snowboarders in the world that the trick they've been practicing and risking life and limb for is banned? They would laugh and do it anyway" (cited in Moran and Gibson, 2010, para. 15). Despite such debates, no constraints were placed on the amplitude or technicality of maneuvers in the snowboarding events at the 2010 Winter Olympic Games.

Many boys and girls, and young men and women, around the world spend countless hours practicing and performing new maneuvers in terrain parks and half-pipes, often attempting to imitate their snowboarding heroes who they see on television, and in the magazines and films. While serious injuries can and do occur in these snowy playgrounds, for the majority of participants (as distinct from elite-level athletes such as Pearce and White) risk is largely perceived rather than real: "Terrain parks and half-pipes are carefully constructed and maintained by trained professionals, they are positioned within ski-resort boundaries, rules and regulations are signposted and policed by resort employees, and, if injury should occur, the ski-patrol and medical facilities are only minutes away" (Thorpe, 2007a, p. 292). In comparison, the risk involved in big mountain riding is very much a reality.

big mountain snowboarding: heroes, helicopters, and avalanches

Big mountain snowboarding is undeniably extreme. In the words of cultural commentator Susanna Howe (1998), "big mountain riding is downright dangerous. Avalanches, sluffs, helicopter crashes, crevasses, rocks, and exposure to the elements take their toll on those who aren't prepared or aren't lucky" (p. 143). According to big mountain snowboarder Rob Kingwill, "big mountain snowboarding is the pinnacle of snowboarding . . . it combines all the other aspects of snowboarding and forces you to constantly adapt to changes in terrain and conditions" (para. 11). Another experienced snowboarder and journalist describes big mountain riding as "scary":

> It can result in the most memorable experiences of your life or it can result in a horrible death by suffocation or bloodied trauma buried under hundreds of tons of moving snow. Snowboarders can reach speeds of over 150km/h as they race down rocky faces, over cliffs, crevasses and outrun avalanches. Snowboarding down mountains in places like Alaska, that are so steep you cannot see more than 10 meters in front of you . . . takes amazing snowboarding ability and a super heightened awareness of the mountain. . . . Unlike freestyle riding, which is heavily visual, big mountain riding relies on feeling, being in the moment and experiencing everything that is around you; the snow, the mountain, the trees, the speed, the wind, the airtime. (Holt, 2005, p. 91)

Indeed, big mountain snowboarding requires a different set of physical, social, psychological, and technical skills. As revealed in the following comments from Eric, a professional Canadian snowboarder, avalanches are a very real source of anxiety for those venturing into the backcountry:

> For me, avalanches are the scariest part of snowboarding. I have seen some massive slides and known people who have died in their tracks. I've been buried once and was dug out within minutes by my friends who were there. Avalanches put you in your place and remind you about how strong and dangerous the mountains can be. Safety and proper equipment is an absolute must whenever you're in avalanche potential territory. You have to trust the awareness and abilities of everyone you're with because your life is literally in their hands and theirs in yours. (interview, 2008)

Even experienced snowboarders can find themselves in trouble when traveling out of bounds or "ducking the ropes" of a ski resort. Todd Richards (2003) recalls following a friend "down a windblown ridgeline . . . the day after a storm" when "Zach threw on his brakes, waving his hands for us to stop":

> We pulled up next to him, peered over a roller, and realized that we were perched on top of an eighty-foot cliff with no way down. Above us was an open slope, and it didn't take a rocket scientist to deduce that if the snow we were standing on slipped, we'd get swept off the cliff. Suddenly we were shitting our pants. Very carefully, we took our snowboards off and hiked, as gently as possible, back up the ridgeline. (p. 155)

Despite such dangers, the backcountry environment has the potential to offer such affective and sensual experiences that it becomes a highly alluring space for many participants.

As a result of spending "years learning about snow conditions and behavior, weather patterns, emergency techniques, and rock climbing," big mountain snowboarders are often "physically different" than freestyle snowboarders and participants from other disciplines (Howe, 1998, p. 140). According to Howe (1998), many professional big mountain snowboarders are "four or five inches taller" than freestyle athletes, with "more bulk on them, so that they can ride a longer, stiffer type of board" (p. 140). The embodied cultural practices (e.g., hair styles, beverage preferences) of big mountain snowboarders are also distinctive. Todd Richards (2003) recalled meeting Alaskan snowboarders Jay Liska and Ritchie Fowler, who he described as "a couple of big, tough looking guys"; they were "notorious big mountain snowboarders who rode big boards, wore their sideburns long, and drank whiskey like water" (p. 157).

Big mountain riding not only "separates the novices from those who have been around much longer," it also provides a space for "real men" to "prove their worth on the steeps" (Howe, 1998, p. 143). Tom Burt is widely regarded as one of these men. A professional big mountain snowboarder for more than 20 years, Burt has laid claim to more than forty "first descents," including Peru's Cordillera Blanca, Nepal's Mount Pumori, Mexico's Mount Orizaba, and Alaska's Mount McKinley, which he ascended and descended with close friend and fellow big mountain legend Jim Zellers. In a biography of professional U.S. big mountain snowboarder Jeremy Jones, *Snowboarding* magazine contrasts the commitment of big mountain snowboarders with those of freestyle athletes; "While many of his piste-confined contemporaries are sipping cocoa in contest lounges and hitting the club after hitting the twenty-stair [rail in the terrain park or urban environment], Jeremy is digging snow pits, dodging slough, and studying images of his next potential unbelievable descent" (Best Big, 2009, para. 1).

Older, highly experienced, and typically white, male snowboarders have dominated big mountain snowboarding. However, a few women, including Julie Zell, Karleen Jeffery, Victoria Jealouse, Tina Basich, and Annie Boulanger, are highly proficient big mountain riders. Early big mountain snowboarder and skier Karleen Jeffery took a proactive approach to educating herself on backcountry safety and developing her skills: "I just love the whole decision-making process. I'm relying on myself for survival, and it's all based on my own knowledge. I can't rely on anyone else to keep me alive. It's a challenge every day, and I study what I do. I'm always researching and trying to preserve my life" (cited in Jeffery, 2008, para. 15).

After riding in the Chilean backcountry with Jeffery, big mountain legend Craig Kelly acknowledged her skills: "I immediately noticed that you carved hard and really well in intense places, where most people would be more likely to chatter out or slow down" (cited in Jeffery, 2008, para. 14). While Kelly welcomed the opportunity to share the big mountain experience with the highly proficient Jeffery, not all male snowboarders share the same sentiment. Victoria Jealouse, one of the most culturally renowned female big mountain snowboarders, for example, reflects upon some of the difficulties negotiating space among her male peers:

A professional female snowboarder performs an impressive cliff drop in the backcountry. (Courtesy of Nikita Sportswear.)

I've been on some film shoots (where of course I'm the only girl) and none of the guys are really friends of mine. They see me as a fifth wheel and they are acting really competitive . . . it super-sucks. It's hard enough to ride well in natural terrain where you don't usually get to warm up, only get one chance to get the shot, and have all the variables of weather, snow, good/bad camera angles, that have to come together, let alone some group-dynamics struggle. You are trying to dare yourself to do something, and there is some comment thrown at you that completely blows your confidence. Those vibes can be so hard to ignore. (cited in Victoria, 2005, para. 8, and para. 27)

Encouraging other women to pursue big mountain snowboarding, Jealouse offers sage advice:

Take a lot of baby steps in order to feel confident in your decision-making. To take too big a step and get sluffed, or get bucked, or have a bad crash or blow it and tumble the wrong way off a cliff, definitely sets you back. . . . don't let any kind of pressure affect your decision-making [and] be really aware of where you are and memorize your exposure and line. Take a picture . . . and spend as much time as you need to be 100 percent sure. As you'll find out, everything looks totally different

from the top. You usually can't see anything, and everything looks
wrong, backwards. I take a lot of time . . . that's the way I have to
do it in order to ride confidently. (cited in Taylor, no date, para. 14)

Despite some initial difficulties, Jealouse's commitment to big mountain
snowboarding, and physical prowess and courage captured in numerous
male-dominated snowboarding films and magazines, have garnered her
much respect within the sport and industry, such that she is popularly
known as the "queen of big mountain snowboarding" (Taylor, no date).

A group of professional female snowboarders hiking into the
backcountry. (Courtesy of Nikita Sportswear.)

Due to the risks involved and the remote locations in which the activity typically takes place, big mountain snowboarding is rarely a competitive endeavor. Yet, some big mountain riders do test their skills in unique events such as the King of the Hill in Alaska, the World Heli Challenge in Wanaka, New Zealand, and the Nissan Freeride World Tour. Developed in 2008, the latter is an exclusive circuit including a select group of the world's best big mountain snowboarders. Events are held in Sochi, Russia; Squaw Valley, California; Chamonix, France; and Verbier, Switzerland. The final event, the Verbier Extreme, is held on the infamous Bec des Rosses, a frighteningly steep and jagged rock face reaching a height of 10,571 feet. In preparation for the event, contestants carefully study the mountain face with binoculars, maps, and weather and snow reports, before carefully planning their descent route. On the day of the competition, participants hike for over an hour to the summit and then ride down one at a time. Their run is judged by a panel of experts who allocate scores based on the "steepness, exposure, snow conditions, difficulty of terrain, obstacles, jumps, control, falls, continuity, pace, smooth transitions, style, technical ability, and energy" of their 1,640-foot vertical descent. Winner of the 2009 Freeride World Tour, Xavier de la Rue, describes the technicalities of such events:

> To throw yourself down a big face with conditions that are not great puts massive pressure on you. No one is totally relaxed. You [can do all the necessary preparation, taking time to plan your line with binoculars or taking photos of the face] but you never know until you ride, it's always gonna be tough. It's the point when all the experience is super necessary . . . to be able to predict where all of the snow is going to go, how the rocks are sticking out. . . . It's heavy! Even just one run can totally destroy you for the rest of the day. (cited in Andrews, 2009, para. 5)

While big mountain snowboarding (and skiing) competitions are gaining popularity, professional big mountain snowboarders gain most infamy via exposure in niche media (i.e., magazines and videos) captured outside competition.

Not dissimilar from their freestyle-focused counterparts, big mountain snowboarders continue to pioneer new spaces and develop more highly technical and courageous approaches. Footage of Terje Haakonsen soaring down the previously unridden 24,934-foot Alaskan peak on the appropriately named blockbuster film *First Descent*, and magazine covers featuring Mike Basich dropping more than 100 feet from a hovering helicopter onto a mountain face, captured the imagination of viewers around the world. According to big mountain filmmaker Mike Hatchett,

> the sport is getting faster. The riders seem to be going down bigger mountains and making fewer turns. Guys like Tom Burt are riding more technically crazy stuff every year, within their ability of course, but they are going down steeper, more exposed, and on more intricate, lines every year. People step it up even more by going further and further into the mountains. (cited in Keoki, no date, para. 17)

Despite the educated and cautious approaches employed by many elite big mountain snowboarders, the niche media often sensationalizes the risk-taking feats of those pioneering these spaces. An article in the *Medium Magazine*'s 1996 "Death Issue," titled "To die for? Has snowboarding gone too far?" accused the media of promoting some dangerous sentiments: "Bigger is always better," "Avalanches can be outrun," and "No matter how many rocks you tumble through, you'll never hit one" (cited in Howe, 1998, p. 144).

Yet, death is a very real threat in this environment, and one that even the most experienced big mountain snowboarders do not always avoid. On January 3, 2003, 19-year-old professional French snowboarder Tristan Picot died from a broken neck suffered in an avalanche in Jackson Hole, Wyoming. Just a few weeks later, Craig Kelly—four-time World Champion snowboarder, legendary U.S. big mountain rider, and backcountry guide—was tragically killed on January 21 by an avalanche while working with Selkirk Mountain Experience (SME), a backcountry ski-touring business based in Revelstoke, British Columbia, Canada. Two more professional snowboarders, Josh Malay and Tommy Brummer, were killed in avalanche-related incidents in 2004 and 2006, respectively. More recently, French snowboarder Karine Ruby—Olympic gold and silver medalist, and six-time World Champion—died in 2009 while training to be a mountain guide at the French resort of Chamonix. For many core snowboarders, the deaths of Kelly, Picot, Malay, Brummer and Ruby, reinforced the extreme dangers inherent in this environment, and prompted some to reconsider (if only briefly) the severity of consequences of backcountry snowboarding and the importance of education and training.

The deaths of a number of high profile snowboarders, however, do not seem to have discouraged less experienced participants from venturing

Signage at a New Zealand ski resort warns patrons of the dangers outside the confines of the resort boundaries. (Courtesy of Holly Thorpe.)

into the backcountry. Rather, with highly affective images of professional snowboarders riding deep powder away from crowded resorts saturating the niche media, the number of snowboarders "ducking the ropes" and heading out of bounds of their local ski resorts continues grow. But many of these participants do not have the necessary backcountry knowledge or skills. A highly experienced backcountry snowboarding guide living in Chamonix, France, Neil McNab (2008), laments these trends:

> Attitudes to off-piste and backcountry riding are today very different from what they where only a decade ago when the untamed challenges of the high mountains where seen as the domain only of the most experienced skier or mountaineer. Back then, after a heavy

snowfall, the motto was, "let the mountains have their day," the snow would be left to settle and nature would find its balance. Today . . . the race is on and extreme fever is upon us. . . . more and more people of all abilities and levels or experience are drawn away from the pistes in search of the excitement of fresh lines and deep powder [and] the push is on to get further and further out there to find those last secret spots in the very heart of the high mountains. (paras. 2–4)

Not surprisingly, as the number of uneducated snowboarders entering the backcountry has increased, so too have the number of avalanche-related accidents. In North America, for example, avalanche fatalities have increased steadily from close to zero in the 1950s, to an average of 28 deaths per year in the United States and 14 per year in Canada. Eighty percent of all avalanche fatalities in the United States happen in Alaska, Colorado, Montana, Utah, and Wyoming. The biggest increase, however, has been in British Columbia, Canada where dangerous back-country terrain is often easily accessible from resort boundaries, and technological developments (e.g., snowmobiles) are increasingly being used to access ever more remote terrain.

In contrast to the carefully maintained piste at most North American ski resorts, European ski resorts often include large areas of terrain without avalanche control such that avalanche fatalities are considerably higher. During the 2005–2006 season, for example, more than 50 people were killed by avalanches in France alone. According to Bruce Tremper (2001), author of *Staying Alive in Avalanche Terrain*, almost all of avalanche fatalities are "recreationists . . . very skilled in their sport, male, fit, educated, intelligent, middle class, and between the ages of 18 and 40" (cited in Avalanche Fatalities, no date, para. 6). Continuing, Tremper notes that although most victims are experienced snowboarders and skiers (or snow-mobilers), their avalanche knowledge invariably lags behind their sport skills. Importantly, in some countries, human error in the backcountry can also have serious legal consequences. In France, for example, if an individual sets off an avalanche that ultimately kills someone on the piste below, they may face charges of manslaughter.

In sum, whether performing a "double cork" in the half-pipe, a 360-degree rotation over a 187-foot jump in Norway, straight-lining a "no-fall" chute in the French Alps, or jumping a 60-foot cliff in the Alaskan backcountry, snowboarders earn cultural status and respect from their peers through displays of physical prowess and courage (Thorpe,

2007, 2011). Traditionally, snowboarders who were prepared to risk it all received the lion's share of media coverage (in advertising, editorial, and video) and prestige. Yet, few contemporary professionals embody this attitude to risk. Snowboarders, particularly athletes wanting to prolong their careers, are increasingly taking safety precautions. For example, many freestyle snowboarders wear helmets and extensive lower- and upper-body padding, also known as "body armor," to protect them from falls in terrain parks and half-pipes. With the deaths of a number of prominent big mountain snowboarders, backcountry boarders are also increasingly enrolling in snow-safety courses and carrying the necessary safety equipment (e.g., avalanche transceivers, probes, shovels) in case of an emergency (see Chapter 6). The mass media and many corporate sponsors continue to attach the moniker *extreme* to all snowboarding in an attempt to sell products, events, and personalities, but, as this book will illustrate, the relevance of the term is limited to a few participants in a minority of styles.

2. origins

the exact date of the birth of snowboarding is unknown and remains hotly contested within the culture. People have long been standing on sleds and trying to slide on snow; recent "discoveries" include a board dating back to the 1920s and a 1939 film of a man riding a snowboard-type sled sideways down a small hill in Chicago (Howe, 1998; Humphreys, 1996, 1997; Reed, 2005; Thorpe, 2007a). Snowboarding, as the activity is understood today, however, emerged in the late 1960s and 1970s in North America with a new piece of equipment that appealed to the hedonistic desires of a new generation of youth. The popularization of the Malibu surf-board and the escapism and hedonism of surfing, with its antiestablishment countercultural values and do-it-yourself philosophies, inspired many of the early snowboarders.

the pioneering years

In 1964, Michigan chemical engineer Sherman Poppen invented the Snurfer by bolting two skis together and adding a rope for stability. The simple design was so popular with his young daughters and their neighborhood friends, that Poppen developed the concept further and went into mass production. More than half a million Snurfers were sold for $10 to $30 from supermarkets and sports stores across North America between 1966 and 1977 (Howe, 1998; Reed, 2005). Although the Snurfer was seen as a gimmick—a children's toy much like the hula-hoop—it inspired many of the early snowboarding pioneers. In Vermont, Jake Burton Carpenter began experimenting with various materials (i.e., foam, fiberglass, wood) and techniques (i.e., steam-bent solid wood, vertically laminated wood) with the goal of making a board that was more maneuverable and faster than the Snurfer (Howe, 1998). In 1978, he established Burton Boards (see Chapter 5). The early Burton boards had a rubber water-ski binding for the front foot which allowed greater control and maneuverability; turns became easier and more stable (Reed, 2005). Thus, Burton modified the board and the action.

Burton was not the only one to experiment with board designs. Other pioneers included Dimitrije Milovick from Utah, Tom Sims and Chuck Barefoot from California, Chris and Bev Sanders from California, and Mike Olsen from Washington who established Winterstick, Sims Snowboards, Avalanche Snowboards, and GNU Snowboards, respectively. As with many of the early pioneers, Olsen's motivation was "just fun" (cited in Howe, 1998, p. 33). According to snowboarding historian Susanna Howe (1998), all of these early board-makers wanted "an alternative" to the elitist culture associated with skiing (p. 31). While an alternative impulse drove these board makers, their plans for the sport and styles of participation varied. Well into the 1980s boards varied extensively in shape, which in turn influenced the style of snowboarding; "It was a period of trial and error, and groups of boarders adopted their own version of snowboarding shaped by local climate and terrain, equipment, and background (e.g., skiing, skateboarding, surfing, BMX biking, or mountaineering)" (Thorpe, 2011a, p. 22). Yet most of these pioneers embodied the idealism of the bygone counterculture and, in direct contrast to the elitist, bourgeois, and disciplined sport of skiing, embraced snowboarding as a fun, creative, and individualistic activity (Humphreys, 1996, 1997; Thorpe, 2011a).

Although predominantly men pioneered the early snowboarding industry, women were integral players. Donna Carpenter, for example, has been an important part of Burton Snowboards since she and Jake married in 1981 (Stassen, 2005). From 1985 to 1990 she was Burton Snowboards' first European sales and operations manager, and later became company chief financial officer, followed by positions as founder and director of Burton Snowboards women's initiatives. Similarly, in the early 1980s, Beverly Sanders co-founded Avalanche Snowboards with Chris Sanders, her boyfriend (and later husband), who made snowboards in his garage. On the weekends, the couple would hike up the slopes at Lake Tahoe's Soda Springs to test these boards, and "every weekend Bev would end up selling them to some curious skiers" (Chris Sanders, cited in Howe, 1998, p. 31).

difficult beginnings

Many ski resorts in North America initially banned snowboarders. According to a *Wall Street Journal* article published in 1988, owners,

Jake Burton Carpenter testing one of his early designs.
(Courtesy of James Cassimus.)

managers, and their skiing clientele defined snowboarders as "13–18 year olds with raging hormones" who liked skateboarding and surfing (Hughes, 1988, para. 11). The national sales manager for Burton Snowboards, David Schmidt confirms that "most people visualize snowboarders as a bunch of skate rats who are going to terrorize the mountain" (cited in Nelson, 1989). Bans made participation difficult, but they did not stop determined devotees, many of whom continued to hike local snow covered slopes to test their latest technologies and develop their skills.

It was not until the early 1980s that small resorts, such as Suicide Six in Vermont and Slide Mountain in New York, began to permit snowboarders access to their chair lifts and slopes. Larger resorts were less keen to allow snowboarders. But, in 1983, Stratton Mountain in Vermont became the first major ski field to open to snowboarders, and many others quickly followed. This newly found access was the result of two major factors. First, a number of snowboarders actively campaigned for access (Howe, 1998). Indeed, some committed proponents worked with resorts to develop certification systems to manage the behavior and skills of snowboarders. Second, skiing had reached a growth plateau; "snowboarding offered ski-fields a new youth market and ongoing economic prosperity" (Thorpe, 2007a, p. 288; also see Humphreys, 1996, 1997). Writing for the *Wall Street Journal*, Kathleen Hughes (1988) described snowboarding as the "biggest boost to the ski industry since chairlifts" (para. 8). Even after gaining access to the resorts, snowboarders continued to see themselves as "different" from skiers. While some tensions developed between the two groups, early U.S. snowboarder Todd Richards (2003) described the interactions between skiers and snowboarders during this period as playful and mostly in good humor: "It was fun to toy with unsuspecting wanker-two-plankers; I'm certain they considered us equally pathetic. Snowboarders were a novelty to skiers, and skiers were old news to snowboarders. There was an utter lack of understanding, which made the early days so much fun" (p. 73). According to skiing historian Annie Gilbert Coleman (2004), a running joke among skiers went: "What's the difference between a boarder and a catfish? One is a bottom-dwelling, disgusting, rejected muck sucker and the other is a fish" (p. 206). But, as the number of snowboarders increased during the 1980s and 1990s, so too did struggles between the two groups.

Skiers and snowboarders shared the same social space, from car parks, to chair lifts, to slopes. However, the two groups were "separated by age, fashion, etiquette, lingo and per capita income" (Heino, 2000, p. 176). Comparing the demographics of skiers and snowboarders in North America during the early 1990s, an early study found that 8.8 percent of snowboarders were university graduates versus 42.1 percent of skiers; 85.3 percent of snowboarders were single versus 60.7 percent of skiers; 73.5 percent of snowboarders were under 25 years old versus 44.5 percent of skiers; and 62.5 percent of snowboarders earned incomes less than Canadian $35,000 versus 46.3 percent of skiers (Williams, Dossa & Fulton, 1994). The differences were such that, as one journalist commented, the skier and the snowboarder typically "ride up the mountain together in chilly silence" (Wulf, 1996, cited in Heino, 2000, p. 176).

Summarizing the cultural divisions during this period, snowboarding historian Duncan Humphreys (1996) wrote that whereas "skiing embodied technical discipline and control," snowboarding "embodied freedom, hedonism and irresponsibility" (p. 9).

Skiers have long had the slopes to themselves, so it is perhaps not surprising that some resisted the arrival of snowboarders who not only tended to dress, speak, and behave differently, but also use the slopes in different ways (e.g., turning across the slopes, jumping off moguls rather than turning around them, "slashing" banks of snow on the sides of runs) (Humphreys, 1996). Physical confrontations and fights between skiers and snowboarders were not unusual as the two groups vied for territory and eminence (Anderson, 1999). But faced with the very real risk of losing access to mountain facilities, many snowboarders abated their unruly behavior, opting instead for symbolic and embodied practices to emphasize their distinctiveness. The most obvious practices involved clothing. One early reporter described "conservative skiers in dull blue and red outfits clutch[ing] their poles and watch[ing] aghast" as two boarders rode past, one wearing a "green leopard-spot bodysuit" and another wearing a "lilac snow jacket, red pants and neon-green glasses" (Hughes, 1988, paras 1 and 3). Male and female snowboarders both readily adopted this dress style. The early clothing practices of wearing bright and mismatched colors helped unite this marginal group of snowboarders and distinguish them from skiers.

In 1985, only 7 percent of U.S. resorts allowed snowboarders and in 1988, snowboarders still comprised just 6 percent of the ski resort population (Crane, 1996). Snowboarding remained a minority activity into the early 1990s, yet participants grouped together to form a unified front. Despite geographical variations in approach, early commentators frequently referred to a pervasive community spirit based on "a fun, non-judgmental scene that valued personal style" (Howe, 1998, p. 23). Although snowboarding was a male-dominated activity during this period, some women found space within this scene. As early U.S. snowboarder and journalist Jennifer Sherowski (2005) recalls, "it didn't seem like gender divisions really mattered. There were so few of us snowboarders, we were all just in it together" (p. 54). Another early U.S. snowboarder Tina Basich (2003) remembers meeting other male and female snowboarders on the mountain and "instantly becoming friends" (p. 36). She also adds that there was "always ... support from the guys" (p. 39).

early competitions

Modern competitive snowboarding began in the early 1980s. In 1981, Suicide Six in Vermont hosted the first U.S. national titles; the resort hosted the first international snowboard race the following year (Howe, 1998). Snowboard competitions during the mid- to late 1980s embodied an inclusive ideology. In her autobiography, professional snowboarder Tina Basich (2003) reflects fondly on these early events, recalling one regional competition in 1986 in which "everybody," from all ability levels and both sexes, competed together. Similarly, Howe (1998) writes that these events acted as "cultural hotbeds" that effectively ironed out any notions of social stratification (p. 51). In other words, these events brought snowboarders from across the country (and countries) together, where they observed, discussed, and shared knowledge regarding skills and technologies and communicated cultural values and lifestyles. Early snowboard competitions were typically poorly organized, often privileging fun over serious competition. Describing these highly festive events, Howe (1998) recalls that many of those in attendance were "drunk and disorderly" (p. 43).

Snowboarding also gained popularity among groups of youths wherever there was snow. The Japanese held their first national snowboarding contest in 1982, and in 1986, the Europeans organized regional events such as the Swiss Championships in St. Moritz. More than 100 male and female competitors from 17 nations competed in the World Championships at Livigno, Italy and St. Moritz, Switzerland in January 1987. At the end of the 1980s, however, the organization of snowboarding competitions was chaotic. For example, two World Championships were simultaneously held in 1987, one shared between Livigno and St. Moritz, the other in Breckenridge, Colorado. However, recognizing the commercial opportunities in developing the sporting side of snowboarding, groups of sporting-inclined snowboarders and manufacturers formed the North American Snowboard Association (NASBA) and Snowboard European Association (SEA) later that year. Their goal was to work together to create a unified World Cup tour, similar to that of skiing. In 1988, devotees formed the United States of America Snowboarding Association (USASA) to standardize rules and organize events in the United States. Similar organizations emerged in snowboarding countries worldwide.

The institutionalization and commercialization of snowboarders in the early and mid-1990s angered many devotees. Some overtly resisted this

process. Jeff Galbriath, Senior Editor of *Snowboarder* magazine, recalls
one Professional Snowboard Tour of America (PSTA) event sponsored
by Body Glove (clothing) where top U.S. snowboarder Shaun Palmer
"hit the main sponsor guy in the face . . . with a hot dog"; Body Glove subsequently "pulled out": "culturally, none of the riders were prepared to
deal with contest structure" (cited in Howe, 1998, p. 56). For some, competitive snowboarding stood in symbolic juxtaposition to "soul boarding"
(Humphreys, 2003; Thorpe, 2007a). For example, in 1990, world champion U.S. snowboarder Craig Kelly retired at the peak of his career from
the competitive circuit because he believed that it was becoming too disciplined (see Chapter 5). Others, however, embraced the new opportunities to test their skills and to earn an income. Debates among
snowboarders over the institutionalization process precipitated social
divisions and fragmentation within the snowboarding culture.

industry growth

The convergence of several factors contributed to the growing number of
snowboarders during the late 1980s and 1990s; more ski resorts opened their
pistes to snowboarders, the mainstream media started reporting more frequently and favorably on snowboarding; snowboarding magazines (e.g.,
Absolutely Radical [1985] renamed *International Snowboarder Magazine*
six months later, *Transworld Snowboarding* [1987], *Snowboarder* [1988],
Blunt [1993]) and films (e.g., *The Western Front* [1988], *Totally Board*
[1989], *Snowboarders in Exile* [1990], *Critical Condition* [1991]) communicated the latest snowboarding tastes and styles to participants around the
world (Thorpe, 2006). Technological advances, economic growth, and further institutionalization, accompanied higher levels of participation.

By the mid-1990s, snowboarding had developed a cohesive industry
complete with its own media, international events and competitions, trade-
shows, fashions, and professional and amateur athletes. In 1995, the North
American snowboard retail industry was worth an estimated $750 million
(Randall, 1995). That same year more than 300 companies peddled
snowboard equipment, apparel, and accessories at the industry trade show,
compared with just 90 companies in 1993 (Randall, 1995). Burton
Snowboards, for example, grew "on average about 100% per year" during
this period (Burton Carpenter & Dumaine, 2002, p. 64) and in 1995,
employed 250 workers and was worth well over $100 million (Bailey,

1998). When Ride Snowboards became the first snowboard company to go public on the NASDAQ stock exchange in 1994, it sold all 500,000 shares in the first two weeks: It then released another 75,000. Within a month the shares had reached $28 each, six times the release price. Industry sources predicted that snowboard market sales would double to $1.5 billion at retail by the end of the 1990s (Randall, 1995).

The growth of the sport and industry attracted an influx of new companies, many of which had their roots elsewhere, in surfing (e.g., Billabong, Rip Curl), skateboarding (e.g., DC, Etnies, Airwalk), skiing (e.g., Rossignol, Soloman, Voikal), and athletics more generally (e.g., Nike, K2, Adidas-Saloman). These companies were very well financed and invested significant amounts of money in their marketing programs. They sponsored groups of elite boarders, and invested heavily in advertising, product design, and packaging. However, with the influx of new companies from outside the culture, perceptions of "cultural authenticity" became a central concern among core boarders. As the president of one mainstream company stated, "it's a difficult category. It's highly technical, and core snowboarders are loyal to core snowboard brands. They are not really open to main stream brands" (Dick Baker, cited in Deemer 2000). To core boarders—the most savvy of consumers—the "authenticity" of a snowboarding company was central to their consumption choices. In an increasingly competitive industry, it was not simply products but the corporate image itself that became essential. Snowboarding companies thus employed various strategies to create and re-create a culturally authentic corporate image (e.g., advertising in snowboarding magazines, sponsoring athletes and events, funding snowboarding videos) and target specific niche markets within the increasingly fragmented snowboarding culture (see Thorpe, 2011a).

"new school snowboarding": punk, hip-hop, skateboarding, and the jib movement

The influx of new participants during the 1990s caused divisions between insiders and newcomers, and various subgroups, within the snowboarding culture. Todd Richards (2003) recollects the emerging divisions during the early 1990s: "There were the experienced alpine snowboarders ... and there were the scrub skater guys ... who wanted to get as much air as possible, mimicking skating heroes of the day" (p. 64). By the end of the decade young core snowboarders rejected alpine snowboarding—a style that privileges speed and carving—which had been the most popular style in

A female "jibber" performs a backside boardslide on a rail. (Courtesy of Nikita Sportswear.)

the mid-1980s; they dismissed alpine riders as skiers on boards. One critic described alpine racers as wearing "skin-tight speed suits and helmets, and rid[ing] boards that hardly resemble anything you'd find on the racks at your local snowboard shop. They wear ski boots for crying out loud" (Berkley, 1998, cited in Heino, 2000, p. 183). New Zealand snowboarder Andrew Morrison defined an alpine racer as "someone . . . [who] carves, carves, carves and carves and carves," adding "I don't have much respect for those guys" (cited in Humphreys 1996, p. 17).

To distinguish themselves from skiers, alpine snowboarders, and the influx of new participants during this period, many young core boarders embraced hypermasculine tastes and styles from skateboarding, punk, and hip-hop cultures. The dominant style of participation during the early and mid-1990s was jibbing—a playful substyle of freestyle snowboarding that involves performing various skateboarding-inspired maneuvers on obstacles including trees, stumps, and rails. Jibbing held the dominant space in many of the new niche magazines and videos, such that the activity quickly gained popularity with snowboarders across North America and internationally.

According to Richards (2003), snowboarders were "soon jumping off anything and everything" such that "resorts began to think twice about where they put their picnic tables" (p. 126). Many young "hard core" snowboarders also subscribed to antiestablishment and do-it-yourself philosophies prevalent within some skateboarding and punk cultures at the time. Ben, an early snowboarder, recalls the anti-establishment mentality among jibbers as "ruining all the fixtures at resorts . . . running into skiers and telling them to screw off . . . " (cited in Anderson, 1999, p. 62). Jake Blattner recollects the do-it-yourself mentality prevalent during this period: "there were no boards being made for what we wanted to do . . . so we took matters into our own hands and cut the noses off our boards" (cited in Howe, 1998, p. 86). As jibbing gained popularity, equipment also changed—boards became shorter and bindings were set further apart to allow a wider stance. The hedonistic snowboarding lifestyle was also integral to the "jib movement." As an early snowboard photographer recalls: "it was all handrails and hip-hop. Everyone would stay out all night, sliding handrails or partying, and then sleep all day" (Markus Paulsen cited in Howe, 1998, p. 86).

Rebelling against the ski industry, young core male (and some female) snowboarders embodied elements of the masculine images of skateboarders, gangsters (e.g., baggy clothing, low riding pants with exposed boxer shorts, gold chains) and punks (e.g., Mohawks, body piercings, studded belts, brightly colored hair), and manipulated these into the stereotypical snowboarder style of early and mid-1990s. In addition, snowboarders often exhibited stoicism and strength by wearing clothing that offered no protection from the snow and cold temperatures. Holly, a participant in an early study, remembers snowboarders "wearing pants that sag down to their knees and flannels . . . covered in snow . . . they care more about the way they look than if they are freezing their butts off" (cited in Anderson, 1999, p. 63). According to Howe (1998), the celebration of the "aggressive" skateboarding-inspired tastes and styles (i.e., participation, clothing, language) during the early 1990s, helped snowboarding "break [sic] through the cool barrier": "No more neon . . . no more dorky ski stuff. . . . As the skate attitude and fashion spread, snowboarding became popular . . . capturing the youth of America" (p. 93).

snowboarding enters the mainstream

During the mid- and late 1990s, television agencies and corporate sponsors began to recognize the huge potential in snowboarding as a way to tap into the highly lucrative youth market. Mainstream companies quickly began appropriating the "cool" image of the snowboarder to sell products ranging from chewing gum to vehicles to both youth and mainstream markets. Snowboarding was one of many action, lifestyle or extreme sports (e.g., surfing, skateboarding, BMX, inline skating) that increasingly became controlled and defined by transnational media corporations like ESPN and NBC via mega-events such as the X Games and Gravity Games during this period (Booth & Thorpe, 2007; Thorpe, 2006; Wheaton, 2004, 2010). One cultural commentator recalls some of the tensions that emerged during the incorporation of snowboarding: "Around 1997 it all changed . . . you started seeing snowboard competitions on . . . major channels like NBC on Saturday afternoons. . . . [But] the media still hadn't figured out how to deal with it really . . . [It took some time before] ESPN found out they couldn't just take guys who covered football and stick them in a booth in front of the pipe and have them announce it on TV . . . " (Stepanek, no date, para. 4). But, as the comments from one early participant suggest, snowboarders were not passive in this process: "We all knew the sponsors and the media had no idea what the sport was about, but if dressing up like clowns and posing for MTV meant a few days of free-riding, most of us were in" (David Alden, cited in Howe, 1998, p. 56). In 1998, ESPN's different sport channels beamed the X Games to 198 countries in 21 languages (Rinehart, 2000). The incorporation of snowboarding into the X Games and 1998 Winter Olympics (see Chapter 4), video games including Xbox "Amped Freestyle" and Ubisoft "Shaun White Snowboarding," and blockbuster movies such as *OutCold* (2001) and *First Descent* (2005), helped further expose the sport to the mainstream, as well as contributing to the creation of the star system (Thorpe, 2006).

In contrast to earlier generations, most current professional snowboarders embrace commercial approaches or, in the more colorful words of Todd Richards (2003), are "milk[ing] it while it's lactating" (p. 178). Some professional snowboarders including Torah Bright, Gretchen Bleiler, Kelly Clark, Tara Dakides, Lindsey Jacobellis, Danny Kass, Hannah Teter, and Shaun White, are attracting major corporate sponsors including Target, Visa, Nike, Mountain Dew, Campbell's Soup, and Boost Mobile. Today, some professional snowboarders are earning seven-figure salaries from their prize monies, corporate sponsors, and snowboard sponsors. Despite the increasing professionalism at the elite level, residual traces of snowboarding's countercultural past remain. Many professional athletes continue to endorse "amateur-like" philosophies (Humphreys, 2003). For example, in an interview with *Rolling Stone* magazine, double Olympic half-pipe gold medalist Shaun White downplays the professionalism of snowboarding: "We are still the dirty ones in the bunch, the sketchy snowboard kids. I don't think I'd have it

Shaun White launches off a rail in the slopestyle event at the Winter X Games. (AP Photo/Nathan Bilow.)

any other way" (Edwards, 2006, p. 45). Of course, neither would the corporate sponsors who "profit from the commodification of snowboarding's perceived irresponsible and uncontrolled image" (Thorpe, 2007a, p. 291; also see Thorpe & Wheaton, 2011).

While a few professional snowboarders are earning multimillion dollar incomes, the majority of participants view money as merely a means to live the snowboarding lifestyle. Most jobs in the snowboarding industry (e.g., snowboard instructor, ski lift-operator, photographer, and journalist) pay subsistence wages. These jobs tend to be held by passionate snowboarders committed to the lifestyle rather than the financial rewards (Thorpe, 2007a, 2011; see also Wheaton, 2000). In the words of top snowboarding photographer Trevor Graves: "If you're shooting to maintain the lifestyle, it's worth it. That's all you can do with the time constraints anyway. It's not a huge cash-maker, like fashion or rock photography. It's really about living snowboarding" (cited in Howe, 1998, p. 107). After professional Canadian snowboarder Leanne Pelosi graduated from college she relocated to "Whistler to be a poor snowboarder while all [her] university friends were making cashola" (cited in Sherowski, January 2005, p. 168). In comparison to "sitting behind a desk working some white-collar job," she is "living [her] dream, meeting amazing people, and snowboarding year-round"; "My choice was definitely better ... I love it" she adds (cited in Sherowski, January 2005, p. 168).

contemporary snowboarding: growth and cultural fragmentation

The mainstream exposure of snowboarding during the late 1990s and 2000s significantly affected cultural demographics. The activity attracted participants from around the world, and from more diverse social classes and age groups. Snowboarding experienced a 160 percent growth in total participation between 1995 and 2007, and a 257 percent increase in frequent participation during this period (Action Sports, 2007). During the early 2000s, snowboarding was one of the fastest growing sports in the United States (Fastest Growing, 2005; Thorpe, 2007a). It was also esti-mated that more than 80 percent of children who practiced winter sports in the United States during the late 1990s had ridden a snowboard by their twelfth birthday (Meyers, 1996).

Approximately 97 percent of ski resorts in North America and Europe cur-rently welcome snowboarders. In March 2008, Taos, New Mexico opened its slopes to snowboarders after 55 years as a ski-only resort, and many boarders continue to actively campaign the three remaining "skier-only" resorts in the United States—Alta Ski Resort and Deer Valley in Utah, and Mad River Glen in Vermont. In December 2007, for example, Burton Snowboards launched the "Sabotage Stupidity Campaign" which encouraged snowboard-ers to "poach for freedom" as a protest against ski resorts that banned their participation; the company offered $5,000 for the best video documentation of "a successful poach job" of these resorts. Interestingly, it was shortly after the announcement of this campaign that Taos decided to allow snowboard-ers. In the United States, snowboarding is particularly popular in the Northeast, North Central, and Western states (Action Sports, 2007). According to one survey, 26.1 percent of California, Oregon, and Washington residents went snowboarding at least once in 2003 (Hard Numbers, 2005, p. 56). Similar trends occurred elsewhere. In Japan, for example, the number of snowboarders grew 87 percent between 1977 and 2000. Today, snowboarders account for 35 to 40 percent of business at Japanese resorts nationwide, and in some places this figure is closer to 90 percent (Karan, 2005).

Snowboarding cultural demographics have changed considerably over the past two decades, but it should be noted that in 2005, more than 75 percent of snowboarders were 24 or younger (NGSA 2005), and 42 percent of snowboarders come from households of more than $75,000 (Action Sports, 2007). In 2001, approximately only 11 percent of U.S. snowboarders were members of racial/ethnic minority groups (NGSA 2001). However, some cultural commentators believe snowboarding has "grayed": in 2010, approximately 60 percent of U.S. snowboarders were over 25 years old and almost 34 percent were over 32 years old (Lewis, 2010a). The female snowboard demographic has also more than doubled in the past decade. In 1994, only 20 percent of snowboarders in the United States were female; by 2003, women made up approximately 34.3 percent (NGSA 2005). As well as targeting the aging snowboarding demographic and the female niche market, many U.S. snowboard companies and ski resorts are also employing an array of strategies to attract more Hispanic customers and patrons (see Lewis, 2010b; Bang, Brooks, Alberto Delaroca & Jiménez, 2010). According to Bob Holme, youth marketing director, "the urban (multicultural) market is a huge untapped resource for resorts. There is a lot of opportunity to reach into that market and give access to get on the mountain and have a ski or snowboard experience" (cited in Bang et al. 2010, p. 8). Certified AASI (Association of American Snowboard Instructors) Latino snowboard instructor Gaby Hernandez sees more Hispanic people "getting involved. People I knew (Hispanics) that did not want to know anything about snowboarding are calling me and asking if I can teach them ... " (cited in Bang et al., 2010, p. 13).

The rapid popularization and commercialization of snowboarding during the late 1990s and early 2000s fuelled cultural divisions within the pastime. Cody Dresser, managing editor of *Transworld Snowboarding*, believes that snowboarding has "outgrown" all notions of a homogenous culture (p. 28). Today, participants range from three to 70 years old, from novice and weekend warrior, to core participant, to professional athlete. Snowboarders demonstrate various levels of physical prowess and cultural commitment, and engage in an array of styles (e.g., alpine, freestyle, big-mountain, jibbing, and snow-skating) in various snowy spaces (e.g., on and off-piste at ski resorts, half-pipes, terrain parks, backcountry, and urban environments). "Core participants" include males and females whose commitment to the practice of snowboarding is such that they organize their lives around snow conditions and seasonal patterns (Thorpe, 2010a; see also Wheaton, 2000). In contrast to core boarders, snowboarders who are less committed—including male and female novices, poseurs, or weekend warriors—have lower cultural status. Rather than demonstrating commitment via participation, poseurs consciously display name-brand clothing and equipment. Clothing plays an important part in constructing a distinctive snowboarding identity, but participants are unable to buy their way into the core of the culture. Pamela, an early snowboarder, captures the emerging tensions between groups of boarders during this period:

> When I started snowboarding it wasn't cool. I had a hard time with all these newcomers who were just doing it because it was cool and I remember thinking, "you fake-asses, what are you doing, this is *our* sport." Some people would just turn up for a season and be "oh yeah, I'm a snowboarder." There's something quite fake about it. That element has grown in snowboarding, and that is something that I find quite unsavory really. (interview, 2005)

Another core snowboarder, Moriah, proclaims that "snowboarding is something that comes from the heart, something that you want to do for yourself, not something you're doing to *be cool*" (interview, 2005). These comments allude to a dominant mode of thinking among "core" boarders, that is, that the "core" snowboarder who demonstrates commitment to the activity itself, not just the snowboarding style, is the only "authentic" cultural identity (see Thorpe, 2011a; Wheaton, 2000).

As the snowboarding culture has become increasingly divided, the relations between skiers and snowboarders have also shifted. In most North American and Australasian resorts, and some European slopes, style of participation (i.e., freestyle, big mountain, alpine) is the primary divide with skiers and snowboarders increasingly sharing terrain as well as styles of talk and dress, training methods, and lifestyles. Young skiers now draw inspiration from the styles of participation, technologies, jargon, and fashion of freestyle snowboarders. "Snowboarding has gained so much respect from the ski world," says U.S. core boarder and ski and snowboard cinematographer Zane, which he attributes to U.S. success in the Olympics:

> Now kids are trying to emulate snowboarding on skis. There has been a rebirth in skiing with freestyle, and skiers are dressing like snowboarders, and snowboarders and skiers are hanging out

together. I think it's a good thing, as long as skiers remember that they hated snowboarders for a long time. (interview, November 2005)

A snowboarding journalist also notes the long-standing "feud" between skiers and snowboarders "fading":

The boom in freestyle snowboarding attracted more skiers to the terrain park areas. Skiers began sliding rails, riding switch and performing huge aerial spins, which served to attract new, young recruits to the skiing crowd. Skiing, like boarding, was once again super cool and a symbiotic relationship was born, with both sports influencing, inspiring, and benefiting from one another. (Baldwin, 2006b, para. 16)

Further illustrating this trend, the 2008 National Sporting Goods Association report showed that approximately 20 percent of snowboarders also ski, and 18 percent of skiers also snowboard (Facts About, 2009). Although these shifts are occurring predominantly at the core level of the snow culture—that is, among the most committed, and typically younger, snowboarders and skiers—this trend is filtering into the broader alpine snow culture, and relations between the majority of skiers and snowboarders are becoming more amicable at many resorts. It is important to note, however, that this is not the case in all locations; the divisions between skiers and snowboarders are still very much in existence in some local, regional, and national contexts where skiing has had a particularly long tradition of dominance (e.g., some regions in France, Italy, and Switzerland).

the snowboarding industry

While some snowboarders lament the divisions within their culture, members of the snowboarding industry welcome growing participation rates and cultural fragmentation as vital for economic growth. "Obviously, for self-interested business reasons I think the more people who snowboard the better," proclaims Jake Burton (cited in Hagerman 2002, 21). Ironically, the commercialization process is directly implicated in the fragmentation of the snowboarding, a process that produces new niche markets necessary for the growth of the snowboarding industry.

Today, hundreds of companies provide snowboarding-specific equipment and clothing in an abundance of styles. The contemporary snowboarding market consists of an array of consumer groups (e.g., children, youth, women, older boarders, freeriders, backcountry, jibbers, alpine). This market fragmentation is evident in the diversification of the snowboarding industry. Many small companies specialize in producing boards (e.g., GNU, Option, Morrow), boots (e.g., 32, Osiris), clothing (e.g., NFA, Bonfire, Dub, 686, Sessions, Holden), women's clothing (e.g., Betty Rides, Nikita) or accessories (e.g., Grenade Gloves, Dragon goggles and sunglasses) targeted at specific market segments. Some of these niche companies are the creations of committed snowboarders attempting to create a career within the snowboarding industry and professional snowboarders seeking to capitalize on their cultural status (e.g., Air-Blaster, Grenade), whereas other companies (e.g., Burton, DC, Quiksilver) target every segment of the snowboarding market by offering various lines of equipment, clothing, and accessories often under the guise of a confederation of small specialist firms. For example, Burton Snowboards and its subsidiary companies—R.E.D. (helmets and body protection equipment), Gravis Footwear (shoes and bags), Anon Optics (goggles), Analog Clothing (casual apparel line), Forum Snowboards (snowboard equipment, clothing, and accessories), Special Blend (snowboard clothing and accessories), Four Square (snowboard clothing), and Jeenyus (snowboard equipment and clothing)—currently controls approximately 40 to 70 percent of the multibillion dollar global market, depending on the specific category of goods (Brooks, 2010) (see Chapter 5).

the snowboarding media

The media is implemented in the fragmentation of the snowboarding culture. A plethora of *mass media* (e.g., television, newspapers, and mainstream magazines), *niche media* (e.g., sport-specific magazines, films, and Web sites), and *micromedia* (e.g., flyers, posters, homemade videos, and online zines), report on snowboarding (Thorpe, 2008a). Attempting to cater for different audiences, these media employ an array of representational styles. Whereas the mass media tends to be produced by non-snowboarding journalists for a mass audience, often with little or no knowledge of snowboarding, niche snowboarding media are typically created by journalists, editors, photographers, and filmmakers who are (or were) active and highly proficient snowboarders. Niche media, including magazines (e.g., *Transworld Snowboarding, Snowboarder* magazine), films (e.g., *Resistance, Commitment*), and Web sites (e.g., www.snowboard.com), are instrumental to committed snowboarders' cultural identity construction

(Thorpe, 2008a). For snowboarding historian Susanna Howe (1998), photographers and filmmakers are "the real image makers" because their work "creates the dream that is snowboarding" and "sells lifestyle" (p. 107). Similarly, Doug Palladini, publisher of *Snowboarder* magazine, proclaims that snowboarding magazines are "not just something you pick up at the airport"; to core participants they are "the bible" (cited in Howe, 1998, p. 104).

Though the niche media resides closest to the culture, commercial processes also complicate their production (see Thorpe, 2011a). In 2004, *Transworld Snowboarding* had a circulation of 207,000 per issue, featured a total of 1,333 pages of advertisements, and generated $21.9 million in revenue, up from $14.9 million in 2000 (Stableford, 2005, para.7). In 2007, *Transworld Snowboarding* magazine had an annual print circulation of 1,380,000, and the magazine Web site hosted more than 2,304,000 visits; 84 percent of *Transworld Snowboarding* viewers are male with a median age of 19 years (Transworld Media, 2007). *Snowboarder* magazine, also produced in California and distributed internationally, has the second largest circulation (approximately 890,000 per year). In contrast, smaller local niche magazines such as Spain's *Snow Planet*, Sweden's *Transition*, and the UK-based *White Lines*, have been described as "labors of love . . . sustained only by the passion of the staff and the avidity with which their generally low readership devours each issue" (Barr, Moran & Wallace, 2006, p. 15).

In his autobiography, *Off the Chain*, early professional Canadian snowboarder Ross Rebagliati (2009) reflects upon the cultural significance of videos during the late 1980s and 1990s:

> Snowboard videos were always playing in [my] house [in Whistler]. The early videos were like primers: how to board, how to look, how to be. The design was gritty and the soundtrack raucous; this rawness, of course, was in keeping with the snowboard ethic. The fact that these videos were so difficult to come by made them even cooler; watching them felt like being a member of an exclusive little club. [We would] watch the same videos over, and over, and over. . . . We even made our own videos, and those were in rotation at the chalet as well. (p. 46)

More recently, snowboarding author Rob Reed (2005) described snowboarding films as "windows into the culture of snowboarding . . . Through these films viewers can connect with the best [snowboarding] personalities,

Cover of *Transworld Snowboarding* magazine. (Courtesy of Bonnier Corporation.)

styles, destinations, and tricks" (p. 114). Niche snowboarding Web sites also offer important spaces for sharing information and communicating across local and national cultures. For example, the world's largest snowboarding Web site, www.snowboard.com hosts 550,000 registered members—313,000 from the United States, 98,000 from Canada, and 144,000 from other countries around the world (Media Man, no date).

Coverage in the niche media, particularly magazines and films, plays an important role in both the financial and social reward systems within the snowboarding industry and culture. As Richards (2003) explains, he wanted to be in these magazines and videos because it paid well, "but it was more about gaining respect from my friends. If a rider pulled a 900 [degree rotation] and nobody saw it, he didn't want to run up and say, 'Did you see that?' . . . The videos did the talking for him. The name of the game was acting like you didn't give a shit, but I think everyone wants to get noticed when they pull off something big. Videos let us maintain that cool facade with minimal outward conceit" (p. 156). Niche snowboarding films and magazines not only communicate snowboarding knowledge across groups of snowboarders in different regions and nations, they also contribute to the construction and maintenance of the cultural hierarchy via the allocation of respect and status.

Some snowboarders also create low circulating *micromedia* (e.g., flyers, homemade snowboarding videos) that target specific groups within the snowboarding culture. Micromedia play an important role in organizing the culture at local and regional levels (e.g., posters for upcoming events). Fanzines and some Web sites also give vent to unruly voices, local slang, moaning, ranting, and swearing (Thornton, 1996). Indeed, it is here that some participants express their angst at other mass or niche forms of snowboarding media. "Why when I pick up a snowboarding magazine must I be confronted with something on about the same maturity level as a frat party," rails Chris in an online zine; "everything is about who is cool and who isn't, we are right you are wrong" (www.yobeat.com, no date). Snowboarders are also employing an array of new social media, such as Twitter, Facebook, YouTube, and iPhone, to share information and images, organize events, and discuss and debate issues ranging from the quality of the half-pipe at a local resort to the effects of global warming on the snowboarding industry.

In sum, the story of snowboarding began a little over four decades ago with a new piece of equipment that appealed to the hedonistic desires of a new generation. Snowboarding developed in a "historically unique conjuncture" of transnational mass communications, corporate sponsors, entertainment industries, and a growing affluent and young population, such that it has "diffused around the world at a phenomenal rate" (Booth and Thorpe, 2007, p. 187). While many early participants regret the changes that have occurred as a result of the processes of commercialization and institutionalization, contemporary snowboarders typically recognize major corporate sponsorships and mass mediated events (e.g., Olympics, X Games) as integral parts of the sport in the twenty-first century. Many current boarders accept that "the snowboarding industry sold itself out to the corporate world" (Question, 2006, para. 2), however, this does not necessarily diminish the enjoyment they derive from participation. Indeed, many acknowledge the benefits offered to athletes and participants in this hypercommercial context (e.g., opportunities for athletes to travel, well organized and widely publicized events, more affordable

The next generation of snowboarders, seven-year-old George Thorpe performs a jump at Snow Park, New Zealand. (Courtesy of Geoff Thorpe.)

equipment, etc). Today, styles of participation and competition continue to evolve as boarders create new and more technical maneuvers, and ski resorts and snowboarding companies invest heavily in the equipment and personnel necessary to cater to the diverse demands of participants. In this context, snowboarding technologies and the skills of professional athletes continue to develop apace, such that every winter we are witnessing snowboarders going "faster, stronger, and higher."

3.   science

the act of standing on a snowboard and sliding down a snowy slope involves balance and coordination, as well as a tacit understanding of some of the basic laws of physics. The Three Laws of Motion developed by Sir Isaac Newton (1643–1727), for example, underpin all snowboarding movement. The first Law of Motion, the Law of Inertia, states that whatever an object is already doing, whether at rest or in motion, it will continue to do so, unless acted upon by some force. One of the key forces acting upon a stationary snowboarder at the top of a slope is gravity (G) which works in two main directions. The normal force (N) is perpendicular (at right angles) to the plane of the slope and works by pushing the snowboarder directly into the mountain. The second directional force (F) is parallel to the slope of the mountain and is responsible for accelerating the snowboarder down the slope. According to the Third Law of Motion, or the law of Action and Reaction, whenever one body exerts a force on a second body, the second body exerts an equal and opposite force on the first. The normal force (N) pushing the snowboarder into the mountain is then cancelled out by the "reaction force" of the snowboarder's body against the mountain. Thus, it is the F force which pushes the snowboarder down the mountain, and as the slope gets steeper the normal component of gravity gets smaller and component F increases. The Second Law of Motion, which states that the force on an object is equal to the mass of the object multiplied by its acceleration, helps explain why the acceleration of a snowboarder down the mountain increases as the force F gets larger on a steeper slope.

As well as the force of gravity, frictional forces are also important in understanding the basic laws of motion in snowboarding. Sliding friction is caused by the interaction between the molecules in the snow and those on the base of the snowboard. The sliding friction in snowboarding is typically very small but, combined with pressure exerted by the board, is sufficient to melt a tiny layer of snow. Lubricated by the water in the melted snow, the snowboard is able to slide easily down a snowy surface. Snowboarders wax their boards to minimize these restrictive forces of friction. The frictional force between the base of the board and the snow is proportional to the normal force (N) and hence, decreases as the mountain slope becomes steeper. But as the snowboarder travels down the slope and gains momentum, his or her body must also push all of the molecules in the air aside, which results in a transfer of momentum. The faster the snowboarder travels, the greater the air resistance acting on the body and thus, the rate of transfer of momentum (i.e., the larger the frictional force or drag). A snowboarder reaches his or her top speed or "terminal velocity," when all of the forces involved balance out and there is zero net force. Of course, the quality of the snowboard, the type of wax used on the base of the board, the water content in the snow, the weight or mass of the snowboarder, and aerodynamics are all part of the equation.

Many snowboarders develop an embodied understanding of the basic physics and biomechanics of the sport through the (often painful) process of trial and error. Others consciously draw upon these principles to further develop their skills and technique. During the mid-1980s, for example, early professional snowboarder and engineering student, Craig Kelly, was among the first to adopt a scientifically informed analytic approach to the sport: "When I train I'm very analytical, and I constantly think about working a certain muscle group or perfecting a particular technique. If my riding doesn't feel technically perfect, exactly the way it should, I concentrate completely on the problem. If I chatter out on a heel turn, I think, 'why did that happen?' Okay, next time put more weight on your rear foot" (cited in Blehm, 2008, para. 17). Developing a highly technical and efficient style of snowboarding, Kelly went on to win four World Championships. He was one of the first to adopt such an analytical approach to performance, but today most snowboard instruction and coaching courses include physics- and biomechanics-informed movement analysis components. Educated instructors and coaches around the world are using this knowledge to inform their teaching at levels ranging from beginners to Olympic athletes. Moreover, as snowboarding becomes increasingly professional and competitive, athletes and coaches attend more closely to the physics and biomechanics of the sport to develop better training techniques for high performance. This chapter examines three scientific aspects of extreme snowboarding: (1) the physics of freestyle snowboarding, (2) avalanche science, as well as (3) some of the socio-psychological aspects of extreme snowboarding.

the physics of freestyle snowboarding

In contrast to the forces acting upon a snowboarder when sliding down a snowy slope, the mechanics of freestyle snowboarding in half-pipes or on purposefully built jumps are considerably more complex (Krüger & Edelmann-Nusser, 2009; O'Shea, 2004). Dynamic balance is central to freestyle performances in which athletes use the laws of gravity to build speed, gain height, and keep their balance, while performing highly technical aerial maneuvers. National Science Foundation (NSF) senior physicist Paul Doherty describes the gravitational forces and kinetic energy involved in elite half-pipe performances:

> As gravity pulls the snowboarder down the half-pipe, they gain speed. At the same time, they are being pushed against the sides by contact forces. Snowboarders push back against the G-forces and build speed by pumping their legs up and down. By standing up against the extra forces in the curve, snowboarders add to their kinetic energy— the energy of motion. It gives them the speed they need to get air off the rim. The faster they go, the higher they go. The higher they go . . . the better tricks they can do. (cited in Science of Snowboarding, 2010, para. 5)

Double Olympic gold medalist Shaun White confirms "you actually feel G-forces when you're going up [the wall of the half-pipe], it's sucking you against the wall" (cited in Science of Snowboarding, 2010, para. 6).

Every snowboarder standing at the top of a half-pipe possesses potential energy. However, it is the snowboarder's ability to convert this potential energy into kinetic energy that affects how much speed and height he or she can gain as he or she travels up and out of the walls of the half-pipe. Competitive male and female half-pipe riders are often of similar height and weight, and thus many possess equal (or similar) amounts of potential energy as they stand at the top of the half-pipe. But snowboarders vary considerably in their ability to effectively convert this potential energy into kinetic energy. Whereas a committed recreational half-pipe rider may be practicing maneuvers three or four feet above the half-pipe walls, the top female athletes have developed skills and techniques to reach heights of 6–15 feet, while the elite male athletes utilize kinetic energy to soar up to 20 feet.

The height of the half-pipe is also an important factor in achieving maximum speed. The transition from half-pipes with 18-foot walls to super-pipes with 22-foot walls, as the standard for international half-pipe competitions, gave way to much more spectacular performances. The additional height of the super-pipe walls enables athletes to store more gravitational energy at the top of the wall, and thus gain more potential energy and kinetic energy (Science of snowboarding in the Olympics, 2010). Shaun White reached a record breaking height of 23 feet on the immaculately shaped super-pipe at the 2010 Winter X Games. With larger half-pipes facilitating increased speed and airtime, snowboarders are also able to perform ever more technical maneuvers such as the Double McTwist 1260 (degree rotation) (also known as the Tomahawk) and the Double Cork 1080 (degree rotation). Describing the laws of physics behind such performances, Doherty explains:

> As a snowboarder moves down the side of the pipe, potential energy gets converted into kinetic energy. The kinetic energy of an object is the energy it possesses because of its motion. When they jump, the kinetic energy is converted back into potential energy. Gravity slows them down in the air, so they lose kinetic energy. At the height of their jump, the snowboarders are at the maximum potential energy. (cited in Science of snowboarding in the Olympics, 2010, para. 8)

The Olympic half-pipe is scored by seven judges with one overall impression score, thus a medal winning performance requires the athlete to consistently and effectively transfer potential energy into kinetic energy on each of his or her five or six "hits" along the walls of the half-pipe. If a snowboarder becomes unstable or falls upon landing any of his or her jumps, he or she will lose kinetic energy and thus critical speed and amplitude on his or her subsequent jumps, and his or her final score will reflect this error.

Performing aerial maneuvers on jumps in terrain parks, in the backcountry, or big air events, also involves complex bio-mechanical processes. A snowboard jump typically comprises various phases—the in-run, flight (or aerial) phase, preparation for landing, and landing—each of which contributes to the length, height, and overall performance of the jump. In general, a freestyle snowboarding jump includes both ballistic and aerodynamic factors. The ballistic factors include release velocity (speed) and release position (body positioning) from the jump takeoff; whereas aerodynamic factors during takeoff and flight influence the gliding properties of the jumper (e.g., velocity, balance, and control of snowboarder in-flight) (Zatsiorsky, Komi & Virmavirta, 2000). According to sport biome-chanist Fred Yeadon (2000), "in the aerial phases of most sporting move-ments . . . the path of the mass center follows a parabola that is determined by the position and velocity of the mass centre at take-off" (p. 273). The takeoff phase is critical for performing a successful snowboard jump as it is here that the athlete is able to increase the vertical lift and simultaneously maintain, or even increase, the horizontal release velocity via the effective co-ordination of specific actions (e.g., performing an "ollie" or "popping" off the ramp by explosively jumping the front and back leg in quick succes-sion) (Zatsiorsky et al., 2000). However, in comparison to sports such as gymnastics, the flight path of the snowboarder is not solely determined by the velocity and body position of athlete at take-off; typically performed in the alpine environment (rather than indoor environments), air resistance also produces drag and lift force during the in-flight phase of the snowboard jump. But, as with gymnastics, the amount and type of rotation of the snow-boarder is "largely under the control of the athlete" (Yeadon, 2000, p. 282).

In freestyle snowboarding, the somersault (e.g., a back-flip) and/or rotation (e.g., 180, 360, 540, 720, 900, 1080 degree spin) is initiated during the take-off phase, while twist rotations (e.g., a "method" grab) may be initiated during takeoff or during the aerial phase by means of asymmetrical arm or hip movements. As Yeadon (2000) explains in rela-tion to acrobatic aerial movements more generally, for simple maneuvers in which the body rotates around a single axis, the angular momentum is the product of the inertia and angular velocity at takeoff. In preparation for a rotational maneuver, a skilled snowboarder will develop rotational force by twisting his or her upper body in the opposite direction of the spin just before take-off, and then "snapping" into the spin upon take-off. Employing highly technical movement sensors and computer graphics to explain some of the scientific principles involved in Shaun White's "Double Cork" half-pipe maneuver, a report produced by the U.S. National Science Foundation focused on "science of the Winter Olympic Games" explained: "The trick begins 9 feet below the lip. In 266 millisec-onds his upper body rotates around his spine. Like a hockey player winds up for a snap shot, Shaun's twist spring-loads the board. As he launches, the board unwinds at an angular velocity of 540 degrees per second" (Science of snowboarding in the Olympics, 2010).

A freestyle snowboarder performing a spin maneuver on a jump or in the half-pipe develops rotational momentum, which is the result of his or her rotational inertia multiplied by rotational velocity. Snowboarders often intuitively control or conserve rotational momentum by moving mass away from or closer to the center of mass. Many snowboarders extend their arms during the run-in phase, and then bend their knees upon take-off, often reaching down to grab their board. In so doing, they are bringing their mass (which includes their snowboard) closer to their center of rotation, which reduces the moment of inertia about the twist axis and increases the speed of rotation; the grab also helps stabilize the snowboarder during the flight phase. The rate of rotation increases when the moment of inertia is decreased (e.g., arms and/or legs are brought closer to the center of mass), and the spin speed decreases when the moment of inertia is increased (e.g., arms and/or legs are extended away from the center of mass). By flexing and extending joints (e.g., hips, knees, shoulders) at appropriate times during the jump, the snowboarder can speed up or slow down his or her rotation. As Yeadon (2000) explains in relation to aerial movements in gymnastics, "asymmetrical arm movements may be used to stop or slow the twist/spin in a twisting somersault, or prevent the build-up of twist in a non-twisting somersault. The control of the twist in this way is possible using feedback via the inner ear balance mechanisms" (p. 282). Similar principles apply in freestyle snowboarding. Among highly skilled snowboarders these corrective movements are often very small. However, if the build-up of twist is corrected somewhat late, a larger arm asymmetry may be required. Excessive corrective arm movements (e.g., "rolling down the windows") typically identify less experienced freestyle snowboarders as they attempt to counteract excessive or unintentional rotational or twisting forces.

Snowboarding maneuvers involving rotations and/or twists about more than one bodily axis are more biomechanically complex, yet the same principle of angular momentum conservation governs these motions (Yeadon, 1993, 2000). In an analysis of Shaun White's infamous "Double Cork" maneuver, an *ESPN* report describes the "rapid spatial reorientation" involved in performing maneuvers with rotations over multiple axes: "...360 degrees around his x axis overlaps with a spin around his y axis, into another 360 around his x axis ... and this all goes down in just 1.8 seconds" (Brenkus, 2010). The report also describes the risks involved in such highly technical inverted aerial maneuvers:

Shaun spends 44 percent of the flight looking up. In other words, for almost half the trick his frame of reference is skewed, and the margin

A snowboarder trying to control G-forces and rotational momentum while competing in the quarter-pipe event at the 2009 U.S. Open in Stratton, Vermont. (AP
Photo/Nancy Palmieri.)

for error is tiny. If Shaun's launch is too vertical, he risks hitting the
deck. Launching back away from the wall creates more flight time,
which means more time to finish the trick, but every foot away from the
wall increases freefall. For example, only two feet out [from the wall
during flight] means another five feet down the wall [upon landing] with
a potential impact of 11,000 pounds of force. Shaun can still land the
trick, but the further the launch from the lip the higher the potential
forces of impact. (Brenkus, 2010)

Clearly, understanding the forces acting on a snowboarder during training
and competition are highly valuable for developing effective technique,
which not only improves performance, but also can help reduce the risk
of injury.

Building facilities that enable professional freestyle snowboarders to perform more technical maneuvers with greater speed and amplitude also
require careful calculations. For example, the 10 meter (32.8 feet) high
quarter-pipe jump built specifically for the 2007 Oakley Arctic Challenge
held in Oslo, Norway, was "designed using groundbreaking computer planning software to help eliminate G-force exposure and make the ride as

The snowboarding LG Big Air World Cup was a key event at the 2010 Relentless Freeze Festival in London, England. Standing over 32 meters high and 100 meters long, with over 550 tons of real snow used, the jump offered athletes the opportunity to perform an array of spectacular maneuvers for an estimated 20,000 spectators. (Courtesy of Holly Thorpe.)

smooth as possible . . . a huge drop-in ramp at the top of the in-run was [also] built on top of the natural slope profile to provide riders with enough speed to showcase their creative streaks, and attempt to quell Heikki Sorsa's (FIN) still unbeaten 2001 World Record, 9.3m air" (Oakley Arctic, 2007, para. 2). The following year, professional Norwegian snowboarder and event founder Terje Haakonson broke Sorsa's record performing a 360 degree rotation 32 feet above the quarter-pipe (Terje Breaks, 2008, para. 1). According to Matty Swanson, marketing manager for Oakley, the design and construction of this jump was based on highly scientific calculations: "by studying the science of transition, Norwegian rocket scientists helped us determine the speed, G forces and transition needed for a rider to break the current world record" (Terje Breaks, 2008, para. 3). As professional athletes continue to push the boundaries of what is perceived as humanly possible on a snowboard, the scientific dimensions of both the snowboarding body and mind, as well as equipment, technologies, and facilities, are garnering more attention and funding.

The 2011 Big Air Snowboard FIS World Championships were held on a specially designed jump of enormous proportions in an indoor arena in Barcelona, Spain. (AP Photo/Manu Fernandez.)

snow science: understanding avalanches

Snowboarders enter an uncontrolled environment when they travel beyond a ski resort's boundaries or into the backcountry. In comparison to snowboarding at a ski-resort where trained professionals carefully manage the slopes, backcountry users must take individual responsibility for identifying, avoiding, or negotiating an array of natural hazards including crevasses, buried rocks, cliffs, and avalanches. Thus, for snowboarders entering the backcountry, knowledge of snow science, and particularly the causes of avalanches, is invaluable. According to Dale Atkins (2010), an avalanche researcher and educator based in Colorado, "staying alive in avalanche terrain not only involves learning about avalanches but also traveling with experienced and practiced companions, carrying rescue equipment and knowing how to use it, obeying ski area signs and warnings, being flexible about when and where to go, and lastly, being able to say 'not today'" (p. 2). A particularly vocal advocate for backcountry education among snowboarders, U.S. snowboard legend Jeremy Jones explains: "learning how to read the mountains is a never-ending quest. You will never know it all but you owe it to yourself, and your riding partners, to keep learning and listening" (Jones, 2009, para. 1).

Simply, an avalanche is a mass of snow sliding down a mountainside. Avalanches range from small slides fracturing less than 30 centimeters deep with a width of 20–30 meters and traveling at 50 km/hour, to large slides fracturing 2–3 meters or deeper with a width of 1,000 meters or more, and traveling at speeds up to (and sometimes greater than) 150 km/hour (Atkins, 2010). Avalanche-related fatalities and incidents involving recreational snowboarders and skiers often garner extensive media coverage, yet avalanches are by no means recent phenomena. Avalanches have been claiming lives of those who travel or live in mountainous regions for thousands of years (Davies, 2009). Records suggest that in 218 BC, the Carthagian military commander and tactician Hannibal Barca lost an estimated 18,000 men (as well as many horses and elephants) as a result of avalanches while crossing the Alps to battle the Roman army. During World War I, thousands of Italian and Austrian troops were killed by avalanches as they fought in the mountain passes between 1915 and 1918. Avalanches were often used as weapons with soldiers bombing snowfields above enemy troops to start snow-slides. According to one Austrian officer, "the mountains in winter are more dangerous than the Italians" (cited in "Soldiers Perish," no date, para. 2). On May 31, 1970, a large earthquake in Peru loosened millions of tons of icy snow from the high slopes of Nevado de Huascarian to produce one of the "worst avalanches in history." Tumbling into lakes and reservoirs, the ice fall caused lakes to overflow sending a wave of mud, ice, debris, and rocks 10 miles down the valley burying the city of Yungay and its 20,000 inhabitants under 100 million cubic yards of mud and rubble; only 92 survived. In 1990, a 7.7 scale earthquake in Iran caused an avalanche that buried many villages, and ultimately claimed an estimated 50,000 lives.

Avalanche fatalities of recreational skiers and snowboarders are small in comparison to such events with a long-term average of 15 deaths per winter. Although the numbers of incidents seems to be growing. The winter of 2003 was one of the deadliest recorded for recreational mountain users in Western Canada with 29 avalanche fatalities (Jamieson & Geldsetzer, 1996). In the French Alps, 55 avalanche-related fatalities were recorded during the 2005–2006 winter, making this the highest number since the 1970s. The increasing number of avalanche fatalities is commonly attributed to the growing "powder fever" among recreational snowboarders and skiers. A long-time backcountry snowboarder, instructor, and Chamonix resident, Neil McNab, says that "major developments in equipment are

An avalanche crashes through a forest near a Swiss ski resort in the southern Swiss Alps, Switzerland, in February 1999. (AP Photo/Fabrice Coffrini.)

making it easier for people to ride and ski off-piste. So, what was once deemed 'the backcountry' is now becoming 'the norm.' As the boundaries are pushed further and further out each year, the potential for dangerous situations to arise obviously increases" (cited in Davies, 2009 para. 16). Similarly, Adkins (2010) notes that, today "anyone who is slightly athletic can easily find himself or herself in avalanche terrain," such that avalanche accidents are increasingly occurring "near ski areas when someone ventures out-of-bounds in search of powder snow and untracked slopes" (p. 3).

Understanding the risk of an avalanche on a particular slope requires consideration of at least three factors—(1) the snowpack, (2) the terrain, and (3) the weather (McClung & Schaerer, 2006)—popularly known as the "Avalanche Triangle." The snowpack consists of several layers caused by the various snowfalls and weather patterns throughout the season; the strength of the bonding between these layers is a critical factor for avalanches. The type of snow crystals in the snowpack directly affects the bonding between layers. Snow crystals come in an array of shapes including the well-known six-sided symmetrical shape, hexagonal plates, columns, and needles. The shape of the snow crystal depends on the air temperature and saturation, and will change throughout the season with new weather patterns or snowfall. Weather changes can either strengthen or weaken bonds, thus resulting in internal snowpack changes, or "meta-morphism." The temperature difference between the surface and base of the snowpack can also have a strong metamorphous effect (What causes avalanches, 2000; McClung & Schaerer, 2006).

To gain an understanding of the different layers that exist in the snow-pack on a particular slope and determine the strength of the bonding between these layers, educated backcountry snowboarders often dig a cross-sectional trench across a suspect slope and then attempt to detect strong and weak layers. In so doing, they will pay particular attention to the presence of loose, sugary snow called "depth hoar" known to cause a very unstable snowpack. Importantly, findings from one snow pit do not translate to other slopes which may have been affected differently by weather (e.g., wind, sun, temperature) and snowfalls. A spokeswoman for the Swiss Federal Institute for Snow and Avalanche Research, Birgit Ottmer, explains the problems with relying too heavily on snow profiling: "In the past, back-country snow users were told to carry out snow profiles and then rely on them for working out whether the conditions are safe or not. But we now know that relying solely on snow profiles can be dan-gerous [because] it's just focused on one spot. A few meters away, the profile could be different—there can be multiple microclimates in one small area" (cited in Davies, 2009, para. 14). Similarly, Karl Birkeland, an avalanche scientist with the U.S. Department of Agriculture Forest Service National Avalanche Center in Montana, concurs: "users must realize that stability tests [are] just one piece of the puzzle for avalanche prediction" (cited in Davies, 2009, para. 14).

The location and gradient of a slope are also key factors in estimating the likelihood of an avalanche. Backcountry enthusiasts are advised to be par-ticularly cautious of slopes on the leeward (protected) side of a mountain because they often receive a lot of wind-deposited snow and thus, may be very unstable. While large avalanches have been recorded on slopes with inclines ranging from 25 to 60 degrees, approximately 90 percent of avalanches release on slopes with gradients of between 30 and 45 degrees (Adkins, 2010). Avalanche-scientists advise that steep slopes, particularly those over 38 degrees, are the most dangerous; 38 degrees is the "angle of repose—the steepest angle a granular substance can maintain without col-lapsing under the pull of gravity. And since snow is a granular substance, its target angle is 38 degrees" (Brodit, 2009, para. 4). While avalanches typ-ically begin on steep slopes, low angled slopes are not without risk; weather and snowpack must also be considered in calculating the threat of an avalanche on a particular slope. Many backcountry-users measure the slope angle with an inclinometer, others "eye ball" the slope by dangling a ski pole by the strap and estimating the angle (Brodit, 2009; What Causes, 2000). As well as slope gradient, the ground cover underneath the snowpack also affects the likelihood of a slide; large boulders, trees, and bushes may help to anchor the snow to the mountain (What causes avalanches, 2000)

Meteorological factors are another key determinant in calculating avalanche risk (McClung & Schaerer, 2006). Backcountry-users are advised to pay particular attention to unusual changes in precipitation, temperature, and wind, and during snowstorms. Research has shown that approximately 90 percent of human triggered avalanches occur during, or within 24 hours of, a storm (McClung & Schaerer, 2006). According to big mountain snowboarder Neil McNab (2008), previous generations of backcountry-users in Chamonix, France took seriously the dangerous conditions presented by storms: "after a big snow fall, the motto was to 'let the mountains have their day,' the snow would be left to settle and nature would find its balance" (McNab, 2008, para. 2). McNab laments the impatience among the current generation of backcountry snowboarders and skiers, "if you leave the mountains alone for one day after the storm . . . you'll just sit in the valley and watch it get tracked out by everyone else" (McNab, 2008, para. 5).

Winds of 15 m/h or more also increase avalanche hazards, particularly on the leeward slopes where the wind often deposits snow picked up from the windward slope. Heavy snowfalls also indicate increased avalanche danger, and extreme caution is advised when more than 12 inches has fallen within 24 hours. New snow tends to settle and stabilize when the temperature is near freezing; lower temperatures typically cause dry snow to remain loose and unstable; whereas higher temperatures can cause snow to lose its cohesive strength as the snow crystals change shape (What causes avalanches, 2000). Many committed backcountry snowboarders study the weather for days or weeks before a scheduled trip, with some carefully recording and analyzing meteorological factors throughout the entire winter season to gain a better understanding of the snowpack and avalanche risks in particular areas.

Two main types of avalanche—loose snow avalanches and the slab avalanches—develop as a result of different combinations of snowpack, terrain, and/or weather. Loose snow avalanches (or sluff) generally occur on the surface in new snow or wet spring snow, beginning at a point and then spreading out as they gradually gain momentum. While loose snow avalanches can be "huge and destructive," slab avalanches are typically "the most fatal types of avalanches" (What causes avalanches, 2000, para. 16). Generally, slab avalanches occur over large areas when a cohesive body of snow separates as a moving slab from more stable snow, often leaving a well-defined fracture line (McClung & Schaerer, 2006). Slab avalanches can be further divided into soft and hard slab avalanches. Soft slab avalanches are caused by the rapid accumulation of fresh snow. If the pull of gravity is stronger than the bonding effect between the layers, the new layer of fresh snow releases before it has time to properly bond to the older surface layer. In contrast, a hard slab avalanche can take with it many layers of snow, and thus, can be especially devastating. Hard slab avalanches are often caused by the formation of "depth hoar" in the lower layers of the snow pack, which can make this type of avalanche particularly difficult to predict.

While "eye-balling" slope angles and digging "snow pits" may seem ad hoc approaches to avalanche prediction, such practices are informed by rigorous scientific research. Avalanche researchers at universities and research centers around the world are "studying avalanche behavior and snowpack dynamics and then converting this knowledge into tools and training for those who live, work and play in mountain environments, as well as the techniques required by those trying to forecast avalanches on a daily level" (cited in Davies, 2009, para. 8). Seeking to "translate a deeper and more accurate understanding of how and why avalanches occur into workable solutions for avalanche management and education" (cited in Davies, 2009, para. 8), avalanche research involves both highly technical scientific research and the practical application of this information. Recent computer technologies have been integral to innovative developments in scientific avalanche-research. According to Birgit Ottmer, from the Swiss Federal Institute for Snow and Avalanche Research, "improved computing power has given us the ability to collect millions of pieces of data and actually process them. It's helped us to get closer to understanding what is actually happening inside avalanches" (cited in Davies, 2009, para. 9).

Researchers also use new technologies in real avalanches. For example, the Swiss Federal Institute for Snow and Avalanche Research opened the world's largest avalanche test site at Vallée de la Sionne (Valais, Switzerland) in 1997 to "study the overall dynamic behavior of dense flow and powder-snow avalanches" and to "measure avalanche impact forces along their path" (Ammann, 1999, p. 3). The site enables researchers to trigger avalanches that can travel up to 3,280 feet, and capture and analyze the activity using an array of strategically placed monitors, including instruments on pylons that measure the pressure inside the avalanche, radars that track its speed and distribution, and cameras that take 3D photographs to identify where the avalanche picks up and deposits snow.

Some researchers opt for less technical methods. Avalanche scientist Karl Birkeland is a strong advocate for what he terms "duct-tape science": "[T]here's a huge amount of practical research that can be done. Basic field-oriented work is essential: you don't need big computers for this. This kind of fieldwork could help develop a simple piece of kit that a ski patroller could take and test for avalanche probabilities" (cited in Davies, 2009, para. 10–11). Over the past decade, the latest research has been used to develop a number of rule-based decision methods and user-friendly "checklists" to help backcountry recreationists identify the risks in a particular environment, including the ABC's, Reduction Method, the Stop-or-Go Method, the SnowCard, the Nivo Test, and the Obvious Clues Method (see McClung & Schaerer, 2006).

Despite extensive research, dedicated forecasting management and rescue organizations, and education and prevention campaigns, the number of avalanche fatalities in North America and Europe have yet to subside. With the growing numbers of skiers and snowboarders heading into the backcountry, and human error accounting for approximately 95 percent of avalanche-related fatalities, this is perhaps not surprising. While many incidents involve inexperienced backcountry users, Ian McCammon of the National Outdoor Leadership School in Wyoming explains that "even trained victims commonly ignore obvious clues and fail to make precautions" (cited in Davies, 2009, para. 19). He attributes decision-making errors to the "trap of familiarity" that many experienced backcountry users fall into: "There is a misconception that most victims are young and careless. But there are a number who are very experienced, but become complacent because they have been in a number of situations where no avalanches have occurred" (cited in Davies, 2009, para. 20). Also acknowledging the danger of both familiarity and egos in the backcountry environment, former director of the Swiss Federal Institute for Snow and Avalanche Research, Andre Roch infamously proclaimed: "Remember, my friend, the avalanche does not know that you are an expert" (cited in Davies, 2009, para. 7).

To avoid dangerous situations in the backcountry, individuals and groups must be prepared to make educated and rational decisions, often in moments of high emotion. Even some of the most experienced and educated backcountry snowboarders struggle to turn away from highly alluring powdery slopes despite recognizing warning signs. World-renown big mountain snowboarder Jeremy Jones reflects upon the importance of rational decision-making amid various social pressures and temptations:

> "Mountains speak, wise men listen" (John Muir). This is one of my favorite quotes that perfectly sums up approaching the mountains. You can take all the avalanche courses in the world but if you do not read the signs it does not matter. Often times there is no room for error in the backcountry and one bad call reading the conditions can erase a lifetime of good calls. Because of this I like to keep on the top of my brain sayings like, "just say no" and "live to ride another day." When approaching a line I always go in with the mind set of, "I am going to *look* at the line," not "I am going to *ride* the line." (Jones, 2009, para. 1, emphasis added)

Jones describes education, discipline, as well as affective and embodied knowledge, as integral to his decision-making practices:

> The mountains are one big feel out. Having a preset agenda is dangerous. I never know if I am going to hit a line until the moment I drop in because my mind and gut are observing the constantly changing conditions and I am always open to turning back at any point. This can be tricky when you are filming or leading a group because so many people have worked so hard to get into position and you may feel like you are letting them down by backing down. The further up a line you get, or the closer you get to dropping in, the harder it is to say no to a line. Saying "no" takes practice. If I have not backed off a line for a long time then I start to question myself and will make an effort to back off a line in the near future just to practice saying no. (Jones, 2009, para. 2)

In contrast to the practiced and calculated approach to risk employed by some educated backcountry snowboarders, such as Jones, others seek out dangerous experiences. A trend among some thrill-seeking snowboarders, for example, is to travel into the backcountry, provoke an avalanche, and then try to "surf" if for as long as possible. The individual who rides the avalanche the longest is declared the "winner," while those who "drown" are obviously the losers (On the wave of death, 2004, para. 2). Given the efforts of researchers, avalanche-awareness organizations, mountain guides and rescue teams, and some professional athletes, it is probably not surprising that such trends have outraged the backcountry community. Tim Egan labels the practice "the intersection of risk and stupidity" (cited in Fry, no date, para. 3). Studying the psychology of such risk-taking behaviors, however, some sport psychologists offer a different set of explanations.

psychology of snowboarding

Psychologists have been attempting to understand and explain the experiences of participants in high-risk sports since the late 1960s (e.g., Huberman, 1968; Hymbaugh & Garrett, 1974). Recent studies have focused on various psychological dimensions (e.g., mood, quality of experience, risk perception, disinhibition, goal orientation, flow, self-efficacy, motivation) of an array of so-called extreme sports, including adventure racing (Schneider, Butryn, Furst & Masucci, 2007), BASE jumping (Griffith et al., 2006), high-altitude rock climbing (Fave, Bassi & Massimini, 2003), skateboarding (Boyd & Kim, 2007), skydiving (Celsi, Rose & Leigh, 1993; Lyng, 1990), snowboarding (Anna, Jan & Aleksander, 2007), and surfing (Diehm & Armatas, 2004). However, the dominant approach has been to establish a relationship between high-risk sports and personality traits (e.g., Goma, 1991; Robinson, 1985). Some psychological studies compare personality traits of experimental groups of extreme sport athletes and control groups as assessed by Marvin Zuckerman's Sensation Seeking Scale (SSS) (Breivik, 1996, 1999; Campbell, Tyrrell & Zingaro, 1993; Cronin, 1991; Diehm & Armatas, 2003; Slanger & Rudestam, 1997). Based on his extensive research on the psychological dimensions of various forms of social and physical risk-taking, Zuckerman identified "sensation seekers" as individuals with distinct personality dispositions; they typically have a need for a wide variety of new and involved sensations and experiences and are willing to take physical and social risks to achieve them. According to Zuckerman, all individuals have an optimal level of arousal, with "sensation seekers" having a higher optimal level of arousal than those measuring low in sensation seeking. Zuckerman also suggests that the disposition for sensation seeking tends to fade with age and is more common among males than females (see Self & Findley, 2007).

Other sport psychologists have employed Frank Farley's series of continuums to measure the degree to which extreme sport participants demonstrate various levels of positive and/or negative, and physical and/or cognitive, thrill seeking characteristics (Self, Henry, Findley & Reilly, 2007). For Farley, individuals with thrill seeking or "Type T" personalities can express their personality in positive and negative ways. Examples of positive Type T behavior include extreme sports participation, firefighting, or entrepreneurship, whereas negative Type T behavior might include excessive alcohol or drug use, smoking, sexual promiscuity, or criminal behavior. Importantly, Farley explains that positive and negative thrill-seeking are not mutually exclusive, and some individuals with Type T personalities readily engage in both. Thrill-seeking can also take the forms of mental (cognitive) thrill seeking (e.g., gambling, investment banking) and/or physical (sensory) thrill seeking (e.g., extreme sports, riding roller-coasters). Individuals with Type T personalities crave novelty, excitement, thrills and risks, and are highly inclined toward extreme sports. Comparing extreme sport enthusiasts to nonparticipant groups, various studies have shown extreme sport participants to have a preference for novel, high risk activities and for high levels of arousal, and thus more likely to demonstrate Type T and/or Sensation Seeking personalities (see Diehm & Armatas, 2004; Straub, 1982; Wagner & Houlihan, 1994). In particular, a recent study showed elite Austrian, Italian, and Swiss freestyle snowboard competitors scoring higher on four key dimensions of sensation-seeking (or Type T) personality—extraversion, openness to experience, compatibility, and conscientiousness—than the general population (Muellers & Peters, 2008, p. 339).

Studies focusing on individual dispositions (e.g., Type T, Sensation Seeking) offer interesting insights into human behavior in high-risk and extreme sports. But, some of these studies reinforce stereotypes of so-called extreme sports as dangerous activities enjoyed mostly by reckless, testosterone-fuelled, adrenaline-junkies. Too often, participants are presented as a homogenous group with similar personality types, motives, and experiences. Many psychological studies of extreme sport are also based on the problematic assumption that extreme sports are indeed more risky than traditional sports. As previously discussed, while there is an element of risk involved in all activities labeled extreme, in most cases risk is a subjective calculation that individuals make in the context of their ability (Booth & Thorpe, 2007). Moreover, there is no evidence that disciples of extreme sport have abandoned concerns for safety. On the contrary, many deny accusations that they are risk takers and insist that they are as conscious of safety as participants in established sports. For example, when a fellow big mountain snowboarder asked Craig Kelly for his opinion on a *Time* magazine article that "described people like us as self-centered adrenaline junkies who don't think about our families and the devastating effect an accident might have," Kelly responded somewhat critically: "I would probably agree with them if they were to publish some kind of statistics that proved what we're doing really is dangerous. Like you said, you research what you do a lot. It's your life and you put everything into it. From riding with each other, we know we're not taking big chances out there. . . . if I get scared, I back off" (cited in The Interview, 2008, para. 26). Many highly proficient snowboarders actively challenge psychological research that ignores individual differences in experience, skill level, education, and cognitive processing, and reduces their behavior to personality types.

Some researchers have extended their investigations beyond personality types to examine the social-psychological motives of extreme sport enthusiasts. For example, Celsi (1992) found that, despite differences in skills, equipment, environments, and physical sensations produced by various high risk sports, when participants describe the more abstract qualities of their experiences, they tend to use a common language. His research showed that BASE jumpers, skydivers, snowboarders, mountain climbers, and surfers, all reflect on camaraderie, timelessness, involvement, and a sense of freedom, as benefits of their respective sports. Celsi (1992) described these as "transcendental" experiences, proclaiming that "while qualities such as thrill and excitement are always desired and enjoyed, it is the ability of high-risk sports to produce both individual and shared transcendent experience that elevates them most of all to the realm of the 'sacred'" (p. 340). For many big mountain snowboarders, the backcountry offers ample opportunity for transcendental experiences. For example, Canadian mountain guide, John Buffery, proclaims:

> The sensations you get out there are just indescribable . . . being in the hills has given me a certain peace . . . having found that connection, that peace in the mountains, I feel that I have a connection between the earth and myself. I can feel a sense of purpose in some way. (cited in Kelly, 2008, para. 10)

Similarly, Craig Kelly, the quintessential "soul boarder," describes the experience as transcending both the physical and mental realms:

> When I go into the backcountry, I sort of feel this elation at being out there and the purity and the freedom that comes with the experience. It sort of lends itself to believing that there is another dimension to everything we do. . . . All of a sudden you have this feeling of clarity. (cited in Reed, 2005, p. 59)

Many big mountain snowboarders also discuss the experience in terms of the "absolute involvement that is demanded, as well as the sense of release, timelessness, and freedom, that coincides with those peak experiences" (Celsi, 1992, p. 638). Hungarian-born psychologist Mihaly Csikszentimihalyi (1974) defines such moments as "flow" experiences:

> [Flow is] a state in which action follows upon action according to an internal logic which seems to need no conscious intervention on our part. We experience it as a unified flowing from one moment to the next in which we are in control of our actions, and in which there is little distinction between self and environment; between stimulus and response; or between past, present and future. (p. 58)

Flow experiences are "the best moments of people's lives" and "occur when a person's body or mind is stretched to its limits in a voluntary effort to accomplish something difficult and worthwhile" (Csikszentmihalyi, 1990, p. 30). As one male snowboarder puts it: "the movement . . . and fluidity of snowboarding . . . feels like nirvana . . . when your snowboard becomes just an extension of your own body" (Bull, 2009, para. 1). Csikszentmihalyi (1990) described the end result of flow as an *autotelic* experience, one that is intrinsically rewarding. Indeed, some snowboarders find the flow experience so pleasurable that it becomes "highly addictive": "To me, the feeling of shredding deep powder is better than any high you can get artificially. And yes—I was addicted after my very first powder turn. Riding deep powder gives you that special feeling; it's like your eyes are blind, but you can see" (Gagnon, 2008, para. 3).

Summarizing the small, but growing, body of research on the psychological dimensions of extreme sport experiences, Mueller and Peter (2008) explain that "the combination of fun and thrill is one of the main motivators" and "the testing of individual limits and experience seeking are the main intentions of extreme sportsmen" (p. 340). Implicit in this comment, however, is the important observation that the majority of psychological studies have focused on the sensation seeking personalities of young men; few have examined women's risk taking practices and performances in extreme physical pursuits.

gender and risk

Extreme forms of snowboarding (e.g., big mountain snowboarding, big air freestyle) have traditionally placed a strong emphasis on male physicality. As is common in many male-dominated sports, snowboarders earn status and respect from their peers through displays of physical prowess, including finely honed combinations of skill, muscular strength, aggression, toughness, and, above all, courage (see Ford & Brown, 2006; Thorpe, 2005; Wheaton, 2000). Traditionally, such attributes have been understood as desirable or "natural" male traits. Not dissimilar from many other sports, biological reductionism featured strongly as an implicit defense of male superiority in the early snowboarding culture. In the words of one male boarder: "Guys are always going to be better. Chicks are only just doing 900s [degrees of rotation on a jump on in the half-pipe]. Guys have been doing 900s for ages. Girls just aren't strong enough. Girls are girls . . . they are always weaker, the average girl is scared to even put on a snowboard and go down the hill" (Tom, interview, 2004). Some women also accepted biological explanations for their "inferior" performances, "even when there is no validity for such explanations" (Bryson, 1990, p. 175):

> Boys are always stronger than girls . . . no matter what, and to be a really good snowboarder you need to be strong . . . strong girls are never going to be as strong as the top guys. (Moriah, interview, 2005)

> I see girls doing almost everything the boys are doing now. But I think girls will always be a step behind the boys. Girls are never going to be leading the sport, never. The big difference is testosterone. . . . To be a really good snowboarder I don't know if you can really be a lady, it's not a ladies' sport. Even though we are really pushing it and trying to make it a ladies' sport, it's a man's sport . . . we are the minority. (Monique, interview, 2005)

> If I think about the whole girl/boy thing, the only thing I find most frustrating is the physical element . . . not pushing yourself or going to the same limits as boys. I always admired how boys could have less fear. Girls have so much more self-preservation. (Phillipa, interview, 2005)

As these comments suggest, some female snowboarders recognize musculo-skeletal differences (e.g., strength), hormones (e.g., testosterone), and cognitive-functioning (e.g., risk-taking), as contributing to gender differences in snowboarding performances. Such beliefs reinforce the assumption that male boarders are more deserving of respect, media coverage, and economic rewards within the culture. When *Transworld Snowboarding* asked readers to respond to the question, "Should female riders get paid as much as the dudes [male snowboarders]?" many correspondents emphasized male superiority: "guys can throw bigger tricks, so why not pay them more"

Professional U.S. snowboarder Janna Meyen spins over the enormous gap-jump at the 2006 Winter X Games in Aspen to win her fourth consecutive gold medal in the women's slope-style event. (AP Photo/Bill Ross.)

(Chelsea, Ontario, Canada); "If the girls are as good as the guys, then yes. But if they're not, then to hell with this equality crap" (Sean, Florida) (In your head, 2005, p. 54).

During the mid-1990s and early 2000s, however, some highly committed and skilled female snowboarders refused to accept gendered arguments for their exclusion, and actively challenged the maleness of snowboarding during this period. For example, when professional U.S. snowboarders Tina Basich and Shannon Dunn were denied participation by the organizers of the 1994 Air and Style Big Air snowboarding contest in Innsbruck, Austria, they dressed in pink outfits and pigtails, hiked up the scaffolding and then proceeded to successfully jump the gap on their snowboards (Basich, 2003; Howe, 1998). In so doing, committed female snowboarders, such as Basich and Dunn, actively challenged assumptions regarding the potential of the female boarding body (see Thorpe, 2005, 2009). Increasingly, male boarders began to recognize and praise their female counterparts for displays of physical prowess, skill, aggression, and courage. After performing a 720 degree spin maneuver at the 1998 Winter X Games, Tina Basich (2003) remembers a few male pro snowboarders "telling me that they couldn't yet do that trick. They looked at me a little differently—they were truly impressed" (p. 134).

In the early twenty-first century, some female boarders are further disrupting conventional social dichotomies by embodying traditionally masculine traits and practices (e.g., risk-taking, aggression, competitiveness, swearing, not "caring" about looking or behaving in traditionally "feminine" ways). When asked whether she considered herself to be "feminine" on the mountain, committed snowboarder, Jamie, replied, "No, the only thing feminine about me on the mountain is my pink goggles. I like to be aggressive, wear big baggy outerwear and don't care what I look like" (interview, 2005). When Hana, a top New Zealand boarder, experiences injury, she says she will "swear and try to keep riding . . . . and then swear some more" (interview, 2006). Similarly, Tara Dakides describes herself on the mountain, as "probably the furthest thing from feminine . . . when I get frustrated and mad, I can't help but throw mini tantrums or yell . . . aggressive sports call for a little aggression at times" (Ulmer & Straus, 2002, para. 5). Dakides confesses that although she tried to conform to gendered expectations and "be nice," it "always felt forced," so eventually she accepted "I just had to be me" (Elliot, 2001, para. 13). The adoption of certain traditionally masculine traits and practices by some female snowboarders does not mean that these women are becoming *like men*. Rather, it suggests that the relationship between gendered social roles and biological sex is more fluid than we have been taught to believe (Newitz, Cox, Sandell & Johnson, 1997).

With the growth of the female niche market during the late 1990s and early 2000s, advertisers and publishers increasingly embraced women's snowboarding, featuring female athletes in more advertisements, editorials, and photos (Thorpe, 2008a). Jennifer Sherowski, senior contributing editor for *Transworld Snowboarding*, observed this trend: "Most companies are keen to [access] the new (or expanding) market area that female snowboarding provides" hence "we are making a really big effort to include women in our editorial, and that's including but not limited to, women's columns. . . . There is a lot more legit coverage of women riders now than there used to be, and more focus on seeing all snowboarders as just 'snowboarders,' not girl snowboarders and guy snowboarders" (interview, 2005, cited in Thorpe, 2008a). Many journalists are also showing greater respect to female boarders, often using gender-neutral language to describe their achievements. In October 2009, professional Canadian snowboarder, Annie Boulanger, gained the most media exposure (editorial and advertising) of any snowboarder in *Transworld Snowboarding* and *Snowboarder* magazines. Reporting on Boulanger's achievement, journalist Mike Lewis

(November 2008) writes: "Boulanger is one of the best snowboarders in the world. Notice that wasn't prefaced with "female," "girl," "woman," or any other adjective; Boulanger straight kills it on some of the biggest, steepest, gnarliest terrain out there" (para. 1).

While female snowboarders and industry members have worked hard to improve the representation of women in the snowboarding media, some men are also actively drawing attention to the various ways women have been, and continue to be, marginalized within the snowboarding sport and industry. For example, Danny Burrows, editor of *Onboard European Snowboard Magazine* and self-proclaimed "manimist/feminist," publicly protested gender disparities in the snowboarding culture:

> Sponsorship deals for girls are minimal in comparison to those of guys. They always draw the short straw when it comes to combined-contests—either having to ride in the dark or once the boys have trashed everything. And even when all goes in their favor and they are riding well, they're served up the ultimate sexist insult: 'Damn, you ride like a guy.' We boys might think this is a compliment, but in reality it suggests that all boys ride better than most girls, which is just not true. There are . . . a hell of a lot of girls who have nuts of nickel whether that be on the rails, in the pipe or getting face shots [powder] in the back-country. See, even the expression for being brave or good, 'having balls' is sexist." (December 2005, p. 15)

The increasing visibility of female snowboarders in the media and on the slopes is challenging some traditional assumptions about women's athletic capabilities. As the following comments from long-time snowboarder, magazine editor, and competition judge, Ste'en Webster, illustrate:

> Of all the sports that I am aware of, snowboarding is the one where girls can compete on a level with the men. So the excuse is gone, you can't say we are all on different levels, because I've seen girls snowboard better than guys. A lot of snowboarding is about strength but it's also about balance and flexibility and state-of-mind, things that girls can excel at over boys. In many ways, snowboarding is a gender-neutral sport. (interview, 2005)

It should be added here, however, that the criteria upon which female snow-boarders are judged by males and females alike, often differs from that of male boarders. Displays of high performance by a female snowboarder are often met with surprise, "whoa, you're a girl? That's amazing" (Moriah, interview, 2005).

In their attempts to explain ongoing gender disparities in male and female sport participation and performance, many feminists and sports sociologists continue to downplay, or deny, biological variables (e.g., hormones, muscle mass), focusing more on the power of social-cultural factors (e.g., media) and structural inequalities. Yet, some highly proficient female snowboarders not only acknowledge, but also celebrate, gendered differences to risk-taking. Many professional female snowboarders discuss the value of admitting their fears and listening to their intuition; few males do the equivalent. Big mountain snowboarder Victoria Jealouse offers other women interested in venturing into the backcountry the following advice:

> never just follow the guys out there, because they say "I'm experienced. We're going to be really careful." That worries me the most because . . . even the guys who are most experienced and educated in safety . . . will say the snow-pit results are yadda yadda, and the temperature is yadda yadda and then (unknowingly) factor in what they don't say out loud, things like . . . "I hiked all the way up here . . . " or "I spent so much money to come up here," or "If I did this line and jumped that cliff, I'd get the shot and be a hero."

Continuing, Jealouse proclaims that:

> girls are much better at isolating the safety factors and making a clear decision, and they also seem to err on the side of conservatism. They tend to not bring the "hero factor" into play. It is important to educate yourself and to know that by being female, you are going to make better decisions than men [because women are] more conservative and will stick more to safety guidelines. (cited in Voskinarian, 2005, para. 14)

Importantly, while Jealouse acknowledges gender differences in cognitive approaches to risk-taking in the backcountry, she does not see these as limiting her potential to perform alongside her male counterparts in extreme places and events.

4.   places and events

constituting almost one-fifth of the land surface of the Earth, mountains have long been places of cultural significance. As Reed (2005) writes, "standing as metaphoric monuments on the grandest scales, [mountains] have captivated the collective spirit and imagination of human kind since the beginning of time" (p. 184). In the late twentieth- and early twenty-first centuries, mountains became important sites of play, pleasure, performance, and desire for snowboarders. Ski resorts, the most common sites of participation, range from small, locally-owned and managed slopes, to exclusive resort destinations hosting a plethora of chairlifts, gondolas, trams, and/or trains accessing hundreds of miles of piste. Boasting more than 600 resorts, Japan has the largest number of ski areas in the world. There are also approximately 500 resorts in the United States, 300 in France, 170 in Canada, 100 in Switzerland, 50 in Australasia (Australia and New Zealand), 7 in Africa, and many more in other European and Asian countries. The world's largest ski area, Les Trois Valléees, is located in the French Alps. With one lift ticket, the resort offers the patron access to more than 370 miles of piste via 196 lifts with a total capacity of 242,000 passengers per hour. While some resorts remain local favorites frequented predominantly by snow-sport enthusiasts from neighboring towns and cities, others become well-known throughout the global snowboarding culture via extensive coverage in magazines and videos, attracting participants from around the world.

Approaching the sport from a position of privilege, many snowboarders travel extensively—locally, nationally, internationally, and virtually—in pursuit of new terrain, fresh snow, and social interactions and cultural connections. According to the authors of *Snowboarding the World*, "Snowboarders are, by definition, travellers. Unless you're lucky enough to live at the foot of a mountain, the typical snowboarding trip means planning a journey ... " (Barr, Moran & Wallace, 2006, p. 3). A recent online survey of more than 2,000 snowboarders from around the world showed approximately 43 percent of correspondents had snowboarded at least once in a foreign country (Poll Results, 2006). In a highly fragmented snowboarding culture, however, it is perhaps not surprising that the travel patterns of snowboarders vary considerably, ranging from budget to luxury national and international holidays (e.g., marginal participants, ex-core participants, or retired athletes), to cyclic seasonal migration between the hemispheres (e.g., core participants working in the sport or tourism industry), to brief international adventures to remote and exotic destinations for competitions, events, or as part of media or contractual obligations (e.g., professional athletes) (see Thorpe, 2010a).

The most traveled snowboarders tend to be professional athletes who are paid to travel to exotic and remote locations to pioneer new spaces and places (e.g., Alaska, Japan, New Zealand); their exploits are then covered in snowboard magazines, films, and Web sites. Coverage of the professional snowboarder's global exploits in magazines and films, and travel stories in various forms of mass media (e.g., newspapers, magazines, television) and niche media (e.g., snowboarding Web sites, magazines, books), have both broadened the range of destinations considered by travelling snowboarders, as well as strengthened the flows of snowboarding tourists and migrants in particular directions.

The authors of *Snowboarding the World*, an extensive guidebook written by two ex-professional snowboarders and a snowboarding journalist, recognize the increasingly diverse demands of travelling snowboarders:

> Fifteen years ago people were just happy to go riding where they could. As resorts became more crowded, the travelling habits of snowboarders correspondingly became more sophisticated as people began to look further afield for something new. . . . Bulgaria, Iran, Poland and Russia . . . As snowboarding destinations, each offers something slightly different to the essentially homogenized riding experience that is snowboarding in Europe or North America. (Barr, Moran & Wallace, 2006, p. 91)

While some adventurous snowboarders seek remote destinations, the majority flock to "fantastic resort destinations," such as—although certainly not limited to—Chamonix, France; Queenstown, New Zealand; and Whistler, Canada (see Thorpe, 2010a, 2011). According to Reed (2005), these places are among "snowboarding's great cathedrals . . .

places of pilgrimage, where likeminded devotees from all over the world congregate during the holy season of winter" (p. 184). Indeed, every year hundreds of thousands of snowboarders travel to these snow-sport "Meccas" where they proceed to "play" in the mountains for days, weeks, months, and sometimes, years. While many are drawn to these sites by the desire to experience new, more challenging, or culturally-infamous, terrain, others are attracted by the opportunities for social interactions with like-minded snow-sport enthusiasts. Arguably, what distinguishes these transnational destinations from other popular national and regional winter locales, is that they each offer a unique combination of social (e.g., quality restaurants, cafés, and nightlife) *and* physical geographies (e.g., snow conditions, weather, and mountain terrain), as well as established infrastructure (e.g., relatively easily accessible via international airports and regional transport; accommodation, user-friendly village design, etc). This chapter introduces four culturally-significant snowboarding destinations, as well as two events, which attract snowboarders from around the world and/or entertain many others.

alaska

Alaska offers some of the biggest and most celebrated terrain in the world. Annual snowfalls average over 1,000 inches in Alaska and five thousand-foot vertical runs are plentiful. According to Israel Valenzuela, senior editor of *Heckler* magazine, there are "cliffs that dot the landscape that are as big as the biggest ski resort in Tahoe and they are merely part of the terrain" (cited in Baccigaluppi, Mayugba & Carnel, 2001, p. 208). Professional snowboarder Tina Basich (2003) describes Alaska as "so intimidating," because "unlike a ski resort, there are no boundaries or clearly marked trails and warnings about cliffs and crevasses or shallow snow. It's up to you to learn the mountain you're riding. Alaska is mother-nature at her most extreme—the weather changes quickly, snow conditions can change within one run—it's vast and steep and bigger than all of us." Basich (2003) highlights some of the perils and pleasures of snowboarding in Alaska in her biography:

> The helicopter dropped us off and we crouched down with our gear and waited for it to lift off. Right after the heli[copter] started to rise our radios exploded with the voice of the helicopter pilot, "it's gone, it's gone! The whole thing is gone!" About seven feet away from where we

were standing there was a fracture line going across the entire mountain. The entire mountain had avalanched. The pressure from the heli[copter] landing had released this fracture, called a climax fracture, which means it cracked off all the snow all the way down to the dirt, rock and ice, sending the entire side of the mountain sliding all the way across the entire bowl. The avalanche had gone 3,500 feet down to the glacier below. We were all very quiet and just waited for the helicopter to come back and pick us up. It was a freaky feeling because if any of us had dropped into that bowl, it would have released and we would not have survived.

The feeling of the untracked powder under my board as I was flying down the run was amazing. The glittering snowflakes flew in plumes off the side of my board as I made my turns. I was so small riding down this huge mountain and had to keep turning, remembering to look back every couple of seconds to see if any snow was moving with me. When I got to the bottom, I sighed with relief that I'd made it down, and what an accomplishment! I named the mountain "T-top."' I looked back up at my turns and the run I had just come down and could barely believe it. I couldn't tell if I was going to cry or laugh, so I just kept smiling.

Snowboarding author Rob Reed (2005) accurately describes Alaska as "a place where mythic lines and narrow escapes give way to snowboarding legend" (p. 66).

Snowboarders have long been hiking into the backcountry and "ducking" the ropes of local ski resorts to access fresh snow and escape crowded slopes. It was not until the late 1980s and early 1990s, however, that Alaska was identified as the new frontier for big mountain snowboarders seeking the ultimate thrill. In Alaska to write an article for *Climbing* magazine, Nick Perata, Shawn Farmer, and Chris Pappas were among the first snowboarders to recognize the possibilities offered by the place when they hiked Alaska's Moose's Tooth and then descended on their boards. However, they were not the only ones captivated by the expansive Alaskan terrain during this period; a number of highly skilled climber/ skiers were simultaneously exploring the Alaskan backcountry. Occasionally, mixed groups of skiers and snowboarders ventured into the Alaskan backcountry together, learning from one another and sharing knowledge (i.e., weather, geography, snow safety, technologies). As Canadian big mountain snowboarder Victoria Jealouse explains, "In Alaska it's always been skiers and snowboarders. We are out there doing it together, and it always has been that way . . . It's cool to be with people that . . . are all thinking the same" (cited in Taylor, no date, para. 4).

The Alaskan heli-skiing phenomenon started in the mountains surrounding Valdez and Juneau during the early 1990s when local skiers and snowboarders convinced local pilots to give them a lift to the top of neighboring peaks. Among the handful of Alaskan snowboarding pioneers were Perata, Falmer, Jay Liska, Ritchie Fowler, Tom Burt, Jim Zellers, and Bonnie Leary (later Zellers). "There were probably only twenty people that were skiing or snowboarding in Valdez," recalls snowboarding cinematographer Mike Hatchett, "there were no guides; it was total cowboy" (cited in Reed, 2005, p. 116). Big mountain legend Jeremy Jones reflects upon the excitement during the early "discovery years":

> A lot of it was always about exploring. From the very first days in AK [Alaska] . . . there wasn't a single dot on the map [a "dot" marks a mountain peak descended], so that feeling of getting in a helicopter and not knowing what's beyond the next ridge was amazing. And with that thought of the best line of my life possibly being right around the corner, the feeling you get from this huge blank canvas is one of the coolest feelings in the world. (cited in Benedek, 2009, para. 10)

A snowboarder or skier who becomes the first to successfully descend a peak is rewarded with the opportunity to name the face and put another "dot" on the map.

In 1993, Mike Hatchett's film, *TB2: a New Way of Thinking*, documented some of the first Alaskan heli-snowboarding footage. By the mid-1990s, numerous snowboarding videos were communicating Alaskan big mountain riding to the broader boarding culture. "When people saw the videos of people making slick powder turns in Alaska, they wanted that. It became a fantasy," says early professional snowboarder Jeff Fulton, but the majority of snowboarders "aren't educated enough to be out there" (cited in Howe, 1998, p. 134). With such highly evocative images flooding the snowboarding media, Alaska quickly became "a destination of choice" for boarders seeking adventure and excitement. Heli-skiing and heli-boarding blossomed into a cottage industry where diehards make the long pilgrimage each spring, and a day snowboarding can cost anywhere upwards of $1,000—a price-tag covering both helicopter rides and the advice of highly trained guides. Today, an array of heli-boarding companies offer teams of professional athletes and wealthy clients access

Jeremy Jones—professional U.S. snowboarder and eight-time winner of the "Big Mountain Snowboarder of the Year" award—on an Alaskan peak during the filming of his big mountain snowboarding film *Deeper* (2010). (Credit: O'Neill/ Greg von Doersten.)

to the Alaskan backcountry experience from the three main "heli hotspots" of Cordova, Haines, and Valdez.

Snowboarding author Tam Leach (2006) offers those interested in travelling to Alaska the following advice:

> Different operators suit different clients. Some specialize in all-inclusive trips well-suited to wealthy holidaymakers with less experience, while others operate more as a mountain taxi-service, with a

mandatory guide to show the way. Lodge or no lodge, heli-time package or pay-per-day, the company of older skiers or pros on a hectic filming schedule: a little bit of web surfing should make it pretty obvious which place will suit your style, your ability and your budget. (p. 342)

Continuing, Leach explains some of the financial and logistical considerations for such trips: "heli-time is either priced by number of runs and/or guaranteed vertical feet per day, or according to the Hobbs (airtime) meter in the helicopter . . . If possible, aim to spend at least twice as many days in Alaska as you'd like to fly, to allow for down days [due to weather]" (Leach, 2006, p. 342). A healthy bank account is not the only requirement for snowboarding in Alaska, courage, physical prowess, and patience, are also necessities.

chamonix, france

A mountain community in south eastern France, Chamonix is situated at the base of the spectacular Mont Blanc. The highest mountain in the European Alps (15,780 ft), Mont Blanc is the third most visited natural site in the world. The infamous Mont Blanc has long held a special allure for mountain climbers and sightseers, but the massive peaks of the Aiguilles Rouges surrounding Chamonix also serve an optimal playground for other outdoor activities, particularly in their more extreme variants (e.g., ice climbing, rock-climbing, extreme skiing and snowboarding, paragliding, rafting, mountain-biking). The physical geography of the Chamonix backcountry offers experienced participants bountiful opportunities for physical adventure, exploring new terrain in unchartered terrain. For those less willing (or able) to engage in such high-risk pursuits, the Chamonix valley offers 12 separate ski areas with 49 lifts, 145 marked ski runs, and access to over 760 acres of skiable terrain. Chamonix also boasts the world's biggest lift-serviced skiable vertical drop of 9,209 feet; one of the world's longest ski runs through the Vallée Blanche at 13.7 miles; and the highest gondola in Europe which transports passengers to an elevation of 12,605 feet and offers views spanning three countries—France, Italy, and Switzerland.

Chamonix has a resident population of approximately 10,000 from more than 40 different nationalities, many of whom are passionate snowboarders and/or skiers drawn by the promise of fresh snow and challenging terrain. Canadian big mountain snowboarder Karleen Jeffery, for example, moved to Chamonix because she "wanted bigger mountains, steeper terrain, unlimited access to all the goods. I wanted to be able to go wherever I want"

The majestic peaks surrounding Chamonix, France are the playground for many extreme snowboarders. (Courtesy of Jose Borrero.)

(Jeffery, 2008, para. 6). In so doing, however, she quickly recognized the need to educate herself of the risks involved in the French backcountry:

> In Europe . . . there are no rules and you watch your own back. Chamonix is a huge valley developed on three sides—all ski resorts. You can go up a lift, ride down into Switzerland and take a train back. You can go down into Italy and take a gondola over. It's just so vast and extensive, and all the resorts are no more than a five- to ten-minute drive from the centre of town. . . . [but] you have to have some knowledge or else there is such danger—you're putting yourself at really high risk. It's more like a personal quest for self-preservation. (Jeffery, 2008, para. 6)

The authors of *Snowboarding the World* (2006) also warn travelling snowboarders of the risks inherent in snowboarding in Chamonix:

> Will I die in Chamonix? Well, it's a good question, and one to which the most obvious answer is "maybe." . . . it's a very scary place up there in the high mountains and people disappear off cliffs and down crevasses all the time . . . you never know when you might need your rope, harness and belay to pull some poor random rider out of a crevasse. (Barr, Moran & Wallace, 2006, p. 119)

A travel journalist describes the "archetypal" figure in Chamonix as a "hard-core mountain man" typically "under 30 [years old] and kitted out in such a way that you immediately know he's an aggressive backcountry animal who'll snarl if you mess with his powder" (Murphy, 2006, para. 6). "The helmet, the Gore-Tex clothing, the ice-axe, harness and transceiver all have a double role. On the mountain, they may save his life; in the bars they announce his toughness to impressed intermediates who wish to God they were like him" (Murphy, 2006, para. 7). For some observers, the clothing and equipment in Chamonix may seem excessive, but for those travelling into the backcountry, it is essential. The gendarmes of the Chamonix Mountain Rescue perform more than 1,300 operations per year. With an annual average of 60 deaths on the slopes, the description of Chamonix as "the death sport capital of the world" (Krakauer, 1997) clearly holds some truth.

queenstown, new zealand

Surrounded by the magnificent Southern Alps and nestled by the shores of Lake Wakatipu, Queenstown is "New Zealand's premier visitor destination and alpine resort" (Queenstown's Official, 2009). Two ski resorts, Coronet Peak and The Remarkables Ski Area—both owned by Southern Alpine Recreation Limited—are located within a short drive of the Queenstown township. Wanaka, located 75 miles northeast of Queenstown, hosts three ski resorts—Cardrona Alpine Resort, Treble Cone Ski Area, and Snow Park. The Central Otago region boasts a thriving international snowboarding scene with each resort hosting a number of highly esteemed snowboarding competitions and events throughout the winter season. The surrounding Alps also offer ample opportunities for heli-boarding. For many passionate snowboarders from the northern hemisphere, travelling to New Zealand offers exciting opportunities to explore new terrain and pursue the dream of the "endless winter"; professional snowboarders often travel to Queenstown, and the neighboring town of Wanaka, for competitions, photo-shoots, and to train for the upcoming competitive season in the northern hemisphere.

A particularly popular destination for highly committed freestyle snowboarders (and skiers) travelling to New Zealand is Snow Park—the southern hemisphere's first "freestyle resort." Established in 2003 by Sam Lee, a passionate young skier and entrepreneur with longstanding family connections with the local region and skiing culture, Snow Park caters specifically to young, core snowboarders and skiers. The resort offers one chair-lift that provides access to an extensive array of well-maintained artificial freestyle features, including a super-pipe, a quarter-pipe, and numerous jumps and rails, and regularly hosts live DJs who deliver music over the entire terrain park via a 5,000-watt sound system. Described as "more like a skate park than a snowboarding resort," and offering a "video-game-like spectacle," Snow Park attracts freestyle snowboarders and skiers from around the world (Barr, Moran & Wallace, 2006, p. 231). In the words of professional snowboarder, Tim Warwood, "this one lift freestyle hotspot is the dream of every snowboard park monkey worldwide . . . jumps, rails and the best pipe in the southern hemisphere. It's perfect!" (cited in Barr, Moran & Wallace, 2006, p. 230). As well as hosting numerous high caliber international freestyle snowboarding and skiing events during the winter (e.g., Burton NZ Open, Billabong Slopestyle Jam, Volcom Peanut Butter Rail Jam), the resort is also frequently hired for the exclusive use of snowboarding and skiing companies and filming agencies seeking to capture high-quality images and footage of their sponsored athletes performing on specifically designed obstacles. With images of professional snowboarders performing on innovative and expertly shaped jumps, half-pipes and rails, gaining extensive coverage in many North American and European-produced magazines and videos, Snow Park has become a key destination for the travelling freestyle snowboarder.

whistler, canada

Every year thousands of young boarders from across the globe make the pilgrimage to Whistler with the dream of "living and breathing" the snowboarding lifestyle for the season; some do not leave. The snowboarding culture thrives in Whistler, such that it is commonly described as the snowboarder's "Disneyland." Indeed, Whistler/Blackcomb is so popular among boarders that it wins the *Transworld Snowboarding* "Resort Poll" year after year because it offers "the complete snowboarding experience on-hill and off— from the perfect corduroy cruisers; long, challenging tree runs; sheer cliffs; and quality of snow, to the epic kickers, rails, and Super-pipe, as well as the restaurants, hotels and nightlife in Whistler Village" (Fast, 2005, p. 24).

Located less than two hours north of Vancouver in British Columbia, Canada, Whistler is home to some of the world's best snowboarding terrain. Two mountains, Whistler and Blackcomb, rise up a mile out of the valley (5,280 feet) and offer access to over 8,000 acres of ride-able terrain. The average annual snowfall is 30 feet, and with a total of 33 lifts, boarders and skiers have the luxury of choosing from over 200 marked runs. Whistler and Blackcomb provide snowboarders with access to five immaculately groomed terrain parks, with some jumps exceeding 100 feet, as well as three perfectly shaped half-pipes. The resorts are also infamous for their natural terrain, the preferred playground of free-riders. Some highly committed snowboarding residents also own snowmobiles which they use to access thousands of acres of backcountry terrain. As local professional snowboarder Jesse Huffman (2006) observes:

> Snowmobiling has become a raging scene in Whistler due to the unprecedented access to terrain. Within a 30-minute drive from town, there are at least a dozen different areas to park your truck and snowmobile into the wilderness. The second reason is the unparalleled quality of the terrain. Again, just a 30-minute snowmobile tour up the terrain delivers the cliffs, spines, peaks, pitches, cornices and other formations that consistently land photos labeled "Whistler Backcountry" in the glossy pages of snowboard magazines. (p. 67)

As Huffman suggests, a significant proportion of magazine and film footage is captured in the Whistler region. In the summer, freestyle snowboard camps, held in terrain parks and half-pipes built on the high-alpine (7,600 feet) glaciated snow on Blackcomb Mountain, are also popular among young snowboard enthusiasts.

But terrain is not the only thing Whistler has in large quantity and variety; "this town likes to party." This is particularly obvious during the 10-day annual World Ski and Snowboard Festival, "the biggest annual gathering of winter sports, music, arts, and culture in North America." According to the event Web site, the event combines "Canada's largest outdoor concert series with an eclectic mix of snow sport contests and anti-contests, fashion shows, film screenings, [and] photography showdowns," concluding: "Take head the festival motto: 'Party in April, sleep in May.'" The legendary big-air event, featuring many of the world's best snowboarders and skiers competing for hundreds of thousands in cash and prizes, is held in the village and draws huge, highly festive crowds. Further illustrating the international caliber of this resort destination, Whistler, with Vancouver, hosted the 2010 Winter Olympic Games, at which snowboarders were a particularly visible feature.

the winter olympics

Snowboarding's debut at the 1998 Winter Olympics signified a defining moment in the history of the sport. The inclusion of snowboarding into the Olympic program was highly political and heavily contested within the snowboarding culture, and the event divided boarders (see Humphreys, 1997, 2003; Thorpe, 2011a; Thorpe & Wheaton, 2011). Many where infuriated by the International Olympic Committee's (IOC) decision to include snowboarding as a discipline governed by the International Ski Federation (FIS) rather than the International Snowboard Federation (ISF)—an organization established in 1990 by 120 snowboarders from more than five nations, and dedicated to hosting elite level competitions around the world. The loudest voice of opposition came from Terje Haakonsen—undoubtedly the world's best half-pipe rider at the time—who argued that this decision demonstrated the International Olympic Committee's lack of understanding of snowboarding culture and consideration of snowboarders' needs: "Snowboarding is not a discipline of skiing" (cited in Olympic Gold, 2010, p. 78). Haakonsen refused to enter the Games, and protested against snowboarders being turned into "uniform-wearing, flag-bearing, walking logo[s]" (Mellegren, 1998, para. 8; Humphreys, 1996, 2003). While Haakonsen's political response garnered the most media coverage, other snowboarders expressed similar sentiments. For example, professional U.S. snowboarder Morgan Lafonte argued: "I think the Olympics are way too big and are going to change snowboarding. They are going to make us fit their mold. They aren't fitting into our mold ... it will create a reality for snowboarding that millions will swallow and accept" (cited in Howe, 1998, p. 151; see Thorpe & Wheaton, 2011).

Some snowboarders, however, embraced the sport's inclusion in the Olympics. "I want to go to the Olympics ... be the first snowboarder to win a gold medal and be written into the history books" proclaimed U.S. snowboarder Jimi Scott (cited in Howe, 1998, p. 151). Similarly, Todd Richards (2003) noted that while "half of the companies and riders were looking forward to the Olympics as the ultimate forum that would legitimize the sport," the other half "didn't give a damn about the Olympics because it reeked of skiing—a stuffy by-the-books sport with an attitude that was the kiss of death for snowboarding's irreverent spirit" (cited in Thorpe, 2009, p. 372).

The incorporation of snowboarding into the Olympic program continued regardless of conflicting philosophies and contrasting viewpoints.

Amid much anticipation (and some anxiety), when snowboarding finally debuted at the Nagano Winter Olympic Games in Japan, it was treated as a "side show" event and athletes were largely perceived as "intruders" in the Olympic program (see Thorpe, 2011a; Thorpe & Wheaton, 2011). For example, one reporter at the Games described snowboarders as "the official curiosity of the Nagano Winter Games": "They're totally new to the Olympics. They look different, they sound different, they are different" (Wilbon, 1998, p. A01). Snowboarding at the 1998 Winter Olympic Games was further shrouded in controversy when Canadian snowboarder Ross Rebagliati tested positive for marijuana after winning the first Olympic snowboarding gold medal in the men's giant slalom event (Humphreys, 2003). With a reading of 17.8 nanograms of marijuana per milliliter (the World Skiing Federation permits a limit of 15 nanograms per milliliter), Rebagliati argued that he must have inhaled second-hand smoke at a pre-Olympic Games party in Whistler. Unsympathetic to Rebagliati's explanation, the International Olympic Committee (IOC) revoked his medal. It was only when Rebagliati's lawyers found a loophole—marijuana was not on the IOC's list of banned substances—that the IOC returned his medal. The incident grabbed headlines around the world. The scandal was the source of much humor for many, but for others it "confirmed snowboarding culture's anti-authoritarian and counter-cultural roots, and offered support for arguments—from snowboarders as well as many mainstream commentators—that snowboarding was not ready to become an Olympic sport" (Thorpe, 2010b, para. 6; also see Thorpe & Wheaton, 2011).

Over the next four years, the IOC, FIS, and television agencies worked towards developing more effective strategies for representing snowboarding and snowboarders, such that the snowboarding events at the 2002 Winter Olympics in Salt Lake City were deemed a resounding success (Thorpe & Wheaton, 2011). According to a Leisure Trends survey, 32 percent (nearly 92 million people) of the U.S. population watched the 2002 Olympic snowboarding half-pipe competition in which Americans won gold, silver, and bronze in the men's event (this was the first U.S. Winter Olympic medal sweep since 1956) and gold in the women's event. Of those viewers, 18.6 million Americans said they wanted to try snowboarding (Snowboarding and the Olympics, 2004). More recently, the snowboarding events at the 2010 Winter Olympics in Vancouver were some of the most widely watched of the Games (Dillman, 2010). According to Ste'en Webster, assistant head-judge for the half-pipe events at the 2002 and 2010 Winter Olympics: "I think it was pretty clear at the Vancouver Olympics, more so than ever before, how much of a draw card snowboarding is . . . . Snowboarding brings viewers to the Olympics, and credibility with the youth culture of today—something I believe the Olympics has been struggling to maintain" (interview, 2010, cited in Thorpe, 2010b, para. 1).

The IOC continues to hold strong on some rules and regulations (e.g., no stickers on snowboards, no large corporate logos on clothing or equipment). But, as Olympic snowboarding events draw growing numbers of viewers and spectators, the IOC seems increasingly willing to negotiate space for snowboarders' expressions of creativity and individuality (Thorpe & Wheaton, 2011). Drawing inspiration from the X Games, the IOC allows snowboarder's to self-select songs to be played during their half-pipe run. Some athletes (particularly the most popular U.S. snowboarders) are also able to define clothing tastes and styles more consistent with snowboarding cultural aesthetic. For example, the 2010 U.S. Olympic snowboard-cross team refused to wear the competition outfit, opting instead for the waterproof blue jeans allocated to the training uniform: "Snowboarding is the cool factor, that's what the sport is all about, so why not embellish it to its limit. To wear jeans in the Olympics? I don't think you can get any cooler than that. [So] we told 'em 'we're wearing these jeans, and there's nothing you can say about it'" (cited in Graves, 2010, para. 4). The blue jeans featured on the podium days later, and quickly became a hot commodity sought by snowboarders around the world.

Despite the increasing professionalism among elite snowboarders, the marriage between the Olympic movement and snowboarding culture remains tenuous. The unique ideologies and value systems celebrated within the broader snowboarding culture sometimes leads to "cultural clashes" with the disciplinary, hierarchical, nationalistic Olympic regime (Thorpe, 2010b; Thorpe & Wheaton, 2011). For example, when U.S. snowboarder Lindsey Jacobellis fell near the end of the boarder-cross course in the 2006 Olympic final in Torino, Italy, the mass media demanded an explanation for why she would willingly risk a almost certain gold medal by performing a showy stunt in the final stages of the race (Thorpe, 2009). Jacobellis' responded by arguing: "I was having fun. Snowboarding is fun. I wanted to share my enthusiasm with the crowd" (cited in L. Jenkins, 2006, para. 18). But her explanation was unacceptable to many journalists, commentators, and members of the U.S. public, who viewed "having fun" and "styling it" to be incompatible with Olympic ideals. *Chicago Tribune* columnist Rick Morrissey voiced these concerns:

Shaun White celebrates his win at the 2010 Winter Olympics
wearing the infamous U.S. Olympic Snowboarding uniform
of blue jeans and plaid jacket. (AP Photo/Gerry Broome.)

It probably would be a good thing if somebody explained to the
snowboarders that once they decided to sit at the adults' table, they
made the tacit agreement to play to win. They made the decision to act
like Olympians, which now means to act professional. (cited in
Snowboard Culture, 2006, para. 15)

Many snowboarders, however, do not "share the same sensibility of
Mr. and Mrs. America when it comes to gold medals" (S. Jenkins, 2006,
para. 15). According to *The New York Times*, Jacobellis "symbolizes
Generation X Games, the dudes and dudettes more interested in styling

The controversial "Lindsey Leap" that cost U.S. snowboarder Lindsey Jacobellis the gold medal in the snowboard-cross event at the 2006 Winter Olympics. (AP Photo/Lionel Cironneau.)

than winning" (Araton, 2006, para. 2). Indeed, in contrast to mainstream U.S. audiences, many snowboarders empathized with Jacobellis. For example, fellow U.S. Olympic team member and gold-medalist Seth Wescott insisted that freestyle snowboarding is "where the soul of the sport lies. It would have been a shame if she didn't go for it" (cited in Teton, 2006, para. 4). As this example suggests, despite the rapid professionalism and institutionalization of the sport, many snowboarders—even some of the most competitive—continue to privilege fun, friendship, and creative freedom (e.g., style) over winning, ruthless individualism, and conformity (Thorpe, 2009, 2010; Thorpe and Wheaton, 2011).

In the contemporary context where snowboarding is a highly institutionalized and competitive sport, many elite athletes are increasingly accepting (though often begrudgingly) the rules and regulations set by organizing bodies (e.g., International Olympic Committee, International Ski Federation) (Thomas, 2009). As Bob Klein, a former professional snowboarder and current snowboard agent, observes, with huge corporate sponsorships at stake, many competitive snowboarders are adopting more professional approaches: "it's gotten a lot more serious in recent years . . . there's a lot less [athletes] smoking weed" (cited in Higgins, 2010, para.

15). The coach of the British Olympic Snowboarding Team concurs: "People think snowboarder's smoke a lot of dope, party all the time and are always drinking in bars. But the actual professionals aren't doing that at all" (cited in Thompson, 2006, para. 6). Yet, there are still "instances where the anti-establishment and hedonistic ethos" inherent at the core of some of the snowboarding culture occasionally "clash" with the strict, hierarchical, and disciplinary regimes of traditional sports organizations such as the IOC (Thorpe & Wheaton, 2011, p. 193). For example, when risqué photos of U.S. 2010 Olympic half-pipe bronze medalist Scotty Lago posing with a female fan at a postevent party, appeared on a snowboarding Web site, the general public and mass media criticized Lago's actions as unprofessional and decidedly un-Olympic. Many core snowboarders, however, celebrated his behavior as evidence of the sport's continued connection with its countercultural and antiauthoritarian roots. "If you invite the naughty kids to the party don't be shocked when someone pisses in the punch. Snowboarders are not the typical Olympians, for better or worse" proclaimed Todd Richards (cited inThorpe & Wheaton, 2011, p. 194).

The inclusion in the Olympic program has certainly exposed snowboarding to broader audiences and prompted economic growth in the sport and industry; snowboarding has also greatly facilitated the IOC's goal of modernizing the Winter Games and making the Olympics relevant to younger generations. In so doing, it has helped create new space for action sports (e.g., BMX) in the Olympic program (see Thorpe & Wheaton, 2011). Nonetheless, many snowboarders remain adamant that the Olympics "need snowboarding more than snowboarding needs the Olympics" (Todd Richards, cited in Lipton, 2010, para. 2). Indeed, while the Olympic Games are the pinnacle in the careers of many athletes from more traditional sports, many snowboarders recognize events such as the Arctic Challenge, the Mt. Baker Banked Slalom, and even the X Games, as more culturally "authentic" (Wheaton, 2005), and thus more valued by core participants.

mt. baker banked slalom

Infamous for its big mountain terrain, harsh weather, and heavy snowfalls, Mt. Baker in Washington has been a popular resort among free-riders and backcountry boarders since the early 1980s. In contrast to many other North American resorts, Mt. Baker embraced snowboarding almost from its inception, and supported the development of one of the sport's most culturally renowned events: the Mt. Baker Banked Slalom. In 1985, Bob Barci—a local BMX, skateboard, and snowboard shop owner and mentor for many young snowboarders, including members of the infamous Mt. Baker Hard Core crew—conceived a slalom-style race through a natural gully with gates positioned high on the walls. At the time, the Burton-sponsored U.S. Open was gaining momentum as a key event on the East Coast. Working with Burton-rival Tom Sims, Barci conceptualized an event that would offer a unique West Coast alternative that embraced the terrain and culture of Mt. Baker snowboarding. Originally titled the "Sims Open"—the challenge was to beat Tom Sims' timed run through the course. After selecting a 2,000-foot-long natural half-pipe on the "White Salmon" run as the venue, the next challenge was to convince Duncan Howat, the resort manager, to allow the event. As Sims recalls, "Duncan was worried about us getting in skiers' way. We decided to have it in that location, but only if we had it on Super Bowl Sunday—the slowest day of the year" (cited in Banked Slalom, 2008, para. 3).

Twenty-eight snowboarders took part in the inaugural Sims Open, but due to the highly technical course, only 17 finished. As one snowboarding journalist writes, "the course was, and still is, a complete leg burner, up and down through giant banked turns—and if it's been snowing, it's a fine line between staying on the narrow path and wallowing in the deep snow. Any rider who has ever stood in the start, looking down at the first three gates in the course knows a whole new world of anxiety, adrenaline, and nausea" (Banked Slalom, 2008, para. 4). The majority of competitors traveled from Tahoe and the East Coast for the event, with the primary inspiration to meet other snowboarders, and particularly Tom Sims. As local boarder Jeff Fulton recalls, "it was great to have riders like Tom Sims and Terry Kidwell come to Baker and be able to show them around. Sims was the legend—we were like, 'Wow, he's the guy who makes our boards'" (cited in Banked Slalom, 2008, para. 5). Sims confirmed his legendary status by winning the event.

Renamed the Mt. Baker Banked Slalom the following year, the event gained infamy within the growing snowboarding culture, and began attracting participants from across North America, and later, the world. Over subsequent years, the program evolved into a full weekend of activities, including a bonfire on Saturday night, complete with baked salmon dinner, board "waxing reunions" at the Mt. Baker Snowboard Shop, live bands, and much merriment at The Chandelier hotel in the nearest town of Glacier. These events became an integral part of the "Mt. Baker Banked Slalom" tradition (Banked Slalom, 2008, para. 7).

The Banked Slalom event was the predecessor of the boardercross event—an Olympic and X Games favorite. Boardercross competitors qualify based on individually timed runs through a machine-made course featuring jumps and banked corners, and then race three or five others in the finals. In contrast, the Banked Slalom is an individual event held in natural terrain with no prize monies offered. According to event organizer (and daughter of the resort manager) Gwyn Howat, "the motivation for winning is [a key] difference, it's a personal accomplishment more than a monetary accomplishment" (cited in Banked Slalom, 2008, para. 8). In 1988, the event did offer a large cash prize ($8,200), and the format was changed to facilitate television coverage. However, Howat now describes these years as "a painful phase": "As snowboarding started to grow, the cash prizes started to get out-of-our league. We couldn't offer a 100,000-dollar purse, and we realized that's not even why people were coming here from the beginning, so we moved to a culture-versus-cash philosophy and tried to have more unique rewards," including commissioned work from local artists (cited in Banked Slalom, 2008, para. 8). Winners also receive the venerated Duct Tape trophy and an embroidered Carhart jacket. Most importantly, however, they win the respect of their peers.

Deftly organized by sisters Amy and Gwyn Howat, a small group of resort staff, and a large group of volunteers, the Mt. Baker Banked Slalom continues to attract nearly 300 competitors from around the world, many of whom are the top athletes in the field. Recently celebrating its 25-year anniversary, one snowboarding journalist reflects upon the cultural significance of this event in the current hypercommercial context: "Snowboarding goes through phases—the cool places, people, fashion, and tricks change. It seems only one place and one event is immune to the ephemeral world of mainstream snowboarding—or maybe it's just above it all" (Banked Slalom, 2008, para. 1). Indeed, this is an event where new heroes emerge, and legends are made. For example, Terje Haakonsen won his sixth Duct Tape trophy at the 20-year anniversary event in 2004, equaling the most successful female snowboarder, Karleen Jeffery. Returning to the event year after year, Haakonsen proclaims the salmon dinner and the exceptional opportunities for free-riding (before and after heats) with friends at Mt. Baker resort, as prime drawcards. For Haakonsen, and many other committed snowboarders, the Mt. Baker Banked Slalom is the antithesis of the Winter Olympics.

5.   heroes

in contrast to its largely homogenous and united beginnings, where "every other boarder was your buddy" (Peter Line, cited in Coyle, 2004, p. 115), the contemporary snowboarding culture is highly fragmented and hierarchically organized. While less committed novices and poseurs typically have the least amount of respect within the snowboarding culture, and recreational and "core" participants make up the majority of participants, the top ranks are held by a select few professional snowboarders who demonstrate the most physical prowess, courage, and cultural commitment. This chapter examines the unique valuation system within the snowboarding culture, and presents biographies of five key individuals who have made significant contributions to the development of the sport, culture, or industry, at particular periods in snowboarding's short history: Jake Burton Carpenter, Craig Kelly, Terje Haakonsen, Tara Dakides, and Shaun White, respectively. Of course, these are just a select few of the many who have contributed to the development of snowboarding over the years. While it is impossible to include the biographies of all these individuals in this chapter, the activities of many others are discussed throughout this book.

In the contemporary snowboarding culture, prestige is shaped partly by appearing in the snowboarding media and films, and success in contests. But in contrast to more explicitly competitive sports, "physical prowess is assessed more subjectively by snowboarders in terms of style, commitment to snowboarding, capability on challenging terrain," and difficulty and range of maneuvers able to be performed in various found (e.g., cliffs, cornices) and constructed (e.g., jumps, half-pipes) snowy spaces (Thorpe, 2009, p. 374; see also Ford & Brown, 2006). Only one's peers confer prestige and honor in the snowboarding culture (Midol, 1993). In his recent autobiography, Olympic snowboarder Todd Richards (2003) described "gaining respect from my friends" as "way more important than the prize money or the trophy" (p. 166). As this comment suggests, peer recognition is the most highly valued reward among committed snow-boarders, many of whom compete among themselves, via the symbolic practices of physical prowess, commitment, skill, courage, and risk-taking, for marks of "distinction" (Bourdieu, 1984). In the words of one male participant, snowboarders earn respect by going "bigger and fatter than everybody" (cited in Anderson, 1999, p. 55). These are, of course, practices exclusive to only the most committed boarders.

Those snowboarders who demonstrate the most physical prowess gar-ner the most niche media (e.g., magazines, films) attention, which in some cases transfers into financial support from snowboarding companies. Snowboard companies maintain close contact with consumers by sponsor-ing a team of professional and amateur snowboarders. According to Zane (pseudonym), a core U.S. snowboarder and cinematographer, the compa-nies "spend so much money on their team because the team influences the kids, and the kids see a team riding a certain type of product, and that sells products" (interview, 2005). Manufacturers and retailers hire riders on the basis of their physical skills, personality, and attitude that reflect positively on the company. The perceived marketability of a snowboarder is also very important—a point alluded to by David Carrier-Porcheron, a professional snowboarder sponsored by Burton: "I've been asking Burton, 'Why don't you pick up Gaetan? He's so sick!' They're like, 'No, we couldn't . . . the name Gaetan Chanut is just not selling'" (cited in Dresser, January 2005, p. 148).

Combining significant physical prowess with bigger-than-life snow-boarding personalities, a few professionals, including Gretchen Bleiler, Torah Bright, Tara Dakides, Terje Haakonsen, Lindsey Jacobellis, Jeremy Jones, Mark Frank Montoya, Hannah Teter, JP Walker, and Shaun White, have become "superstars" in the snowboarding culture (Is snowboarding a religion?, 2002, para. 3). In an increasingly mediatized culture, some professional snowboarders become iconic; they hold the highest position within the culture. According to Zane, professional snow-boarders have a "ridiculous influence on the kids" (interview, 2005):

My friend Robbie [professional snowboarder] started wearing jeans [while snowboarding], and now everyone wears jeans on the mountain. . . . A couple of days ago we went up to Brighton [Salt Lake City, Utah] and you could tell who each little kid's favorite pro rider was because of what they were wearing, some even had the same haircut as their favorite pros, it was that easy to tell. It was kinda funny but it made me realize how much these pro riders influence the kids. (interview, 2005)

Typically, it is male professional snowboarders who define the snowboarding styles of dress and participation. Observing the influence of professional male snowboarders on the actions of other male boarders, particularly younger males, professional female snowboarder Morgan Lafonte asked: "Why do boys worship men so much? All the men in snowboarding look the same, have the same mannerisms, talk the same and ride the same . . . I can't tell the difference and I'm inside the sport" (cited in Howe, 1998, p. 118). Increasingly, however, some professional female snowboarders, particularly who have been embraced by the snowboarding industry and media (e.g., Torah Bright, Gretchen Bleiler, Erin Cromstock, Tara Dakides, Gabby Maiden, Hannah Teter), are establishing their own space within the snowboarding culture and legitimizing and defining practices and styles for the next generation of female (and male) boarders.

The representations of idyllic transnational lifestyles (i.e., travel to exotic snowboarding destinations, financial independence, partying) of professional male (and some female) snowboarders—particularly big mountain and freestyle athletes—promoted by snowboarding companies and media (e.g., advertisements and videos), work to create a compelling mythology for many cultural participants (also see Frohlick, 2005; Kay & Laberge, 2003). According to Chris Sanders, CEO of Avalanche Snowboards,

> The dream is basically what the kids see when they look in the magazines and see Damian [Sanders] or Terje [Haakonsen]. They are great lifestyle icons. They have it great. It looks like their lives are 24-hour-a-day adventure. You get handed these plane tickets, you hang out with cool photographers, dye your hair however you want to, and you're making money so your parents have no say in your life. It's all sex, action, and glamour. To an 18-year-old snowboarder, this is the dream. (cited in Howe, 1998, p. 68)

While most of the media and snowboarding companies work hard to (re)create the "dream" of the snowboarding lifestyle via extensive coverage and sponsorship of traveling professionals, in reality such opportunities are only afforded a select few. While a handful of North American, and some European, professionals are making six- and even seven-figure salaries, such opportunities are certainly not available to all professional snowboarders.

The notion that professional snowboarding is the "dream job" continues to pervade the snowboarding culture. While professionalism certainly bestows travel, lifestyle, status, and prestige, a recent promotional document sheds some light on the harsh realities of professional snowboarding that include "repetitive risk, lack of health insurance, shortness of careers, and lack of any type of pension" (Northwave, Drake, & Bakota, Winter 2004/2005, p. 16). Snowboarding journalist Jennifer Sherowski (2003) observes that professional snowboarding is increasingly "dangerous," with "riders . . . put[ting] their lives on the line to get the gnarliest footage and photos" (p. 48). In another article, Sherowski (2008) points to some more sober realities: "[Y]our livelihood and sense of self-worth are based completely on the delicate well-being of your physical body, along with something much less tangible—your marketability. You know, hot one second, gone the next. These variables can, and often do, come together to create a system of pressure so intense that it eats people alive" (para. 1). Professional U.S. snowboarder Mike Basich also exposes the risks when he says, "I worry about making it through the day without breaking a bone or getting stuck in an avalanche (knock, knock). Your body takes a beating" (cited in Baccigaluppi et al., 2001, p. 95). Professional snowboarder Travis Parker sums up the situation when he says that we "have to risk our lives to make a paycheck" (cited in Sherowski, 2003, p. 48).

In the contemporary context, however, with significant sponsorships on offer, many boarders happily embrace commercial approaches. The rewards from selling one's labor power are alluring, as Richards (2003) makes clear: "I wanted to make more money, stay ahead of the other guys, drive the nicest car, and have the nicest house" (p. 270). Similarly, professional snowboarder Tara Dakides describes her good fortune as simply "amazing": "I never thought in a million years that I would be able to buy things that I'm able to buy [a new home, a condominium, a new sports-utility vehicle]" (cited in Roberts, 2002, p. A1). Professional snowboarder Kris Jamieson observes "some people making so much money and some so little" in the snowboarding industry (cited in Howe, 1998, p. 101) and draws a perceptive conclusion: "It just goes to show you that snowboarding is just like any other capitalist venture. People don't get what they deserve. They get what they negotiate" (cited in Howe, 1998, p. 101).

Of course, "negotiating" salaries with sponsors or "employers" can be difficult:

The whole business aspect has been an obstacle for me . . . [I have] learnt the hard way . . . I've often just jumped into things, or signed a contract without reading it or understanding it and having enough confidence in myself to tell someone that I'm worth a certain amount. (Megan Pischke, cited in Hakes, 2000, para. 5)

When I first started out professional snowboarding . . . it was a big party . . . I was riding, getting product, and starting to get paid. But now . . . being a professional is serious . . . because I'm dealing with a higher level of everything. The people that are interested in snowboarding now and the people that you want to appeal to are big corporations, people that have PhDs and they don't even snowboard, they don't ski, they go to the gym for their workout. Try to go from working with people that snowboard to people that have absolutely no idea, who have never even seen snow. They are the people that are making all the decisions now and you have to market yourself to them. Being a pro snowboarder means being versatile, kind of like an entrepreneur of your own talent. (Morgan Lafonte, cited in Baccigaluppi, Mayugba & Carnel, 2001, p. 96)

When asked if she receives adequate financial compensation, Lafonte replied,

God, no! Hell, no! K2 thinks my niche is backcountry, [but] anybody that goes into the backcountry is putting [themselves] at risk right away. For someone like K2 to ask me for a film segment in Hatchett's movie, I gotta be out there bustin' my ass. I've gotta be one up on the guys. You know, whoever gets up there first gets it. For what you do to your body and yourself, no, you're definitely not paid what you need to be. (cited in Baccigaluppi et al., 2001, p. 96)

Notwithstanding the essential roles of the sponsored athlete to company success, professional snowboarders are also vulnerable to the processes associated with capitalist accumulation. As pro-snowboarder Tom Burt remarks, sponsored snowboarders are often "the first . . . to hit the floor when companies fall . . . [they're] just a marketing tool" (cited in Baccigaluppi et al., 2001, p. 97). Todd Richards (2003) sums up the plight of the sponsored snowboarder during the economic crisis of the late 1990s: "[F]or the average pro-snowboarder trying to make a living, it meant, 'Damn, my royalty check sucks this month.' Or worse, 'What do you mean, you're restructuring the team? Oh, I get it, I'm fired'" (p. 217). Perhaps not surprisingly, similar processes are underway during the more recent economic recession of the late 2000s and the early 2010s.

As snowboarding becomes increasingly institutionalized and commercialized, professional snowboarders are not only becoming more aware of their individual commodity value, but also their power as a group. Many professional snowboarders now work with sports (or celebrity) agents to better market themselves and to create further opportunities for sponsorship and media coverage. Others are organizing to ensure better working conditions for competitive snowboarders. In 2011, for example, a group of professional snowboarders from around the world founded "We Are Snowboarding" (W.A.S) in response to concerns that "the way snowboarding events are being run now is unhealthy for the athletes who compete within the circuit on a yearly basis" (WAS Launch, 2011). The group has publically expressed concerns over the increasingly "hectic" international competitive schedule. For example, between December 2010 and March 2011, there were more than 27 major competitions scheduled across the globe—i.e., Ticket to Ride (TTR), Burton Global Open Series, FIS World Championships, Dew Tour, and the Winter X Games—with little time scheduled for rest and recovery. The members of W.A.S. are also frustrated by the organization of some these events which prioritize the needs of television and sponsors over the safety of athletes. They are actively challenging:

> competitions that take place at twilight when riders can't see landings or during severe storms when riding conditions are obviously unsafe. Baseball stops in the rain, golf delays during thunderstorms, and ski jumping is postponed when the winds hit specific speeds. Snowboarding events should follow the same rules. (WAS Launch, 2011)

According to the official Web site, W.A.S. was established with the aim to:

> give riders a voice within the competitive snowboarding arena in order to help facilitate a positive, mature progression of the sport. W.A.S. seeks to align the interests of event organizers with those of competitive snowboarders in order to help establish a healthy competitive schedule that benefits the competition circuit, the sport, the athletes, the sponsors, the media, and also the end viewer. (see http://www.wearesnowboarding.com/)

The culture, industry, and sport of snowboarding have undergone rapid changes over the past four decades. While the snowboarding culture has always celebrated those men (and some women) who demonstrate the most physical prowess on the mountain, the personalities and lifestyles of the most culturally exalted "heroes" have been specific to the trends and developments in the broader sociocultural-political context. The remainder of this chapter presents biographies of five individuals who have significantly contributed to the development of the sport, culture, or industry, at particular periods in snowboarding's short history. As noted previously, there have been, and will be, many others who have made, and will make, unique contributions to the development of snowboarding.

jake burton carpenter (1954–)

Born in Manhattan and raised on Long Island, Jake Burton Carpenter (later Jake Burton) describes his upbringing as "a middle class deal," he enjoyed summers at the beach, and family skiing holidays during the winter. He spent the summers envying those riding waves, but during the winter his family traveled to the mountains where he learned the joys of skiing. "From day one, I just got into it and dug the sensation [of skiing]" (Burton, 2008, para. 5). However, two tragedies early in Jake's life—the death of his older brother in Vietnam and his mother to leukemia—shattered his childhood innocence and redefined his personality. "Dealing with all that shit at that age made me very independent. Since then, I've never been comfortable in a closed group of people . . . I like to operate with a certain level of independence" (Burton, 2008, para. 11). While attending boarding school in Massachusetts, these individualist tendencies took the form of adolescent rebellion: "I was basically a f—k off as a kid. I started to learn to beat the system at a very young age and took pride in that. My role models were f—k offs, and I was basically following in their footsteps. I was smoking cigarettes and smoking dope and f—king around, just doing the bare minimum in classes" (Burton, 2010, para. 3).

It was during this time that he first developed a passion for sliding sideways on the snow: "We'd get high and go out on the local sledding hill and ride Snurfers straight down. It was a rodeo-type thing. Just fourteen or fifteen years old, bombing down and taking horrendous wipe-outs" (Burton, 2010, para. 14). At age 15 he was expelled from boarding school and subsequently enrolled in a small private school in Connecticut close to Mohawk Mountain ski resort. Here Jake joined the ski team and rechanneled his energies: "I sort of turned things around and decided I really didn't want to be an underachiever for the rest of my life" (Burton, 2010, para. 16). After finishing high school, Jake started a landscaping business with a friend, enrolled in (and subsequently dropped out of) University of Colorado, and then moved back to New York where he began working for a small business broker company in Manhattan. It was here that he first began to imagine himself as an entrepreneur: "I was talking to all these successful entrepreneurs and realized that it's not impossible to get a business going. The people I was dealing with didn't bowl me over with their capabilities. They seemed like normal people, and I was like, 'Shit, I could've done that'" (Burton, 2010, para. 23).

Combining his newly acquired business acumen and passion for snowsports, twenty-three-year-old Jake Burton Carpenter established Burton Snowboards in 1977 in Londonderry, Vermont. Having recently graduated from New York University with a degree in economics, and together with his work experience in Manhattan, Burton was ready to start his own business. An avid Snurfer in his teenage years, Burton saw the activity as an untapped opportunity for capital accumulation (Helmich, 2000). Indeed, he confessed that his primary drive was to "create a successful business" (Burton, 2003, p. 403) and "make a good living...like 100 grand a year or something" (Burton Carpenter & Dumaine, 2002, para. 12). He calculated that by producing 50 boards a day, he could make at least a comfortable living (Burton Carpenter & Dumaine, 2002). Only now does Jake admit to being "blindly optimistic" (cited in Helmich, 2000, para. 5): "I didn't do any market research; I didn't talk to any competitors. I just brought a little saber saw and started making boards in my apartment. I didn't know what I was doing...It was trial and error" (Burton Carpenter & Dumaine, 2002, p. 64). Burton worked mostly alone, relying on some part-time help from high-school students. After making the boards, he became a "travelling salesman," loading his station wagon and driving to ski and sports stores across the eastern states trying to market and sell his product (Bailey, 1998, para. 28). Within the first year, the fledgling company had sold 300 boards for $88 each, but many complained that the price tag was too high. Burton responded with a cheaper version, the "Backyard," which sold (without bindings) for $45. The following year, he sold 700 boards but continued to struggle financially. In his own words: "I started the business as a get-rich-quick scheme, but very soon I had even less money than when I started" (Burton cited in Morris, 2008, para. 5).

By 1981 Burton had spent his $120,000 inheritance and was $130,000 in debt, but orders for his boards climbed into the thousands over the next few years. In the early and mid-1980s, Burton shifted his focus from selling boards to promoting snowboarding as a physical activity. To create a market, Burton also lobbied the local ski resorts to open their slopes to snowboarding. Paul Alden, who worked for Burton Snowboards from 1984 to 1990, recalls that Burton "spent hundreds of thousands of dollars to put this sport on the map" (cited in Bailey, 1998, para. 32). In 1983, Stratton Mountain in Vermont became the first major ski field to open its piste to snowboarders as a result of Burton's lobbying. Others quickly followed. Sensing the growing momentum, Burton turned his attention back to his product. With financial backing from his wife's family, he developed binding technologies and added a high-tech base and steel edges to his boards, thus making the boards more maneuverable (Randall, 1995). Burton continued to develop snowboarding technologies, and to improve his marketing and distribution practices. In 1984, sales of Burton Snowboards reached $1 million.

Burton Snowboards was not alone in the early snowboarding industry and his plans for the activity and styles of participation diverged from some other early board-makers, particularly Tom Sims. Snowboarding historian Susanna Howe (1998) distinguishes between Burton's vision of snowboarding informed by his "reserved . . . but determined East Coast personality and ski racing background" and that of Tom Sim's which was grounded in "the Californian lifestyle" and "a decade in the volatile skateboard industry." The latter also had good contacts in the media which he used to promote "a personality-driven, hero-worship" snowboarding machine (p. 23). Burton and Sims hosted two major annual contests, the Nationals and the Worlds respectively, in the early 1980s. Not only did such contests contribute to fostering a larger national and international community, they also had a significant impact on the commercial success of their companies (Howe 1998). The rivalry between Burton Snowboards and Sims Snowboards continued to grow and as the competitive arena opened up in the 1980s, Burton and Sims regularly butted heads. Tom Hsieh, editor of the first snowboarding magazine, *International Snowboarder Magazine* (established in 1985 and now defunct), became caught up in this struggle: "I would get calls at three in the morning from those guys. Jake would call up and say that I had too many guys in the air, not enough guys on the ground. That basically meant that I had too many Sims (freestyle) riders [in the magazine] and not enough Burton (alpine) riders" (cited in Howe,

1998, p. 46). According to Howe (1998), however, the "Sims-Burton, West-East coast rivalry" ultimately proved "healthy for snowboarding's advancement" (p. 23).

The potential for growth in overseas markets was considerable during this period and Burton Snowboards established offices in Innsbruck, Austria in 1986 and Tokyo, Japan in 1995. Brad Steward, an employee at Sims Snowboards, recalls that everyone thought Burton was "nuts for going to Europe" (cited in Bailey, 1998, para. 34), but he admitted that Jake "always had vision" and knew how to "look at the much bigger picture" (para. 34). Through geographical expansion, Burton Snowboards became the leading snowboard company in North America, Europe, and Japan (Burton, 2008). Today, Burton Snowboards is a good example of a successful "transnational company" (Pries, 2001). From their offices in Australia, Austria, California, and Japan, and headquarters in Burlington, Vermont, Burton Snowboards currently distributes via independent Burton representatives to authorized specialty retailers in the United States, Canada, 28 countries in Europe, two countries in South America, and Japan, Korea, Australia and New Zealand (Fact Sheet, 2003). In 2009, Burton Snowboards and its subsidiary companies employed almost 1,000 people globally (Burton Reports, 2009). Burton Snowboards also recently expanded into the broader board-sports industry by founding Channel Islands Surfboards and acquiring DNA Distribution, an umbrella company for various skateboarding brands including Alien Workshop, Habitat Skateboards, and Reflex. Doing business in over 35 countries, Burton Snowboards claims to conform to strict ethical global production guidelines (Burton Goes, 2005).

The structure and organization of Burton Snowboards continues to be informed by some of the philosophies inherent in the snowboarding culture. Employees at the headquarters in Burlington, Vermont are given a free season pass to Stowe Mountain Resort and flexibility in their work regimes. For example, if it snows two feet overnight employees can take a few hours off in the morning to go snowboarding, but are expected to work late in the evening. The work environment accommodates young employees; the dress code is casual, dogs are allowed, and a skateboard ramp is available for use during breaks. Despite the appearances of a relaxed workplace, a former employee asserts that Burton Snowboards is famous for "burning out the bright-eyed young workers who flock to the company" and adds that "there is nothing light about it, the work is serious as hell" (cited in Goodman, 2003, para. 19). The labor structure of Burton

Snowboards relies heavily upon part-time, temporary, or subcontracted work arrangements. As numerous social commentators proclaim, such labor structures are necessary for companies to remain flexible in a highly volatile industry. For example, in 2002, following the September 11 terrorist attacks and a poor snow year in North America, Europe, and Japan, Burton Snowboards underwent restructuring and laid off 102 employees (Snowboard Shocker, 2002, para. 6). Burton conceded that while "the people side of these moves suck," such changes were necessary to remain competitive in a capitalist system (Snowboard Shocker, 2002, para. 5).

Despite a recent downturn in the snowboarding industry, Burton Snowboards continues to hold a lion's share of the market such that perceptions of being too commercially successful exist in some quarters. To core boarders—the most savvy of consumers—the "authenticity" of a snowboarding company is central to their consumption choices, and many shy from companies that appear too commercially successful. For example, anti-Burton sentiments regularly appear on snowboarding Web sites: "I personally do not like [Burton] because they're trying to take over the sport and they're only in it for the money that's not what snowboarding is all about" (posted by grrlboarder, on October 30, 2004, www.snowboard.com); "It's rad that Jake Burton still owns em and they've been around for so long but it just seems lame how they dominate sh*t so much, even though that is business, they just seem too geared towards the dollar" (posted by SsKnAoTwE on July 18, 2004, www.snowboard.com). Not surprisingly, competitors help fuel this sentiment. For example, at a 2004 tradeshow, Ride Snowboards posted a banner stating: "The worst thing about riding a Burton is telling your friends you're gay" (see Buzinski, 2004). Shortly after, Ride Snowboards publicly apologized for this homophobic banner. However, the company continued to produce stickers for individuals to place on their snowboards with "the unBurton" printed on them.

While some are critical of his involvement, many others appreciate Burton's contribution to the development of the sport and culture, and the opportunities his company offers its sponsored athletes are second to none: "Burton made snowboarding. Lots of people don't want to believe that because Burton has lots of money. But without Burton, snowboarding would not be as progressive as it is today. Burton pays its riders so well. Every single one of the Burton riders is on the snow 200 plus days a year. Jake is on the snow every day, the guys from Salomon aren't. Jake is the man" (Moriah, interview, 2005).

Core snowboarders base their consumption decisions on "values such as loyalty and commitment" (The principles of snowboarding, 2002, para. 2).

According to one snowboarding journalist: "Riders will typically consider the nature of the company: Is the company committed to snowboarding? Does the company truly understand snowboarding? Companies that are seen to have ulterior motives or as not part of the snowboarding culture will generally be boycotted. Such companies cannot be trusted" (The principles of snowboarding, 2002, para. 2). Recognizing the importance of demonstrating "cultural commitment," Burton Snowboards has always invested heavily in the development of the sport and culture. In 2006, the company established the Burton Global Open Series, which includes some of snowboarding's most prestigious events, including the long-standing Burton U.S. Open, and more recently, the Burton Canadian Open, Burton European Open Snowboarding Championships, Nissan X-Trail Nippon Open, New Zealand Burton Open, and the Burton Australian Snowboarding Open Championships. Although figures of such investment are unavailable, the total prize money for the Burton Global Open Series ($700,000) is indicative of the company's economic investment. The company also invests heavily in the highly esteemed Arctic Challenge and established the novel Burton Abominable Snow Jam (Mt. Hood, Oregon).

Further raising the visibility of the company, Burton Snowboard's recently partnered with various ski resorts—Killington Ski Resort, Vermont; Northstar, Tahoe; Avoriaz, France; The Remarkables, New Zealand; and Flachauwinkel, Austria—to develop an original series of "organic" snowboard terrain parks known as the "Burton Stash" series, which feature natural obstacles such as rocks, stumps, and logs (see www.thestash.com). Burton Snowboard's also partners with various media agencies to produce snowboarding films (e.g., *The B Movie*), television programming (e.g., "Burton TV"), and interactive Web-based media (e.g., Burton Studios with iTunes) to further "showcase Burton's vast history and knowledge to new and expanded audiences" (Press release, 2004). Burton Snowboards, and its subsidiary companies, also sponsor over 100 snowboarders worldwide, approximately 30 of who are women, including U.S. Olympic half-pipe gold medalists Kelly Clark and Hannah Teter. Burton Snowboards also conducts an annual "World Tour" marketing campaign, traveling to major cities throughout North America, Europe, and Japan with a selection of its top athletes. Burton Snowboards also has a philanthropic bent. For example, Burton Snowboards raised and donated $152,000 to disaster relief efforts to help those affected by the hurricanes in North America and earthquakes in Pakistan during 2005, and has also established "Chill," an international, nonprofit intervention program for at-risk inner-city youth aged 10–18.

Unlike the majority of other snowboarding companies, Burton Snowboards remains privately owned by Jake Burton and his wife. While they do not release financial information, a recent industry review estimated that Burton Snowboards currently controls approximately 40 to 70 percent of the multibillion dollar global market, depending on the specific category of goods (Brooks, 2010); foreign sales account for 60 percent of volume, with a very profitable Japanese segment (Burton history, 2005). With diversification into the surf and skate industries and the opening of several brand stores, some suggest that the Burton conglomerate could be worth $1 billion in five years. Jake, however, is "not hung up on that number. I'm not the kind of guy who gets up every morning and says, 'we have to get to $1 billion'" (cited in Horovitz, 20010, para. 17). Recently developing a group of senior managers and dividing up the functions of the company, Jake is increasingly stepping away from the day-to-day running of the business, and spending more time on his board.

> I don't work like I used to. I don't work weekends anymore, and I'm not working 70-hour weeks. Instead, I'm out riding. I'm thinking about it, living it. I've taken my success as an opportunity to get more involved in the sport than I've ever been. I ride alone a lot, get on the chairlift with some kid and talk about what's going on. I realized that the only way I was going to be effective was to immerse myself even more in riding. . . . I can't imagine myself being happier. (Burton, 2010, para. 54)

Spending more than 100 days per year on mountains around the world, Jake Burton confirms his enduring commitment to the sport, and garners respect from some of the sports current heroes; "when [Jake's] in the trees, he does ripping turns. He's a wild man" proclaims Olympic champion Shaun White (cited in Horovitz, 2010, para. 27).

craig kelly (1966–2003)

Craig Kelly, four-time World Champion snowboarder, legendary big mountain rider, and backcountry guide, grew up in the north western town of Mount Vernon, Washington not far from Mt. Baker Ski Area. He tried snowboarding for the first time in 1981, and was among the first snowboarders allowed on Mt. Baker the following year. During the 1980s, the teenage Kelly was part of a tight-knit group of snowboarding friends including Jeff Fulton, Carter Turk, Eric Janko, Dan Donnelly, Amy Howat, and Mike Ranquet, commonly known as the Mt. Baker Hard Core Crew. The infamously harsh weather and varied terrain of Mt. Baker helped nurture this group into all-round free-riders. During the winter of 1983, Tom Sims, early pioneer and owner of Sims Snowboards, "discovered" Kelly during his first trip to Mt. Baker. "When I saw Craig ride," Sims remembers, "I knew he was special" (cited in Blehm, 2003, para. 11). Sims quickly signed Kelly to his snowboarding team.

After finishing high school, Kelly began studying for a degree in chemical engineering at the University of Washington while simultaneously pursuing his snowboarding career. After spending the week at classes at the university, he would drive to Mt. Baker to "train" on the weekends. In 1985, at age eighteen, Kelly took fourth in the inaugural Mt. Baker Banked Slalom event, two years later he won his first half-pipe World Championship. During this time, Kelly became known as "the sport's first truly professional athlete" (Blehm, 2003, para. 26). In the late 1980s, Kelly accepted a generous offer for sponsorship from Burton Snowboards and terminated his contract with Sims. In so doing, however, he became embroiled in a complicated legal battle between Vision (the parent company of Sims Snowboards) and Burton Snowboards due to a supposed breach of contract. While the case was pending, the judge required Kelly to ride his Burton snowboard without graphics; this lead to the ingenious marketing of the first signature board, the "Mystery Air" (Blehm, 2003). Images of Kelly riding the graphic-less "Mystery Air" snowboard caused much cultural controversy. When the suit ultimately ruled in Burton Snowboards' favor, the "Mystery Air" was replaced with the "Craig Kelly Air" which quickly became one of Burton's best-selling snowboards; some commentators rank this as the most culturally renowned snowboard ever built. With his new sponsor offering a six-figure salary, Kelly quit his studies (despite being only a few credits short of graduation) to focus wholeheartedly on his career as a professional snowboarder. Kelly proceeded to win three more World Championship titles and three U.S. Open titles, along with the Baker Banked Slalom in 1988, 1991, and 1993.

At the peak of his career, however, Kelly retired from competitive snowboarding. Exhausted by the "negative energy and stress" of competition, he refocused his attention on backcountry snowboarding (Blehm, 2008, para. 30). In his own words:

Snowboarding is something that I think should be done on your own terms. Society is full of rules, and I use the time I spend in the mountains as an opportunity to free myself of all constraints. . . . competing on the World Tour restricted the freedom that I found with snowboarding in the first place, so I decided to try a year with very little competing. . . . This is not retirement. I am simply revolving my snowboarding around free-riding rather than competing. (cited in Reed, 2005, p. 59)

Kelly told Jeff Galbraith, founding editor of *Frequency: The Snowboard Journal*, that he sought not "the most dangerous line but the one that feels the best—the grooviest" (cited in Reed, 2005, p. 57). For Kelly, snowboarding in the backcountry offered new opportunities for self-expression and transcendental experiences:

My favorite part of the backcountry experience is the freedom aspect . . . the concept of the pu'u in Chinese means the uncarved block, or the clean slate . . . and that's what the backcountry represents to me. Even through you can't go everywhere—you're gonna find a cliff or avalanche danger or whatever—but in general you are so much more free in the backcountry to carve the line you want or pick the route you want. And you get to express yourself in whatever way feels comfortable out there. . . . In the backcountry is when I feel most artistically inclined, without inhibitions. Especially without cameras around. (cited in Karleen, 2008, para. 13)

Tom Sims labeled Kelly "a Zen snowboarder" and said that he "sacrificed material wealth to seek oneness with his riding and the backcountry." Certainly, Craig Kelly was the quintessential soul-boarder.

At the time, many in the sport and industry deemed Kelly's career radical; he was among the first to attempt to pioneer a career solely from big mountain snowboarding. Nonetheless, he convinced his primary sponsor—Burton Snowboards—to trust his decision to refocus his energies. While Kelly no longer competed in snowboarding competitions, he maintained his relationship with Burton Snowboards as a sponsored team rider and spokesman. Highly evocative images of Kelly's backcountry exploits—carving down steep mountain faces, or jumping off rugged cliffs—regularly appeared in snowboarding magazines and films, such that he continued to act as a highly effective "media tool" for Burton. He also combined his extensive snowboarding knowledge and technical background to work closely with Burton

Snowboards' designers and engineers to produce new technologies, including a splitboard designed specifically for ascending backcountry terrain. Jake Burton recognizes Kelly as making not only a unique contribution to the development of snowboarding style, technique and technologies, but also to the "success of Burton as a brand" (cited in Reed, 2005, p. 57).

But, on January 21, 2003, Craig Kelly was tragically killed by an avalanche while working with Selkirk Mountain Experience (SME), a backcountry ski-touring business based in Revelstoke, British Columbia, Canada. Reed (2005) likened Kelly's loss to snowboarding to "the passing of a Pope or the untimely death of Princess Diana" (p. 61). "I can't think of a bigger loss to the sport and to all of us personally" said Jake Burton, "Craig was the epitome of core" (cited in Reed, 2005, p. 62). In 2007, *Let it Ride*—a film produced by Jacques Russo and narrated by Metallica front man James Hetfield—documented the life of Craig Kelly. With original interviews of Kelly speaking candidly about his experiences and visually stunning footage of him performing in various snowy environments (i.e., half-pipes, backcountry), juxtaposed with heartfelt interviews with various key cultural participants, the film was acclaimed by snowboarders and mountain-film festival audiences alike. The film won numerous awards, including Best Film Mountain Culture award at the Whistler Film Festival, and Best Film and Best Soundtrack at the X-Dance Film Festival in Salt Lake City, Utah. Dano Pendygrasse, the editor of *Future Snowboarding Magazine*, says the film is particularly significant because it tells the story of "snowboarding's last great leader."

terje haakonsen (1974–)

Five-time World Champion snowboarder, Terje Haakonsen grew up in the Telemark region of southern Norway in the village of Romot. He learned to crosscountry ski at age three and alpine ski when he was five. But it was not until the winter of 1987 that he first tried snowboarding. Within three short years, Haakonsen had mastered the sport; he had signed a sponsorship deal with Burton Snowboards, and begun competing at the highest level. He made his debut on the international snowboarding scene at the 1990 U.S. Open, as professional boarder Todd Richards (2003) recalls "a little fifteen-year-old kid from Norway" dropping into the half-pipe and wowing the crowd with "big airs that seemed even bigger because of his size": "Everybody who watched him ride that day suspected they might be watching the next Craig Kelly" (p. 100). Haakonsen went on to fulfill these expectations, winning multiple World Championships, three U.S. Open Half-pipe Championships, and five European Half-pipe Championships. In the half-pipe, he performed the most difficult maneuvers with huge amplitude and a sense of ease. Highly creative in his approach to snowboarding, Haakonsen developed a new aerial maneuver called the Haakonflip. He further solidified his mythic status in 1998 when, at the infamous Mt. Baker Banked Slalom event, he rode through the challenging course fakie (backwards) and still finished fourth in the qualifying round. The following day he won the event (see Chapter 4).

Not only did Haakonsen win nearly every major half-pipe competition at least once during the 1990s, he also played an integral role in redeveloping big mountain riding. He was among the first snowboarders to perform freestyle snowboarding maneuvers on natural terrain in the backcountry. Always searching for new challenges, Haakonsen was also refining his skills on a surfboard. In his own words, "surfing has made me look at the terrain a little differently. The way I do power turns in the critical point in the mountains is similar to surfing. I think surfing has helped my snowboarding" (cited in Galbraith & Marcopoulos, 2004). Certainly, his combination of freestyle, free-riding, and surfing styles helped redefine big mountain riding. During the mid- to late 1990s, Haakonsen shifted his focus from competition to filming and continued to expand his legend with "unbelievable performances" in videos such as *RoadKill*, *The Garden*, and the *Totally Board* series. He then redefined the meaning of "going big" in *Subjekt Haakonsen* (1996) and *The Haakonsen Faktor* (2000). According to snowboarding journalist Jeff Galbraith, these videos reinforced Haakonsen's "feline propensity for landing on his feet from any height and any position" (Galbraith & Marcopoulos, 2004). It is for this reason that he is popularly nicknamed "The Cat."

Haakonsen was undoubtedly the world's best half-pipe rider when snowboarding was included in the Winter Olympics. But he fervently opposed snowboarding's inclusion into the Games. He criticized the International Olympic Committee's lack of understanding of snowboarding culture or consideration of snowboarders' needs. "The fact is that the big wigs ride in limousines and stay in fancy hotels while the athletes live in barracks in the woods," he argued (cited in Humphreys, 2003, p. 421). Not surprisingly, he refused to participate. In so doing, he singlehandedly called into question the validity of a gold medal.

In 1999, Haakonsen backed up his convictions by cofounding the Arctic Challenge, an annual snowboarding event held in a traditional

Norse village, that prioritized the athletes over all else. He listened to riders' wants and needs and tailored the competition accordingly. Haakonsen's influence goes beyond rethinking jump and quarter-pipe dimensions, and event organization. For example, wanting to underline the connection between good sporting achievement and quality food, the event serves only organic food and refuses to offer any form of fast food. Furthermore, the event provides opportunities for competitors to enjoy other leisure pursuits during their time in Norway, including fishing and surfing. The event continues to be one of the most innovative and respected titles in the sport.

After stepping away from competitive snowboarding for a few years, Haakonsen returned with a vengeance in 2008 when he won the Arctic Challenge quarter-pipe title with a world-record breaking 360 degree rotation performed 32 feet above the specially designed jump (Terje Breaks, 2008, para. 1). Snowboarding Sports marketing manager, Matty Swanson, declared this "one of the most significant days in snowboarding history . . . There is no question that Terje is the icon of our sport and will be for many years to come" (Terje Breaks, 2008, para. 3). Similarly, Reed (2005) describes him as "a master of all trades"; he "goes the biggest, wins the most, rides the fastest, and just does everything the best" (p. 126). While Haakonsen rarely competes anymore, he continues to feature in snowboarding films, and recently starred in the blockbuster snowboarding movie *First Descent* (2005). In the words of journalist Jeff Galbraith, Terje Haakonsen has "defined snowboarding's attitude, style and soul like none other" (Galbraith & Marcopoulos, 2004).

tara dakides (1975–)

Three-time World Champion snowboarder and five-time X Games gold medallist, Tara Dakides grew up in Laguna Hills, California. Dakides' childhood revolved around sports, including gymnastics, horse-riding, skateboarding, and soccer. She started snowboarding in her early teenage years and found solace from a messy home life in the terrain park. In her own words, "I was never a good student and I always got in trouble. I was definitely a rebellious kid" (cited in Reed, 2005, p. 163). At fifteen she left home, and by sixteen she had found her way to Mammoth Mountain Ski Area, California where she proceeded to live the snowboarding lifestyle. Dakides actively pursued a snowboarding career by riding in local competitions, promoting herself at industry trade shows, and producing "sponsor-me" videos.

During this period she worked the occasional part-time job to "support the habit," but recalls getting fired from both her position as a cashier at an Ace Hardware store for turning up with her lip pierced with a safety pin, and her job at a gourmet sausage place when she failed to show up after her boss refused to give her time off to attend a snowboard contest. With her efforts focused elsewhere, Dakides became one of the most progressive female snowboarders riding rails and jumps in the early 1990s. Sponsors took notice and in 1994 she turned professional, leaving her menial part-time jobs behind for good.

Dakides fundamentally changed women's snowboarding when she performed her revolutionary back-flip—a trick no woman had previously attempted in competition—during the Big Air finals at the 1998 Vans Triple Crown competition at Breckenridge, Colorado. Demonstrating exceptional physical prowess and courage, Dakides helped challenge popular perceptions that female riders were less capable than their male counterparts. According to snowboarding journalist Jardine Hammond (2000), Dakides has "taken not only the standard for women in sport, but the standard of riders of either gender to the next level." Almost every article acknowledges her role in narrowing the gap between genders. "It used to be that women had to measure themselves against the dudes, but not anymore," says fellow professional Barrett Christy, "Tara is a big reason why" (cited in Elliot, 2001). During the late 1990s and early 2000s, Dakides dominated many of the contemporary disciplines including big air, slope style, and rails. Her extensive list of wins includes five Winter X Games gold medals and three World Snowboarding Championships. Dakides' powerful, "aggressive, hard, and fast" styles gained the respect of her peers who voted her Best Female Freestyle Rider in 1999, 2000, and 2001, Best Overall Female Rider in 2000 and 2001, and Best Female Rail Rider in 2001, at the *Transworld Snowboarding* Rider's Poll Awards. Dakides was also *Snowboarder* magazine's Female Snowboarder of the Year in 2000, 2001, and 2002.

Tara Dakides demonstrates a fearless attitude to snowboarding. In her own words, "if it scares me then I just want to do it more, I don't like being scared and I don't like thinking that I'm not going to do something because I'm scared of it" (cited in Watson, 2001). She "rides with the same level of confidence and courage as a guy does," says Jake Burton, "although there have been other women along the way who have done that, it's never been in this sort of technical, freestyle way with rails and big airs. The way she charges is freakin' impressive" (cited in Reed, 2005, p. 158). Indeed, Dakides provided a much needed source of inspiration for many female boarders. According to one core female snowboarder, "I was never really inspired by girls until Tara Dakides in 1998. I really looked up to Tara, not only did she rip, but she was also a gorgeous girl. I think it's important to be able to step it up on the hill and still have a bit of femininity too" (interview, 2006). Professional Canadian snowboarder Leanne Pelosi also admits to "totally idoliz[ing] Tara Dakides." As a role model, Dakides has proved to males and females alike that sex is not a limiting factor in snowboarding. Dakides aggressive style of riding has challenged the "maleness" of snowboarding and, in so doing, she has helped shore up space for women within the sport, culture, and industry.

While Dakides proclaims to appear far from feminine on the mountain, she also enjoys "being a girl. There's nothing wrong with being an athlete and a beautiful woman" (Ulmer & Straus, 2002, para. 5). As well as demonstrating a traditional "masculine" capacity for aggression and dominance, Dakides simultaneously mastered the traditionally-defined "feminine" arts of image management (Thorpe, 2008a). Indeed, part of Dakides' market appeal was her "sexy bad-girl" image. As Reed (2005) writes, "though she may ride (and cuss and spit) like a guy on the snow, that's where it ends. There's no question, she's sexy with a capital X. Indeed, her unique combination of skill and sex appeal helped to cross yet another threshold—that of mainstream pop culture" (p. 164). During the late 1990s and early 2000s, shirtless quartets of admiring males with T-A-R-A spelled across their chests would greet her at finish lines, while online chats often left Dakides fending off marriage proposals, along with more salacious offerings.

A fearless attitude combined with a marketable image contributed to making Dakides "arguably the most popular snowboarder at the Winter X Games" (Seelenbrandt, 2001). With her sporting success Dakides gained eminence in the broader U.S. popular culture, with major corporate sponsors including Mountain Dew and Campbell's Soup, as well as a range of product sponsors including Jeenyus Snowboards, Billabong, Von Zipper, Vans, and Pro Tec Helmets, all using her signature on their designs. Dakides has also achieved broader celebrity status featuring in *Rolling Stone*, *Sports Illustrated*, and *Maxim*. After appearing on its cover (in nothing but body paint), *FHM* readers voted Dakides one of the "Top 100 Sexist Women in the World." She also featured on the cover of *Sports Illustrated for Women* and was named "The Coolest Sports Woman in 2001." She has judged the Miss Teen America pageant and in February 2004 she appeared on the "Late Show with David Letterman." The latter, however, did not go as planned.

A massive wooden snow-covered ramp was constructed outside the studio in the middle of 53rd Street; it was supposed to launch Dakides over the twenty-foot gap between the takeoff and landing. However, warm weather melting the snow and the pressure of a big-time production, diminished Dakides chances of successfully completing the backside 360 degree maneuver she had planned. Standing atop of the jump, Dakides casually laughed and joked with Letterman on live television, but she was unaware of the changing conditions. When it came time to perform the stunt, her board sank in the soft snow covering the run-in and she was thrown off-balance. Soaring off the side of the jump, Dakides collided with a cameraman before falling on asphalt from an estimated height of 25 feet. Dakides was knocked unconscious and split her head in front of a stunned crowd and live national audience. Letterman cancelled two shows scheduled later that night because of this "horrific, miserable tragedy" (cited in Troetal, 2004, para. 1). The mass media pounced upon the event. "It just spread like wildfire" says Dakides: "I woke up the next day on the cover of the [*New York] Post*, the *New York Times*, and the *Daily News*. Paparazzi were trying to climb on the roof and sneak in through the top of the hospital . . . it was *crazy*" (cited in Reed, 2005, p. 161; italics in original). The event was covered by every major U.S. newspaper and it became the lead story on local news programs across the country.

Dakides later returned to the "Late Show with Letterman," sans snow-board, and appeared on "Last Call with Carson Daly," "The Early Show," "Deborah Norville Tonight," and the "The Howard Stern Show." Much to the dismay of many inquisitive snowboarders, Letterman banned any further reruns of the incident, obviously wanting to "erase this little mishap from everyone's minds" (Roenigk, 2004b, para. 1). According to Dakides, footage of the accident was censored because it challenged assumptions held by mainstream U.S. viewers about appropriate risk-taking for young women: "[N]obody wants to see a girl hit the concrete, hard, on *David Letterman*. Is that supposed to be funny?" (cited in Roenigk, 2004b, para. 7). An unforeseen benefit from this incident, according to Dakides, was that "a lot more people know my name now" (cited in Roenigk, 2004b, para. 12). But, Dakides also observed the risks for the athlete within this highly mediated context: "[T]hey build these big obstacles to watch us do gnarlier and gnarlier tricks, and I'm risking my entire season and all my other goals . . . laying in bed for a month is not fun" (cited in Roenigk, 2004b, para. 4).

Adopting a courageous and competitive approach to snowboarding, Dakides has experienced her share of injuries, including a fractured back, dislocated elbows, torn ligaments in each knee, a broken fibula, as well as numerous concussions. Despite numerous surgeries and extensive reha-bilitation programs, Dakides continues to compete. She also satiates her thirst for adventure with a serving of other "extreme" sports; she is an avid surfer and skateboarder, races motocross, and drives a variety of race cars including shifter cars and formula race cars. In 2006, she became the first woman to complete the Baja 1000, traveling 200 miles across the Mexican desert behind the wheel of a custom Baja race car for a total of 43 hours. Tara Dakides surely embodies "extreme."

The significance of her contributions to the development of snowboard-ing, and her personal battles to achieve such successes, have been captured in *Against the Grain: A Documentary on the Life of Tara Dakides*, which went on to win the Best Biography award at the 2008 X-Dance Film Festival, and the Best Sports Documentary at the San Diego International Film Festival that same year. According to Dakides, the motivation for pro-ducing this film—in which she shares her personal journey through parental divorce, depression, drug and alcohol use, suicidal attempts, involuntary confinement to a psychiatric ward, her participation in skateboarding and punk-rock cultures, her competitive snowboarding career, mainstream celebrity, a relationship break-up, and numerous injuries—was to "inspire kids who maybe don't have some sort of guidance or mentor . . . to find the tools to guide themselves" (cited in Bengal, 2008, para. 8).

shaun white (1986–)

Double Olympic half-pipe gold medalist, ten-time Winter X Games gold medalist (five gold medals for slope-style and five for super-pipe), and Summer X Games gold medalist (vert skateboarding), Shaun White was born with a congenital heart defect for which he underwent two open-heart operations before the age of one. Growing up in Carlsbad, California, White took to skateboarding not long after he could walk, and started skiing shortly thereafter. Following in his older brother Jesse's footsteps, he started snowboarding when he was only six years old; he was doing jumps and land-ing them on the same day. According to Jesse, "Mozart was supposed to play piano," it was "that kind of deal for Shaun" (cited in Reed, 2005, p. 170). White was part of a "supportive and tight-knit family" and every weekend during the winter his parents drove three hours to the ski areas near Big Bear Lake, California. "I'd go up and learn like five new tricks and come back down, and every time I was just more and more excited about snowboarding" recalls White (cited in Reed, 2005, p. 172). He started competing, and winning, at age seven. In addition to dominating junior competitions, he made appearances in a number of snowboarding films. With sponsorship from Burton Snowboards, White turned professional at the 1998 U.S. Open, age twelve. He was the sports first "prodigy" and was nicknamed "Future Boy" for his potential to take snowboarding in new and exciting directions.

This is exactly what he has done. In the early twenty-first century, White has become an undeniable force in half-pipe, slope-style, and big-air competitions. In the 2005–2006 season, 19-year-old White became the most successful snowboard competitor in the history of the sport, with 12 consecutive wins, including two X Games gold medals, an Olympic gold medal in the half-pipe, and victory in the U.S. Open Half-pipe and Slope-style Championships. White's huge amplitude, technical abilities, and style in the half-pipe, and on jumps and rails, appear to be an unbeatable combination. According to Tom Zikas, a snowboarding judge and photographer, what separates White from his fellow competitors is that he "makes it look so effortless": "White holds his board-grabs longer, plus his combinations are more gnarly. White will throw consecutive 1080s, then a backside 900, while other boarders space out difficult stunts" (cited in Norcross, 2006, para. 18). Skateboarding legend Tony Hawk describes White as "one of the most amazing athletes on the planet. He's got his own style—plus he can do tricks five feet higher than everyone else" (cited in Edwards, 2006).

With his sporting successes White has gained eminence in the culture. He received the most snowboarding media print coverage (editorial and advertising) in the two major international snowboarding magazines— *Transworld Snowboarding* and *Snowboarder* magazine—during the 2002–2003 and 2005–2006 seasons. Furthermore, he is the first snowboarder since Terje Haakonsen to be the subject of a full length video. *The White Album* (2004) provides a spectacular display of White's snowboarding, and skateboarding, skills. White also starred in the blockbuster film *First Descent* (2005) which featured him performing in half-pipes and on jumps of gigantic proportions (95 feet) in the backcountry, as well as riding death-defying lines in Alaska.

It was White's Olympic success, however, that propelled him most powerfully into the public spotlight. His winning performance at the 2006 Winter Olympics in Turin, Italy grabbed headlines across the country, and he has since made numerous guest appearances on television and radio talk-shows. "The Flying Tomato" rapidly became a household name. He featured on the cover of *Rolling Stone*, which declared him "the coolest *kid* in America," and Ubisoft quickly signed White to a worldwide video game deal. His signature video game "Shaun White Snowboarding: Road Trip" was released in 2007. According to *CNN Money*,

> experts in the field generally point to snowboarder Shaun White as the one break-out star of these Games in terms of endorsement potential. His gold medal win, coupled with his personality, his now famous bright red hair and his memorable nickname—The Flying Tomato—all give him a great profile. He did everything right in Turin. He was even crying on the medals stand. He lived up to the hype. He's clearly comfortable on camera. You'll see a lot of him.

Similarly, *ESPN.com* declares White "one of the biggest financial winners from the games."

Four years later, White was identified as the "most popular" and "recognizable athlete" attending the 2010 Winter Olympic Games in Vancouver (Ebner, 2009). Analyzing online discussions during the Vancouver Olympics, U.S. media analysis firm Neilsen Company revealed White as the second most "buzzed about" athlete at the Games (Skaters and Snowboarders Most Buzzed about Athletes at Olympics, 2010). According to a report by *Forbes* magazine, with an annual salary of more than $10 million from prize money, and his relationships with an array of mainstream (i.e., Red Bull, Target, HP, Mountain Dew, Ubisoft) and board-sport (i.e., Burton, Oakley) companies, White was the most highly paid athlete entering the 2010 Winter Olympics. After winning the gold medal in his first run of the finals, White proceeded to dazzle audiences with "a victory lap that would be remembered" (White, 2010). He described his final performance as "a once-in-a-lifetime feeling," and speaking specifically to his joy of riding the Olympic half-pipe: "there's this amazing moment when you're not going up anymore and not coming down . . . you're just floating . . . it's like flying. . . . it's the best feeling" (*60 Minutes*, 2010).

White is also a passionate and extremely skilled skateboarder. When he was only thirteen years old, he started touring with Tony Hawk's famous Boom Boom HuckJam demo tour during the summer; Hawk has been a supporter ever since. He rode his skateboard "strictly for fun" until the 2003 Slam City Jam skateboarding event in Vancouver, Canada, where he joined the professional ranks. In 2005, he won a silver medal in the vert ramp skating competition at the Summer X Games, becoming the first extreme athlete to win a medal in both the Winter and Summer Games. The same year White won his first skateboarding gold medal at the Dew Action Sports Tour; he then won his first Summer X Games gold medal in the 2007 skateboarding vert event. Just months after his success at the 2010 Winter Olympics, White won a silver medal in the vert skateboarding event at the Summer X Games in downtown Los Angeles. In the words of snowboarding author Rob Reed (2005): "by pushing the envelope in both snowboarding and skateboarding, White has established himself as an action-sport figure beyond compare" (p. 178). This is particularly true in the eyes of corporate and television sponsors. In addition to lucrative sponsorships from transnational board-sport companies such as Burton, Oakley, and Volcom, White also endorses Mountain Dew, Sony Playstation, and Target, appearing in television commercials and sporting their logos.

Immersed in the board-sports industry from a young age, White has become a savvy businessman. He is critically aware of the economic value of both his ability to perform huge gravity defying maneuvers in half-pipes and terrain parks, and the appeal of his "alternative" image to corporate and television sponsors, and the general public alike. In an effort to maintain some credibility in the eyes of his peers, White works closely with key staff to produce marketing campaigns that are consistent with his personal style and cultural values; he also partners with companies to design and develop his own signature products, including goggles with Oakley, snowboarding equipment (e.g., snowboards, bindings, boots), clothing (e.g., jackets, pants) and accessories (e.g., helmets, gloves) with Burton, and a line of urban-style clothing sold in Target stores throughout North America. He was also actively involved in developing the second edition of his signature video game "Shaun White Snowboarding 2: World Stage."

White is explicitly aware of the importance of "cultural authenticity" (Beal and Weidman, 2003) among the highly discerning snowboarding market, and thus carefully protects his image by refusing to be associated with companies or projects that could damage his appeal to young consumers: "A lot of people will just put their name on anything, and you can tell. I just can't do that" (Shaun White, cited in Ebner, 2009, para. 18). According to White's previous agent, Mark Ervin, "every week we get presented with a big opportunity from someone. Shaun turns down a lot of money" (cited in Ebner, 2009, para. 17). Since his second Olympic medal, White has transitioned from action-sport superstar to mainstream celebrity. Reflecting his interest in pursuing new opportunities in music, television, and film, White recently ended his long-term relationship with IMG agent

Mark Ervin, signing a new contract with the more theatrically-focused agency CAA who have dedicated a team of agents to manage his sporting and entertainment deals, and marketing (Mickle, 2010).

Despite White's best efforts to maintain his cultural credibility, his successes have alienated him from his peers, many of whom criticize his individualistic approach to training and competition, and his embrace of mainstream celebrity. During a *60 Minutes* interview in the lead up to the Vancouver Olympics, the interviewee cited one of White's competitors: "He's just got his self, and he's in his own world, and he's doing his own thing. But we all have each other, and it's really quite sad," to which White responds: "Yeah . . . I'll admit . . . I definitely find it a bit lonely sometimes." A snowboarding superstar without peer, White's influence on the sport is undeniable. While he may have become estranged from some of his current snowboarding compatriots, Shaun White is surely inspiring the next generation of snowboarding heroes.

6. technicalities

the early equipment used by the snowboarding pioneers was rudimentary. Boards, boots, and bindings were often homemade or modified by participants themselves. Snowboarding historians such as Susanna Howe (1998) and Rob Reed (2005) have described the early 1980s as a highly experimental time with small groups of snowboarders scattered throughout North America, the majority of whom were developing their own equipment and styles of participation based on trial and error: "each group of backcountry hikers had its own version of snowboarding, shaped by local climate and terrain, equipment, and roots (e.g., skiing, skateboarding, BMX biking, mountaineering, and surfing) . . . boards were all different shapes, with all different features: rocker, multiple fins, swallow tails, fish tails, and all different kinds of side-cut" (Howe, 1998, p. 28). Often credited with developing the modern carving snowboard Mike Olson, founder of Gnu Snowboards, recalls his initial inspiration: "I remember sitting in our backyard drawing a sketch for a skateboard and dreaming about surfing. I remember suddenly looking down thinking how great it would be if I could make a huge skateboard/surf board/ski thing out of the picnic table bench" (cited in Howe, 1998, p. 33). In South Lake Tahoe, Chris Sanders made snowboards in his garage. On the weekends, he would hike up the slopes at Lake Tahoe's Soda Springs with his girlfriend to test these boards, often selling their prototypes to inquisitive skiers (Howe, 1998).

As snowboarding gained popularity among local groups of young board-sport enthusiasts across North America and various European countries, some of the earlier pioneers began developing new technologies with a sense of urgency. Early competitions became important spaces where pioneers showcased both their skills and latest wares. For example, at the 1982 National Snowsurfing Championships at Vermont's Suicide Six ski area, Tom Sims challenged assumptions about what a snowboard looked like and could do: "I went down to the thrift store, the Salvation Army, and brought a pair of skis for five bucks. I unscrewed every metal edge, routed my snowboard, screwed on every little piece, filled it up with epoxy, and sanded it down—so it had metal edges" (cited in Reed, 2005, p. 35). Reaching speeds of 50 miles per hour, Sims won the downhill event, which gave his company and product that much more credibility among his peers. The technical developments and physical performances of the early pioneers at these events had cultural significance.

As the sport and industry continued to grow, snowboarding equipment—boards, boots and bindings—developed quickly during the 1980s and 1990s. Summarizing this period of rapid growth and technological change, snowboarding historian Susanna Howe (1998) writes: "contests threw progression into hyper-speed. Riders were pushed to go faster and jump higher. Board-makers were more aware than ever that there was a future in making snowboards, and more inspired than ever by their inventive colleagues" (p. 50). By 1986, the majority of snowboard makers recognized the value of ski technologies—metal edges, P-text, camber, and side-cut—and some (e.g., Olson, Sanders, and Burton) started making boards in Austria, "capitalizing on its advanced ski engineering, rich alpine heritage, open-minded attitude, and favorable exchange rate" (Howe, 1998, p. 50).

Snowboarding technologies (e.g., board shape, boot lacing systems, binding design) developed quickly during the 1980s and 1990s; such advances made learning easier and attracted more participants to the sport. Many of the latest developments, however, continued to emerge from the riders themselves. For example, Jake Blattner recollects the do-it-yourself mentality prevalent among snowboarders during the early years of the "jib movement" in the early 1990s: "[T]here were no boards being made for what we wanted to do . . . so we took matters into our own hands and cut the noses off our boards" (cited in Howe, 1998, p. 86; see Thorpe, 2007a). Recognizing this trend, some snowboard companies promptly retooled to produce an array of snowboards designed specifically for jibbing (e.g., shorter boards, wider stances, less aggressive edges, twin-tips). In the late 1990s, technological developments slowed, such that new snowboards, boots, and bindings, did not radically change the snowboarding experience. The following comments from Ste'en Webster, Olympic judge and editor of *New Zealand Snowboarder* magazine, are insightful here:

> During the late 80s, and to an extent the early 90s as well, technological developments were rapid fire. . . . These developments

directly influenced the performance factor of what we were doing, so we did anything we possibly could to get our hands on the latest equipment. This has not been a relevant factor of snowboarding for at least 10 years, maybe longer. These days the so-called technological developments have a fraction of the impact of the ones we grew up with. For instance, when the 4-hole insert pattern started to become available, we no longer had to drill holes in our boards to get a wider stance! (interview, 2008)

In an effort to sustain snowboarders' desire for the latest products, companies began investing more strongly in marketing and graphics. Today, companies offer a plethora of boards, bindings, and boots, designed, packaged and marketed specifically for different niche markets (e.g., youth, women) and consumer groups (e.g., freestylers, backcountry). They also produce an array of snowboarding clothing (jackets, pants, beanies, and undergarments), accessories (goggles, gloves, helmets, and body armor), bags (urban bags, snowboard packs, travel bags, and board bags), footwear and casual clothing (t-shirts, long-sleeve shirts, sweatshirts, and caps), for all participants, ranging from novice to professionals. While the "technological developments are a very important and interesting aspect of snowboarding's history" (Ste'en Webster, interview, 2008), this chapter focuses more on some of the technical aspects of the more extreme variants of snowboarding, particularly big jump construction and performance, and big mountain snowboarding access and rescues.

constructing terrain parks

As equipment has developed and the skills of freestyle-oriented snowboarders have continued to progress, so too have the demands on ski resorts to build larger and more challenging facilities. Attempting to attract the highly lucrative snowboarding demographic, ski resorts around the world are investing millions of dollars on expensive equipment and personnel to build high quality half-pipes and terrain parks. In contrast to the early half-pipes which were hand-built by small groups of passionate freestyle snowboarders, today pipe construction typically begins during the summer with extensive earthworks, followed by careful and time-intensive shaping at the beginning of the winter, and nightly maintenance and regular reshaping throughout the season. Many resorts use a Pipe-Dragon—a hydraulically-powered snow-shaping device that is attached to a snow-cat and used to form the half-pipe's curved transitions and vertical walls. Other designs include the Super-pipe Dragon, which creates a pipe on a steeper slope with 15–17 foot walls; and the Pipe Master, which pulls the snow from inside the pipe relocating it elsewhere in the pipe to fill holes and take out bumps. Similar technologies such as the Snow Turbo Super-pipe Grinder, the Pipe Magician, the Scorpion, and the Zaugg Pipe Designer, can cost up to $250,000. Half-pipe dimensions vary across resorts, depending on equipment, snow conditions and geography, and personnel. But international competition half-pipes must meet strict dimensions. A FIS (International Skiing Federation) World Cup super-pipe must feature 6.5 meter (21 ft) high walls, be 120–165 meters (394–541 ft) in length and 19.5 meters (64 ft) in width, and on a slope of 17.5–18.5 degrees. A super-pipe of these dimensions built for the 2010 U.S. Snowboarding Grand Prix event took 550 gallons of snow and approximately $115,000 to create (Kinkade, 2010).

During the late 1990s, many resorts began developing terrain parks which were gaining popularity among young, freestyle-oriented snowboarders. According to professional U.S. snowboarder Todd Richards (2005), ski resorts "slobbered over snowboarders in an effort to attract dollars" during this period, with many going to great lengths to cater to the increasing diverse needs of snowboarders:

> Kids wanted an entire playground, not just a jungle gym, so ski resorts hired snowboarders as consultants [to construct] snowboard parks. In the quest to build the best park, mountain managers signed off on huge kickers, roller-coaster rail slides, welded-metal rainbows, gaps to jump over, and buses and Volkswagen beetles to jib—all the things that were previously forbidden for insurance purposes. (p. 220)

Today, some resorts are culturally renowned within the global snowboarding community for their efforts to cater to the demands of freestyle snowboarders and skiers (see Chapter 4). The annual *Transworld Snowboarding* "Resort Poll" publishes the results of thousands of online votes for the best three North American resorts visited during the previous season, with more than 20 categories including quality of terrain parks and half-pipes. While Whistler/Blackcomb often wins the "best terrain park" category, numerous resorts in California (i.e., Bear Mountain, June Mountain; Northstar-at-Tahoe, Mammoth Mountain), Colorado (i.e., Breckenridge, Buttermilk, Cooper, Keystone, Snowmass), Oregon (i.e., Mt. Hood Meadows), and Utah (i.e., Park City, The Canyons) are regularly recognized for their highly

A snowboarder "jibs" a rail during a slope-style competition held in a terrain park at a ski resort in New Zealand. (Courtesy of Brook Thorpe.)

innovative terrain parks and/or pipes. These resorts make huge investments in freestyle snowboarding. Northstar-at-Tahoe, for example, employs 20 full-time staff (12 day crew and 8 night crew) to build, maintain, and manage, eight terrain parks and a super-pipe.

In their efforts to develop highly innovative terrain parks, some resorts have turned to professional terrain park design companies such as Snow Park Technologies (SPT). With 10 full time employees and more independent contractors spread across North America, SPT builds terrain parks and provides consultation for ski resorts in ten different states. Organizers also hire the company to build courses for the Winter X Games, the Dew Tour, and the U.S. Open, as well as events in Europe, Japan, and New Zealand. Building terrain parks since 1992, Chris "Gunny" Gunnarson, owner of SPT, identifies some of the logistical considerations when building a slope-style or half-pipe course for an international-level competition:

> We put our heart and soul and blood, and sweat and tears into trying to make it as good as it can possibly be . . . but we usually have a defined window of time, maybe its 10 days to build a slopestyle course. If there's not enough snow or the weather conditions get rough, or the snowcats are breaking, or any number of factors, that can cause a

normal build to become a really, really, long and ugly, 20-hour-day for
10-days-straight build. (cited in Sullivan, 2010, paras. 15–16)

Some events are more intensive than others; building the course for the
2010 Winter X Games in Aspen, for example, took Gunnarson and his team
29 consecutive days (and nights) to build. In contrast to the early half-pipe
and jump builders who spent hours digging their own snow playgrounds
before ski resorts allowed them on their slopes, today terrain park construction is a highly lucrative business. As Gunnarson explains, "building parks,
of course, is a really fun, cool and creative process and I get to do something
I love, but at the end of the day, it's really, truly a business . . . resorts aren't
doing this for charity work. It's a viable business." Continuing, he explains,
building terrain parks is "a lot more involved than most people would
actually think. It's not just pushing some snow around and creating a terrain
park. It's everything to do with the fun part, the safety part, the liability part,
and the marketing part, all integrated together" (cited in Sullivan, 2010,
para. 6).

legalities of big air

As terrain parks have become increasingly technical, the severity and rates
of injuries incurred in terrain parks have also increased. A number of highly
controversial legal cases following serious injuries in terrain parks have
prompted many North American resorts to rethink the management of terrain parks. A particularly significant case occurred in 2007, when a snowboarder paralyzed from a fall in a terrain park at Snoqualmie Ski Area in
Washington State received compensation of $14 million, marking the larg-
est jury award levied against a U.S. ski resort. The verdict sent shockwaves
throughout the ski resort industry. Attempting to minimize terrain-park
injuries and avoid expensive liability claims, some resorts proceeded to
limit the size of jumps and difficulty of obstacles; many made helmets mandatory, while others set about educating users about terrain-park safety
practices and etiquette. Terrain park development manager for Boyne
Resorts, New Hampshire, Jay Scambio reveals some of the financial, mana-
gerial, and legal considerations for ski resorts:

> You have to build a place that is attractive to teens, which means it has
> to be perceived as something just for them and away from the
> mainstream. Then you have to say, "O.K., but there are rules here."

It can be a little tricky. You really want this age group because they are the biggest growth sector, but you can't just let them do whatever they want in your parks. (cited in Pennington, 2010, para. 6)

In the United States, Burton Snowboards worked with the National Ski Area Association (NSAA), to develop Smart Style, "a breakthrough program to encourage terrain park safety at resorts nationwide" (Burton and NSAA introduce terrain park safety program, 2008, para. 1). After consultation with terrain-park builders, lawyers and snowboarders, and ski resort managers, Burton developed four simple safety messages: (1) Make a plan, (2) Look before you leap, (3) Easy Style it (Start small and work your way up—Inverted aerials not recommended), and (4) Respect Gets Respect. Burton then worked closely with a design firm to construct print-ready signage templates to help resorts create banners, stickers, and in-park signage, as well as a Web site hosting safety information and educational videos presented by some of Burton Snowboards professional athletes. Ski resorts across North America, as well as Australia, New Zealand, and Europe have since adopted The Smart Style campaign.

In an effort to protect themselves from expensive personal injury and fatality-related lawsuits, many ski resorts in North America have also introduced release waivers to be signed by patrons before entering terrain parks. Access to Whistler-Blackcomb's (Canada) "highest level terrain park" is restricted to "advanced and expert riders" whom must display a "highest level pass" at the entrance. The passes can be purchased for a small fee (approximately CDN$15), but more importantly require the participant to sign a waiver that states: "I freely accept and fully assume all risks, dangers and hazards associated with using the terrain park and the possibility of loss, personal injury or death resulting there from." Adopting an even more radical approach, the Resorts of the Canadian Rockies, Inc. (RCR), undertook a self-proclaimed "industry-leading initiative" by "eliminating all man-made snow jumps" from all six of its ski resorts across Canada (i.e., Lake Louise Mountain and Nakiska Resort in Alberta, and Fernie Alpine Resort and Kimberly Alpine Resort in British Columbia). According to senior director of business development for RCR, Matt Mosteller, "When we are making decisions about safety at our resorts, the big jumps in the terrain parks always come into question. We decided to make a change. . . . We believe we have a strong moral obligation to not compromise the safety of our guests" (cited in Press Release, 2007, para. 2). Some local snowboarders, however, interpreted this decision differently. "What a 'we got our asses sued' piece of bullshit!" protested one online user (cited in Press Release, 2007, para. 9). Others actively challenged the decision by creating petitions, writing letters to local newspapers, and organizing groups of snowboarders to boycott the resorts. The key point here is that, within the current hyperlegal milieu, terrain parks (particularly in North America) are becoming increasingly regulated and controlled. In this context, many professional snowboarders proceeded to head into the backcountry to build jumps according to their own specifications.

building backcountry jumps

Groups of committed and professional snowboarders often "duck the ropes" and go "out of bounds" of ski resorts, or hike or drive snowmobiles into the backcountry, where they spend hours finding the right location, building a jump (also known as a kicker, booter, cheese wedge), and then practicing and performing an array of maneuvers. As the *Board the World* Web site explains:

> Kicker riding has become one of the most popular and progressive parts of snowboarding. The beauty of kicker riding is you often don't need to spend your hard earned cash for a lift ticket, and its super fun. All it takes is a group of friends, some imagination and a bit of hard work. (What makes a good kicker?, 2000, para. 1)

The Web site also outlines the cultural etiquette regarding jump building, and offers some basic safety advice: "If you build a jump, crowds will pop up out of nowhere as soon as you have finished. The golden rule is 'if you don't help [build it], you don't use it.' Also, make sure you pick a landing with a good gradient, or you will end up with stuffed knees and your knees in your mouth every landing . . . and look out for rocks and stones in the landing" (para. 9).

Some destinations have become particularly well-known for building backcountry jumps. Professional snowboarder Jesse Huffman (2006) describes the appeal of the Whistler backcountry:

> The terrain is ideal for snowboarding on an epic scale: the landings are all steep, and because the elevation is just a matter of snowmobiling further, the powder is almost always good. . . . which is why the place has come to be a bit of a professional circus. The production line quality of snowmobiling in Whistler means that on any

given sunny mid-winter day, you could find seven different film crews in the same backcountry spot. (Huffman, 2006, p. 67)

Expanding upon some of the cultural politics involved in jump construction in an increasingly competitive industry with limited natural resources, a *Board the World* journalist writes:

In the perfect world, you hike half an hour or so into the backcountry, stumble upon the perfect jump location, agree on the angle and type of jump, and then construct the most perfect backcountry booter into a powder, pillow landing. Given the dramatic increase in the level of snowboarding, this perfect outcome is becoming less and less a possibility. . . . These days hiking out into the backcountry can be one of the most stressful and un-fun experiences. Often your search for a good booter location can be cut at the knees because all the good booter locations have been taken. Nowadays to find and session a good booter you need to get up earlier after the last snowfall and head out [to] stake your claim. Film crews such as Mack Dawg have been known to send out a lone scout at day break to stake out jump locations. Other film crews spend days on ski-doos searching out new jump locations deep in remote mountain ranges. (Ouse, 2005, para. 2)

Tensions frequently develop between group members once a site has been located and jump construction begins: "Most riders these days," says Australian snowboarder and co-founder of the *Board the World* Web site, "have strong opinions . . . about what constitutes a good and bad jump. . . . some riders may be after a hip style jump rather than a cheese wedge. Some riders may think the jump isn't 'tech' enough to show them in the best light [on film or in photos]. . . . with so many egos floating around there is [also] the potential that everyone becomes the foreman . . . so again, another round of bickering occurs" (Ouse, 2005, para. 5). He concludes, however, by stating: "[G]enerally, once the jumping begins all previous hours of arguing [are] forgotten and everyone experiences the true fun of riding a backcountry booter" (Ouse, 2005, para. 6).

Attempting to distinguish themselves from other highly proficient professional snowboarders and gain more niche media coverage, some freestyle athletes are attempting to set records on backcountry jumps of gigantic proportions. Such jumps can take many weeks to prepare and construct. For example, Norwegian "legend snow cat master" Lars Eriksen scouted, designed, and then spent three weeks building, the enormous

130-foot jump in the Hemsedal backcountry on which fellow countryman Mads Jonsson set the world record (187 feet) for the longest snowboard jump on May 9, 2005. The location was carefully selected for its long, steep run-in that enabled Jonsson to gain enough speed under his own propulsion. A snowboarding journalist describes the series of events leading up to this momentous occasion:

> After fine tuning the [jump] in the cat with Lars, and testing the speed several times, Mads stepped up with a solid straight air that put him perfectly into the now shaded landing. Quick sled shuttle up, another test straight air, and then BAAMMMMM, Mads lit up the glowing evening sky with a rock solid backside 180 that threw the collected group of riders and lucky observers, not to mention the photographers and cinematographers, into an exclamatory rage. 57 meters (187 feet). Stomp. Silence. Intensity. Stoke. (World Record, 2005, para. 3)

When U.S. professional snowboarders Travis Rice and Roman De Marchi became the first snowboarders to successfully jump the culturally infamous 120-foot "Chad's Gap" located in the backcountry canyons of Salt Lake City, Utah, they also gained much cultural kudos and extensive niche media coverage. In an interview appearing in *Transworld Snowboarding* magazine, Rice revealed some of the cultural considerations and politics involved in constructing and performing on this jump: "The jump took us three solid days [to build] ... We shoveled until after sunset every day building it. We wanted to make it so perfect that there was no way we could hurt ourselves"; "We didn't really talk about [who would hit the gap first] until it was time to hit it. Romain had just guineaed [acted as the 'guinea pig'—first to ride a newly constructed jump, testing speed, angle of take-off, quality of landing, etc.] the Dirksen Gap a couple days before, and I was like, 'So, Romain, you want to hit this thing or what?' He looked at me and was like, 'It's your turn, buddy'" (Trice, 2008, para. 17).

Travis recalls some of the psychological processes involved in preparing for the first jump:

> You can't really think it out too much; you've got to feel it. I applied all my knowledge, [all] my experience from the past kickers. I found the spot where I thought I needed to drop from to make it over. I was more worried about not clearing it than clearing it by too much. ... I did a backside 360 to feel it out [but] went almost 200 feet ... I signaled up to Romain that I went way too big, and then he hit it and also went way

too big. We looked at each other and were like, "All right, at least that's over with." It was session on. (Trice, 2008, para. 19)

The "session" lasted for many hours, with both Travis and Romain performing an array of increasingly technical maneuvers, including various 180, 540, and 720 degree rotations. At the conclusion of the photoshoot, they destroyed the jump citing both political and safety concerns: "There were some other snowboarders who wanted to hit it the next day, and we were like, 'F-k this, we put all of our time and effort into it, what's a little bit more time to go tear it down?' If people really want to hit it that badly, they can spend their own time building it up. [Also] it's dangerous to leave that shit up. Some kid's going to come and try to hit it and just work himself" (Trice, 2008, paras. 17–19).

Gaining global coverage in an array of niche snowboarding magazines, Web sites, and films, Chad's Gap quickly became a key destination for freestyle snowboarders and skiers. But tensions emerged between "crews" of professional snowboarders and skiers and filmmakers and photographers, as groups struggled over territory and eminence. As one ski journalist writes:

From the best of the best to the grovelingly inexperienced . . . [Chad's Gap] is now on every jibber's [freestyle skiers and snowboarders] "To Do before I Die" list. But with stardom comes territorialism. The real hucksters don't talk. They want to keep the Gap secret . . . not [out of] a fear that someone will crunch a bone or stick a pole through their face but that the inexperienced will desecrate the sacred takeoff ramp. . . . Building the ramp takes as much motivation, energy and skill as it does to actually huck [jump]. Two to three full days of six people's labor go into polishing the in-run. If it's not "just right" you could miscalculate your life into the deceased skier's hall of shame. Often, however, the countless hours spent building the jump are laid to waste the next day by poachers or film crews taping the glory and stomping out the evidence. (Adler, no date)

However, when X Games freestyle ski champion Tanner Hall broke both ankles and "nearly died" during an unsuccessful attempt at Chad's Gap, many were prompted to reevaluate the risk involved, at least temporarily. The exact location of this culturally infamous location continues to be carefully protected.

As professional snowboarding becomes increasingly competitive, athletes and filmmakers are employing an array of technologies to both enhance performance and minimize unnecessary risk. Some committed snowboarders use snowmobiles (also known as sleds) to tow one another into jumps that would otherwise be impossible to naturally get enough speed to cover the distance between the takeoff and landing (e.g., due to wet snow conditions, lack of run-in distance, or gradient); some are also practicing highly technical maneuvers over airbags and wearing protective "body armor" under their snowboard clothing; radar guns are also being used to help monitor speed. Professional U.S. snowboarder Bjorn Leines reflects upon the value of a radar gun for performing a 900 degree rotation over Chad's Gap:

> That jump was a big ordeal; we had to build it for five days and there was a crowd and ski patrol. It is a technical jump, as far as getting the speed dialed in. . . . The skiers we were with had [a radar]. They were going 61 mph backwards into it. We figured we had to go 55 [mph] at the takeoff to clear it. You need to be able to tell the difference between going 45 and 55, and the radar gun got us dialed in on that. With it, we could always go back and check how fast we were going like, "Ok, I went 51 on that trick and it felt good and I dropped from that spot." (cited in Bridges, 2005a, para. 26)

Leines reveals some of the cognitive processes involved in preparing to jump over a 120-foot gap traveling at 55 miles per hour: "It is mental at that point. . . . You have to know what you can do and see yourself doing it. I just pictured myself going into the takeoff, being calm, snapping into the trick and knowing what my eyes were going to see when I was coming out of it" (cited in Bridges, 2005a, para. 25). Recognizing the risk involved in such performances, Leines states matter-of-factly: "You've got to get into that zone of 'I'm going to nail this!' Not to be cheesy, but it's nail the trick or put a nail in your coffin. You hit your head . . . or snap your neck off something like that [and] you're going to be all done" (cited in Bridges, 2005a, para. 29). Certainly, as backcountry jumps continue to grow in size and become increasingly technical, so too do the risks involved for participants.

   To develop the strength and flexibility necessary for such performances, and to minimize the potential of injury, professional snowboarders are increasingly engaging in highly structured and disciplined training regimes. Freestyle snowboarder and U.S. Olympic half-pipe silver medalist Gretchen Bleiler comments on the ideological shift among professional snowboarders in relation to training:

When I first started snowboarding, nobody trained off-hill. People weren't going to the gym and getting stronger. Snowboarding was more self-expression, like skateboarding. It was just something you went and did, it wasn't something you trained for. [But today] you have to be strong, and you have to know how to use your body properly and how to fire the correct muscles. (cited in Branch, 2010, para. 2)

Sponsored by the U.S.-based health club chain, 24 Hour Fitness, Bleiler typically begins her day with yoga or "dynamic stretching," then after four or five hours training on the mountain, she heads straight to the gym where she spends half an hour "spinning" on the stationary bike: "If you're up on the hill training for four hours, your body definitely builds up some lactic acid," she said. "So it's important to come down, stretch, get on the bike. Getting on the bike and spinning is just kind of pumping out that lactic acid, so the next day you're not as sore" (cited in Branch, 2010, para. 20). Her spinning routine is followed by weight-training and/or other snowboarding-specific exercises on the balance ball, with a ladder, or on a trampoline. "All of these things are great for injury prevention. Not just that, but also confidence. When you're up on the hill and you know you're as strong as you can be, you're more willing and able and confident to go and do bigger and harder and more technical tricks" explains Bleiler (cited in Branch, 2010, para. 20). When training in Park City, Utah, she also takes advantage of the 85,000 square-foot U.S. Ski and Snowboard Association's Center of Excellence in Park City. Opened in 2009, the facility features a vast weight room, as well as skateboard ramps, trampolines, and a landing pit filled with foam cubes. As with many professional freestyle snowboarders, Bleiler regularly uses the trampoline and a landing pit to develop air awareness and practice new aerial half-pipe or big air maneuvers: "The trampoline is a really a good place to test [my tricks]. The more I can do them here, the more I know how it should feel, and how it should look on the hill" (cited in Branch, 2010, para. 27).

technicalities of big mountain snowboarding

In contrast to performing in artificially constructed terrain parks and half-pipes, or backcountry jumps, big mountain snowboarding takes place in an uncontrolled and dynamic natural environment. Top Canadian freestyle competitor turned big mountain rider, Annie Boulanger, explains some of the unique challenges posed in the backcountry:

> When you ride backcountry, all your skills come into play. You have to be so on it and work at it really hard. The terrain changes every day. You have to know how to ride everything, from cliffs and lines to transitions and jumps. You need so much board control and confidence, because you never know exactly what you're dropping into . . . and there's no way back. The snow might be terrible—it might all slide, or the cliff might be bigger than expected or the landing flat. Or it might just be perfect, and all those years of riding come together impeccably in that one line or drop. (cited in Sherowski, 2008, para. 8)

Boulanger compares competing in a freestyle contest "with a huge crowd, blaring music, and judges watching you intently" to the "pure, solitary, soulful" experience of snowboarding in the backcountry where "there's a simple 'man versus mountain' thing going on" (cited in Sherowski, 2008, para. 10). Big mountain snowboarding requires a combination of advanced snowboarding skills, board control on varying terrain, avalanche awareness, and basic mountaineering skills, as well as "a super heightened awareness of the mountain": "Unlike freestyle riding, which is heavily visual, big mountain riding relies on feeling, being in the moment and experiencing everything that is around you; the snow, the mountain, the trees, the speed, the wind, the airtime" (Holt, 2005, p. 91).

While the freestyle boarder and the big mountain rider may use the same basic equipment—a board, boots, bindings, goggles, helmet—the training, technologies, and skills required for successfully and safely performing in these environments vary considerably. Backcountry snowboarders typically prefer to use longer boards and adjust their stance by moving their bindings slightly toward the tail of the board. Putting more weight on the tail of the board helps the rider keep the board floating above the powder. Some committed participants purchase boards designed specifically for backcountry snowboarding (e.g., swallowtail backcountry board). Snowboarders venturing into the backcountry also carry some (or all) of the following additional equipment either in their backpack or on their body: first aid kit, food, hydration packs, sunscreen, extra clothing in case of a weather change, detailed map of resort and/or surrounding mountains, a compass or GPS, cellphone, avalanche transceiver, probe, and/or shovel. Depending on the route, terrain, and weather, some also carry trekking poles to help navigate difficult terrain, snow-shoes for crossing deep powder, belays and harnesses for climbing, ropes for crevasse rescue and/or rock and ice climbing, crampons and/or ice axes for icy surfaces and ice climbing. Of course, carrying such equipment is useless if it is not accompanied by the knowledge of how and when to use it effectively.

In contrast to extreme surfers who require considerable paddling strength and technique to access big waves, snowboarders do not need high levels of skill to access extreme terrain. As the following comments from Craig Kelly illustrate, snowboarders can access, often unwittingly, dangerous off-piste spaces with very little experience:

> My first backcountry experience was probably my third day snowboarding at Mt. Baker in 1981 . . . we hiked across this little valley to Mt. Herman, which is just out-of-bounds at Mt. Baker. I remember hiking up there for the first time with Jeff Fulton and Dan Donnelly. I knew nothing about avalanches, and that day we were hiking up the main gully when this big rumbler [avalanche] came down just beside us. We just thought of it like lightening (sic), "Oh, we just got so lucky." (The interview: Karleen Jeffery and Craig Kelly, 2008, para. 5)

Following the deaths of a number of high profile big mountain athletes and the increasing diffusion of information regarding the risks in this envi-ronment (e.g., Web sites, magazines), recreational snowboarders are increasingly enrolling in avalanche and snow-safety courses. Many seri-ous backcountry snowboarders continue to educate themselves and keep updated on the latest technologies and techniques by reading books and Web sites, and/or working closely with experienced mentors or guides. For example, even after many years of snowboarding experience and multiple world championships, Craig Kelly completed a seven-day inten-sive level-one Canadian Avalanche Association course and worked closely with "a lot of qualified backcountry guides" (para. 8) throughout· his career, proclaiming that "everybody who steps outside the ropes" should complete at least a short recreational course on avalanche safety (para. 8). In her "personal quest for self preservation," experienced big mountain snowboarder Karleen Jeffrey describes making a strategic effort to "ask guides and more-experienced riders a lot of questions." She always carries a copy of *Mountaineering: Freedom of the Hills*: "It's basi-cally the bible of mountaineering, and it covers everything from what kind of clothes you should be wearing right through crevassed rescue and anchors for rock climbing . . . so any day when I'm out there and I forgot to ask a question, or I feel intimidated, I just look it up" (cited in The Interview, 2008, para. 9).

Big mountain and backcountry snowboarding is highly weather dependent. Thus, committed big mountain snowboarders typically pay careful attention to weather patterns, often spending many hours analyzing weather maps in an effort to predict storms, fresh snowfalls, and periods of clear (and thus filmable) weather. Big mountain snowboarders then organize their travel schedules around such predictions. Professional U.S. snowboarder Erik Leines describes some of the difficulties for athletes whose salaries are based on their ability to capture the most evocative video footage and/or photos within a short, and sometimes fickle, winter season: "When you film your video part, you are at the will of nature. When nature says it's going to snow three feet in Canada, you better be there at 6 a.m. with your snowmobile ready so you can get those sick shots. It is a crazy scramble to film a video these days" (cited in Bridges, 2005b, para. 13). In the same interview, Erik's older brother and fellow professional snowboarder Bjorn Leines, describes the research-intensive, highly flexible, organized approach that led to a particularly successful filming season: "[2005] was the most productive and fun season I've had . . . We rode Utah, Tahoe and around the West Coast. We had good luck with the weather and did a lot of research on the Internet. We would check the weather for a 500-mile radius around Salt Lake City" (cited in Bridges, 2005b, para. 27). As the following comments from Victoria Jealouse illustrate, however, regardless of how much research one does, some winters pose more environmental challenges than others:

> I spent almost the entire year snow-camping in my camper van on the side of a mountain pass up in the Yukon, Canada . . . about 2000 miles from home . . . I drove up there with my crew to film. We went there to avoid the warm temperatures across British Columbia and the western states, but the Yukon had these frequent little rain spatters that would wreck the snow for us, often. We pretty much battled, sledding up to high elevations to find dry snow. We worked super hard, snowmobiling and maintaining our camp which was about a two hour drive from any service stations/stores. We had to keep fuelled up on diesel and propane and food to keep warm, and keep the sleds gassed up. Every day we'd burn through a tank each, so we had to fill up lots of gas cans

and an extra big tank. We wouldn't shower for a week or more. When we arrived in the Yukon, it was –40 degrees and we almost froze in the camper. But then it turned to 0 or +2 on and off [ruining snow conditions]. (cited in Skoglund, 2005, para. 1)

In a highly competitive industry where professional big mountain snowboarders' salaries depend on their ability to capture high quality footage of ever more courageous and creative performances on new and challenging terrain, successful athletes must be highly organized and dedicated to not only preparing themselves physically and psychologically, but also to reading weather patterns, working with film crews, and managing the logistics of frequent national and international travel.

modes of ascent

Before experiencing the thrills of carving down a powdery mountain face, the backcountry snowboarder must first get to the top of the desired peak or slope. Access is a key practical and philosophical issue for backcountry and big mountain boarders. Participants employ an array of different "modes of ascent" (i.e., hiking and climbing, helicopters, snowmobiles, or snow-cats), depending on cost, accessibility, time, safety, knowledge and ability, weather, and motives. Hiking and climbing were the original methods employed by early snowboarders banned from ski resorts, and hiking remains the dominant approach employed by recreational backcountry snowboarders around the world. While many casual backcountry-users hike carrying their snowboards under their arm or behind their back, more experienced backcountry snowboarders often use snowshoes or approach skis (short skis used for ascending) to facilitate faster and more efficient travel on top of the snow. In some countries, the culture of hiking and the "earn your turns" philosophy is widely celebrated. This is particularly true in some European countries, such as France and Italy, where the use of helicopters and snowmobiles for recreational purposes is either limited or banned due to concerns that such technologies disturb the environment and cause a great deal of noise in relation to the number of people who can benefit from the activity.

New technologies such as splitboards—popularly termed the "poor man's heli"—have greatly facilitated the laborious task of hiking in deep snow. Developed in the mid-1990s, splitboards enable the snowboarder

Three snowboarders hiking out-of-bounds of a ski resort to access fresh snow and new terrain. (AP Photo/Peter M. Fredin.)

to travel up a slope on ski-touring type technologies, which can be reassembled at the top to form a snowboard for the descent. In contrast to snow shoes or approach skis which require the snowboarder to carry the additional weight of their snowboard on the way up, and then the snow shoes or skis on the way down, splitboards facilitate much faster access and a lighter load. Early splitboard equipment was rudimentary and many participants expressed concerns over the quality of the descent experience on such technologies. John Buffery, a splitboard guide in a remote backcountry touring lodge in the Canadian Rockies, explains: "What I've heard from other people is that they don't trust it, they don't feel that the board will hold up to their speed and jumping" (cited in Kelly, 2008, para. 7). Yet some professional big mountain snowboarders (i.e., Craig Kelly, Jeremy Jones) and guides have worked closely with snowboarding companies to develop and market splitboard technologies such that sales doubled during the 2008 and 2009 winter seasons (Huffman, 2009). Splitboards, however, remain a small niche market and equipment is still relatively expensive; the board, mounting kit, and bindings, sold separately, start at $1,000, and skins and poles are an additional $250 (Huffman, 2009). The user must also be prepared to assemble and disassemble the equipment themselves. In contrast, other professional snowboarders and wealthy enthusiasts use heli-copters, snow-cats, and snowmobiles (or sleds), and in a few cases small planes, to access new terrain. Each of these methods for ascending a slope has advantages (e.g., access, number of runs/day, environmentally friendly) and disadvantages (e.g., cost, pollution, noise, safety, weather dependent) for the individual and the overall experience.

Interestingly, after many years using helicopters to access remote peaks around the world, Jeremy Jones recently made a conscious decision to pursue a more environmentally conscious approach to big mountain snowboarding. As part of his strategic effort to "reduce my impact on the environment in all aspects of my life," Jones has become a strong advocate of the splitboard (cited in Huffman, 2009, para. 20). In his own words, "splitboarding is such an intimate experience, and so much goes into each run. You mix the endorphin high on the way up with the adrena-lin on the way down, and you've got one of the best feelings in the world" (cited in Huffman, 2009, para. 20). According to Jones, accessing back-country terrain under one's own power has the potential to offer a more rewarding experience:

> Exploring new terrain is essential to me, but it's also the feeling of being out there by yourself. I mean, a helicopter is a pretty disruptive deal. When you're out hiking, really immersed in the mountains and able to approach a big face and look at it on the way up for hours and hours of hiking, it's such a different experience. Mapping out every turn, maybe even sleeping on the face—it just builds and builds and builds. You're having this all-day experience, and after ripping down it you get hit with this feeling . . . It's really like nothing I've felt before. (Jeremy Jones, cited in Benedek, 2009, p. 10)

For some, Jones' approach may seem radical, particularly in the current hypercompetitive snowboarding industry where one's salary is directly related to coverage in films and magazines. However, he follows in the tradition of many other big mountain snowboarders who preferred quality, rather than quantity, backcountry experiences. For example, legendary big mountain snowboarder and a key advocate for the development of split-board technologies, Craig Kelly, believed that, as professional athletes "we've got the freedom to use helicopters, snowmobiles, ski lifts, snow-cats, whatever. But when it's all said and done, I really feel better about that one run if I earned it" (cited in The Interview, 2008, para. 17).

Other big mountain snowboarders are developing alternative, highly innovative approaches to accessing new terrain. For example, a few are dropping out of hovering helicopters to access slopes otherwise inaccessible by hiking or climbing, and/or without a safe helicopter landing zone. Professional Canadian big mountain snowboarder Victoria Jealouse describes the logic that led her to experiment with this unique:

> We started doing that last year. It's way faster and efficient to sit on the edge with your board strapped on. It's good to sometimes just hit something fast . . . maybe the lights going. It's really fun too. It's definitely a little scary. The rotor wash is pretty gnarly—way more wind pressure than I thought. You get arm burn . . . that's when I started getting kinda scared, because after a few minutes of holding on and flexing my arm as hard as I could, it started to burn and I started wondering if I could get bucked off. It was one of those things that I would think, "oh, I would never do that." Then when I was there, it just seemed perfectly normal. (cited in Taylor, no date, para. 14)

Professional U.S. snowboarder Mike Basich performed a particularly extreme example of the "heli drop" when he dropped approximately 120 feet from a helicopter hovering above a steep mountain face below. Culturally renowned for his highly creative approach to both the practice and art of snowboarding, Basich initially set up the stunt in an effort to capture a thought-provoking "self portrait"; he set up a camera with a remote on an adjacent slope, and as he jumped out of the helicopter he used the remote to capture a spectacular image that later appeared on the covers of a number of international snowboarding magazines. The almost unbelievable photo of Basich dropping from such a height prompted many snowboarders to question both the authenticity of the image, and the next step in progressive big mountain snowboarding: "Was the image Photoshopped?" "Where to from here? Is it humanly possible to go any bigger than this?"

in preparation of descent

In preparing for a challenging big mountain descent, professional snowboarders often spend many hours reading topographical maps, analyzing photos of the slope, and identifying potentially dangerous obstacles, safe points, and escape routes. Memorizing the slope and their planned route is essential. Professional French big mountain snowboarder and freestyle

Mike Basich performs a 120 foot "heli-drop" from a hovering helicopter in Alaska. The result of both Basich's artistic and physical skills, this "self portrait" appeared on the cover of various snowboarding magazines. (Self-portrait, Mike Basich.)

competitor, Xavier de la Rue, describes the technicalities of preparing for a challenging big mountain descent: "You look at everything from as many different perspectives and then try and put it all together as best you can, like a jigsaw puzzle. There's an enormous amount of work behind each line. It's a total mental thing though; controlling yourself, knowing your abilities, studying the environment" (cited in Andrews, 2009, para. 5). Victoria Jealouse concurs:

> A lot goes into choosing a line, the days and weeks before. We don't just get in a helicopter the day after a storm, slide up to what looks good and drop in. I think some people think that we're just rolling the dice. It's more like days of progression, digging pits and testing slopes slowly. So by the time you're actually about to drop in, a lot of the emotional curve that you go through is kind of over. When you're standing at the top of your line, looking down, you already understand its full potential. (cited in Kurland, no date, para. 2)

In another interview in *Powder* magazine, Jealouse reveals some of the psychological processes before a first descent:

> I like riding lines when I have fallen in love with them . . . [Where] there's good energy and I've taken the time to look at a line and . . . check the safety and snow stability. That's the only time I get really courageous and feel like I'm going to do something better than I've done before, but it takes a lot of things to fall into place. I work my way up slowly into the terrain. I'll blow off days or an entire trip if things just aren't right, or conditions are sketchy. At least I can come back if I'm still alive. (cited in Taylor, no date, para. 11)

She also reveals the cultural considerations involved in her big mountain decision-making and cognitive processes:

> I am always very sure about what I will do and what I won't do. I feel like I'm at the point where I can read terrain and know if it's over my head. And I definitely won't do anything because of pressure. I'm almost the opposite; if someone tries to pressure me, I won't do it. I would never let pressure enter my decision. I want to do this [snowboarding] for a really long time and I know if I make decisions based on the safety aspects, how I feel, and my riding, I'll make good decisions. When you start letting in pressure or thoughts like "It took a long time to get here and a lot of money" or "I can look like a hero . . . ." when anyone factors in those thoughts, you're not going to make consistent safe decisions. (cited in Taylor, no date, para. 11)

Despite extensive training, research, and experience, however, the back-country is a dynamic and dangerous environment where accidents happen to even the most prepared or cautious participant.

communication and team-work

In comparison to the more individualistic style of snowboarding in terrain parks and half-pipes, safe and successful big mountain snowboarding depends upon effective communication and teamwork. Big mountain snowboarders often work with a partner to facilitate informed decision making, help coordinate helicopter drop off and pickups and camera activity, provide immediate information via two-way radios regarding changes in the terrain that could compromise the rider's planned route, or to help navigate the rider through danger zones and to safety spots. Effective partnerships depend upon open communication, knowledge of a partner's physical abilities and psychological strengths, limitations, and motives, as well as mutual trust and respect. According to professional Canadian big mountain snowboarder Karleen Jeffrey, a good working relationship is essential for a safe and productive descent:

> I have been riding with Matt for over three years now. We try and get in the same groups every day up in Alaska, just because we really trust each other, talking each other down on the radio or that kind of thing. I try to keep the same partners or groups. When you go to Alaska, you don't want to go switching people every single day because you could be putting yourself at risk. You want to know how much knowledge each partner has. (The interview: Karleen Jeffery and Craig Kelly, 2008, para. 9)

A certified ski and snowboard guide with the Canadian Association of Mountain Guides, John Buffery, also recognizes the importance of establishing open communication, clear goals, and hierarchies, among groups hiking into the backcountry: "Everybody should agree upon an individual to lead. In any backcountry party ... make it clear before you go that everyone knows the objective, the general route plan, and if somebody wants to head back, don't send them back alone" (cited in Kelly, 2008, para. 22). Effective communication and teamwork is particularly important for professional snowboarders working with filmcrews.

capturing the action

Many professional big mountain snowboarders' salaries depend almost entirely upon their ability to work with highly specialized big mountain photographers and cinematographers to capture their performances on film. In the current highly competitive industry, cinematographers and professional athletes employ an array of innovative technologies to produce the most highly affective representations of big mountain snowboarding. For example, a recent video part featuring Jeremy Jones was further brought to life for audiences via the use of a camera installed on his helmet. After watching the film, fellow professional snowboarder J.P. Walker enthused: "I was on the edge of my seat. The helmet cam shots put it in perspective. So gnarly, all of that slough on loose snow pulling his board around while he's on top of some crazy spines" (2008 *Snowboarder* magazine).

Filming in such extreme environments, however, is highly technical and typically performed under financial and time duress. Communication and teamwork is essential to making the most of expensive helicopter-time and optimal weather conditions. Victoria Jealouse describes the benefits of developing good working relationships with fellow athletes and filmmakers:

Filming this year with TGR [Teton Gravity Research] in Haines . . . we have been working for three years as the exact same crew and we are getting really tuned into each other and it goes so smoothly. Heli filming is super, super hectic. Even very experienced crews will tell you that. There is a lot of pressure . . . from the safety aspect, the money aspect, the weather aspect and then there is group dynamics. Everyone has to work well together, make fast decisions and give a lot (Jealouse, 2005, para. 26).

In another interview, Jealouse reveals some of the pressures facing athletes within this high stress environment:

[S]ometimes the helicopter can't quite get you to the beginning of the line. You may have to hike up some really dangerous ridgeline. You're huffing and puffing, you know someone else is being filmed right now, you can hear people on the radio, [and] you're letting them know how you're doing. You get to your spot, you look over the edge, you figure out how you're going to drop in, and as you're putting your board on you hear: "Okay, we're coming to shoot you now, you ready?" And you know the helicopter is flying around . . . very expensively in circles. The whole group is waiting for you, two people are dangling outside the heli, and it is super freezing . . . That moment, just before you're about to drop in, can be quite hectic, when the clouds are coming in or the heli's already in the air and logistically it would help everyone if you just hustled and dropped in fairly quickly—although no one expects you to do anything stupid. You may be like, "Look, I don't feel good right now. I can't see my line. I want you to put the heli back down on the ground, everyone just chill I need five or ten minutes to catch my breath." (cited in Kurland, no date, para. 3)

Understanding that not all snowboarders deal well with such stresses, experienced big mountain snowboarder and highly esteemed cinematographer Mike Hatchett carefully selects the athletes he invites to participate in his films:

I want to film someone who [has] steep mountain savvy behind them. . . . They have [to have] ridden on the steeps and have respect for the big mountains and can hopefully bale out if something goes wrong. I have to bring people up here who know what to do in a potentially dangerous situation. . . . it is a real team effort when you are out there. I need to bring people up here I know and trust; also people who are aware of the hazards of big mountain travel, and are willing to play it safe and play as a team. (Mike Hatchett, big mountain filmmaker, interview, para. 17–18)

As these comments suggest, capturing big mountain snowboarding performances on camera is a highly professional endeavor with little room for individualism or uncalculated risk.

rescues

For any individual caught in an avalanche, some basic strategies may increase the chances of survival. An article in *National Geographic* offers the following advice:

If caught in an avalanche, try to get off the slab. Not easy, in most instances. Skiers and snowboarders can head straight downhill to gather speed then veer left or right out of the slide path. . . . No escape? Reach for a tree. No tree? Swim hard. The human body is three times denser than avalanche debris and will sink quickly. As the slide slows, clear air space to breathe. Then punch a hand skyward. Once the avalanche stops, it settles like concrete. Bodily movement is nearly impossible. Wait—and hope—for a rescue. (Avalanches, no date, para. 4)

The speed of rescue is central to surviving an avalanche. Recent studies show that victims rescued within 15 minutes of burial have a 92 percent survival rate; this number drops to approximately 30 percent within 35 minutes (Falk, Brugger & Adler-Kastner, 1994; Van Tilburg, 2000). Inevitably, deeper burials are associated with longer and more difficult extraction. According to Bogle, Boyd and McLaughlin (2010), "victims buried deeper than 200 cm have a probability of survival of only 10 perecnt compared with 80 percent for those buried less than 50 cm" (p. 28). With a very short window for survival, all members of a backcountry group must be prepared to perform their own search and rescue operations. For victims wearing an avalanche transceiver, a signal will be sent out to help the group identify the location of the body. While professional rescue teams should be notified as soon as possible, the remote locations of some backcountry expeditions mean that it is the responsibility of group members to use their own transceivers (all set to a common frequency) and to locate the body (or bodies) as quickly as possible. After the visual search, the group uses portable, collapsible probes (stored in their backpacks) to localize the buried victim and give exact depth of the body. As the snow deposit is often too dense to dig with bare hands, shovels become essential tools for excavating the victim. While some less prepared backcountry participants use their snowboards to help dig, these are less effective and efficient. The familiarity with equipment and ability to use it in high stress situations can be the difference between life and death in the backcountry. Thus, many experienced backcountry users engage in regular group training and practice sessions to ensure all members are confident and able to effectively perform avalanche rescues.

New technological developments are also being employed to minimize risk and facilitate avalanche rescues. Recent examples include the Avalanche Airbag System (ABS) and the Avalung. After a first-hand avalanche experience in Canada, Peter Aschauer developed the avalanche airbag in the mid-1980s, and his company continues to develop airbag technologies. Victims caught in an avalanche will often be pushed below the surface of the moving snow; when the snow stops they are buried under deep debris which sets, almost immediately, like concrete. Thus, the airbag is designed to provide flotation and keep the tumbling victim on the surface of the avalanche motion. The system is built into a rucksack-like device that is activated when the individual pulls a ripcord at the start of their fall. Once the ripcord is pulled, a canister of compressed air inflates two balloons within 2–3 seconds, thus helping the victim stay on or near the surface of the slide. The Swiss Federal Institute for Snow and Avalanche Research, an independent avalanche research center, reported that the ABS avalanche airbag reduced the likelihood of complete burial from 39 percent to 16.2 percent, and lowers the mortality rate from 23 percent to 2.5 percent (Brugger & Falk, 2002). Wireless technologies have also been employed, such that some ABS products now offer remote controlled activation. Such developments are particularly useful for guided backcountry expeditions, enabling the more experienced guide to activate group members' packs upon the first signs of an avalanche. ABS Airbag backpacks cost approximately $1,000, not including canister and trigger, and the latest wireless technologies cost approximately $1,300.

The Avalung is another technological development designed to prolong the survival time of those victims who experience a full burial situation. The Avalung is a lightweight harness worn on top of the clothes to assist breathing for at least one hour when trapped under the snow. Using a mouthpiece attached to a ventilation system, the Avalung extracts air from the snow, redirects carbon dioxide away from the victim's oxygen-intake zone, and reduces ice masking and CO_2 poisoning of the oxygen supply. With a pricetag of approximately $130, the Avalung is a relatively cheap safety device, yet some technical challenges may limit the usefulness of an Avalung. In particular, the system requires the victim to locate and keep the mouthpiece in his or her mouth while moving with the avalanche. With the Avalung and ABS airbag serving different purposes, they are often used in conjunction by serious backcountry participants.

While new technological developments may improve the chances of surviving an avalanche, whether such equipment will actually reduce the number of fatalities is yet to be seen. Research on the introduction of other safety devices—e.g., seatbelts in motor vehicles, automatic activation devices (AADs) among skydivers, sponsons on kayaks—show that these do not necessarily result in a reduced number of fatalities (see Self & Findley, 2007). Psychologists developed the "risk homeostasis theory" to explain this phenomenon (Peltzman, 1975; Self & Findley, 2007). According to the risk homeostasis theory, safety devices provide an increased sense of confidence such that some individuals respond by subconsciously introducing more risk to the situation. For example, many drivers responded to the introduction of compulsory seatbelts by increasing their speed; skydivers using AAD's took to attempting more technical and risky maneuvers; and sponsons gave paddlers a false sense of confidence such that some took on situations that were beyond their skill levels. Similar research has yet to be conducted on the use new avalanche rescue devices by backcountry snowboarders. However, the authors of *The Avalanche Handbook* draw upon the "risk homeostasis theory" to warn that avalanche transceivers are "pushing people toward more thrilling [and hence more dangerous] experiences" (McClung & Schaerer, 2006, p. 152). Neil McNab, a committed backcountry snowboarder and coach living in Chamonix, France agrees:

> There are several new products on the market that are supposed to increase your chances of survival if caught in an avalanche, and they are becoming increasingly popular. For me, the danger is that these products will make people feel that they can take more chances and they might put themselves in situations of greater risk than before. If you're riding a slope where you consider it necessary to have a breathing tube such as the Avalung in your mouth, perhaps you should be thinking about riding a different slope. (cited in Davies, 2009, para. 21)

It is also important to keep in mind that, while new technological developments may prolong the survival time, or facilitate the rescue, of avalanche victims, most avalanche deaths happen during the fall either by being carried over cliffs, being crushed by the weight of snow, or hitting rocks or trees. While avalanches are the most notorious risk in the backcountry, natural obstacles such as buried rocks, cliffs, or crevasses, are also potential hazards.

Backcountry snowboarding can also compromise the safety of others, particularly rescue groups. The following narrative, featured in a recent issue of *Australian and New Zealand Snowboarding* magazine, describes the dangers imposed on the professional and volunteer mountain rescue team by a group of inexperienced snowboarders:

> Recently, a story came to our attention; a tale of Auzzie can-do, mateship, [and] larrikinism . . . It's the story of some blokes who decided to take themselves on an impromptu tour through the backcountry of the Zillertal Mountains in Tyrol, Austria. Ill-prepared and ill-equipped, the lads trekked boldly through a deadly environment . . . Deciding unanimously that radios and provisions are for chicks—it was therefore up to the local rescue teams to locate and save their sorry hides when

foul weather set in and the lads became lost. After a night in the cold, they were found the next day. . . . [The Australians were taken to safety] but two members of the Austrian rescue team were forced to wait behind . . . Cue avalanche. Both men were harnessed and roped together, with one anchoring the other. The latter fell off a ledge, the rope becoming taut, and so took the full force of the avalanche on his body with the harness breaking his back. (Cotsios, 2005, p. 15)

As a fellow traveling snowboarder, the male Australian magazine editor publicly condemns the reckless actions of his countrymen. In some cases, victims are not only charged with the cost of rescue, which can be thousands of dollars, but may also face legal ramifications—if their actions are deemed negligent—as well as the wrath of local residents.

Backcountry rescues are also increasingly being facilitated by new telecommunication technologies. As cellphone reception improves, snowboarders and skiers are using cellphones to call for help when injured or lost in the backcountry. For example, when two young British entrepreneurs and snowboarding enthusiasts, Jason Tavaria and Rob Williams, became lost in a snowstorm in the Swiss Alps, the entire search and rescue operation played out over Twitter and other social networking sites. Friends of the duo sent messages and updates from the lodge while they waited for word on their rescue (Becker, 2009). Some of the Twitter messages posted read: "2 of our ski party been missing since 4PM. Conditions terrible"; "Urgent: If anyone has or knows Rob Williams of Dolphin Music's mobile, please send. Mountain rescue in progress"; "Rob's number rec'd via Twitter; Jason now found using GPS/Google maps and phone; still working on finding Rob." As the latter message alludes, Tavaria determined his location using the GPS satellite navigation signal on his iPhone which he then posted using his Twitter application. Rescue teams were able to quickly locate Tavaria, who was found trapped yet unharmed. Unfortunately, his companion was not so lucky; disoriented and blinded by the snowstorm, Williams fell over a 60-foot cliff and died. Clearly, while new technologies are opening up the backcountry to increasing numbers of snowboarders and, in some cases, facilitating more effective backcountry rescues, they are a poor substitute for experience and education. As the above examples suggest, the lack of either can have dire and long-lasting consequences.

7. futures

since its emergence in the late 1960s and 1970s, snowboarding has evolved from a marginal activity for a few alternative youth to an Olympic sport with millions of participants worldwide. Over the past four decades, snowboarding has grown rapidly in many western, and some eastern (e.g., China, Japan, South Korea), countries. Participants ranging from five to seventy-five years of age engage in an array of styles and demonstrate varying levels of skill and commitment. Today, the sport, culture, and industry of snowboarding is dynamic and in a constant state of flux. Technologies and styles of participation and competition continue to evolve as boarders create new and more technical maneuvers, and search for new spaces to practice and perform their skills. This chapter outlines six recent trends and future directions for snowboarding as it continues to develop into the twenty-first century.

styles of participation: from noboarding to b.a.s.e jumping

Since its emergence in the 1970s, the practice of snowboarding has continued to mutate rapidly as devotees add new twists to established styles, or draw upon existing sports to spawn new variations. A popular trend during the late 1990s and early 2000s, for example, were snow-skates (skateboards for the snow). While snow-skates were mostly used off the ski resorts, on slopes of gentle gradient, or in snow-covered urban spaces (e.g., car parks), some North American ski resorts responded to this trend by developing specially designed snow-skate parks. Another hybrid activity is snow-kiting, an offshoot of kite-surfing, that involves snowboarding with a kite. A particularly extreme development is the amalgamation of snowboarding and B.A.S.E jumping. In 1996, Dave Barlia completed the

Dave Barlia prepares to release his chute during a successful snowboard B.A.S.E jump in Switzerland. (Courtesy of Dave Barlia. Photo by Matt Small.)

first successful snowboard B.A.S.E jump when he soared off a jump constructed on the side of a 1,500-foot cliff in Lauterbrunnen, Switzerland. Once airborne he released the shoot from his backpack to land in the valley. The following year, he broke his own record when he completed a 3,000 foot jump in Norway.

Others have been less successful. One experienced B.A.S.E jumper, but less competent snowboarder, crashed into the cliff face when jumping off a 550-foot cliff in the Canadian Rockies, British Columbia. Lucky not to be killed by the accident, the jumper waited over ten hours on a two-by-two foot ledge at 9 degrees Fahrenheit before the search and rescue team reached him. The survivor anonymously writes about his experiences on a Web site:

> My canopy opened facing the wall . . . I reached up and pulled hard. Too late; looking down, here comes the rock, brace for impact, stick my snowboard out . . . I slammed into the cliff face . . . bumped down a guestimated fifty feet and came to a sudden stop in my harness. . . . I leaned forward a little more so I could reach a hold and take some weight off my harness . . . I grabbed my cellphone and called my groundcrew to let them know I was okay. . . . After that I climbed out of my harness to a little ledge about seven feet higher (Snowboard base cliff strike, 2007, paras. 13–15).

After rearranging his clothing and equipment, and using his canopy as insulation, the jumper "waited . . . and waited . . . and waited some more . . . All the while doing my exercises, hugging my legs, trying to remain my grip on the ledge, and staring at the stars and lights in the distance" (para. 43). Reflecting upon the accident, he concludes: "It is scary how quickly after an ordeal the brain filters out the negative parts and leaves just a great story. [But] let there be no mistake about it; the whole thing sucked" (para. 76).

In contrast to the highly technical and dangerous pursuit of B.A.S.E jumping, other snowboarders are reverting to the origins of the sport with NoBoarding, a concept not far-removed from the original act of Snurfing. Despite its historical roots, NoBoarding has been described as "a young sport that replaces traditional snowboard bindings with a knobbed polymer traction pad and a heavy-duty bungee rope . . . Without high-backs to lean on or straps to hold feet in place, the pad prevents slipping, and a firm grip on the rope keeps the board in place" (Huffman, 2008, para. 2). The original NoBoard was developed during the 1999–2000 winter season by injured Canadian snowboarder Greg Todds as an attempt to "relieve both stress on his knees and impending boredom" (Anderson, 2008, p. 161). With long-time friend Cholo Burns, Todds experimented with screws, wax, and lids from garbage bins to produce the first NoBoard prototypes; they tested their latest developments in the backcountry in the Kootenay Mountains in British Columbia, Canada. The following winter they cofounded the NoBoard Company and continued to experiment with new technologies (e.g., steel molds for the pads) until they had produced a range of operational NoBoard prototypes. But, when Todds was tragically killed in an avalanche in January 2005, Burns became even more determined to "finish what Greg started back in 1999." With increasing coverage in the niche media, and the first *Noboard Magazine* and video released in 2007, NoBoarding drew the attention of small groups of boarders across North America.

Recognizing the potential of this new activity, Burton Snowboards entered a partnership with Burns. In 2008, Burton became the official manufacturer and distributor for NoBoarding, while Burns maintains "full creative control" (Anderson, 2008, p. 161). The activity continues to gain popularity among snowboarders interested in exploring new terrain and new challenges. Indeed, the activity requires some initial patience and skill. "NoBoarding is kind of like rediscovering snowboarding. At first it's a bit of a challenge, and then the moment it clicks it's the most exhilarating thing," explains professional snowboarder and recent NoBoard "disciple" Jon Cartwright (cited in Anderson, 2008, p. 159). As with surfing and skateboarding, the NoBoarder must move their feet and center of gravity to adapt to pitch and snow conditions. "It's really loose and extremely wild . . . It feels kinda like surfing" proclaimed professional snowboarder and first-time NoBoarder Erik Leines (cited in Huffman, 2008, para. 2). Similarly, Bjorn Leines, brother of Erik, explains:

> There's a freedom that comes with it. . . . it makes me feel younger and it's more of a challenge. It reminds me of those early days when I first started snowboarding, but now that I can turn on a snowboard and skateboard and surf, I just put it all together. I find myself looking at terrain I wouldn't think twice about snowboarding on, but with a NoBoard it looks totally fun again. (cited in Anderson, 2008, p. 159)

With the recent partnership between NoBoard and Burton expanding the "reach and accessibility of the NoBoarding movement," Burns is excited about the possibilities of the activity:

> The big progression will come when younger kids see what we're doing and take it to man-made jumps and school yards. It's hard to say where it's going to go, but the right people are behind it and the seed has been planted. It's going to help snowboarding progress, but it's also going to open a whole new door to a new feeling, the feeling of NoBoarding. (cited in Anderson, 2008, p. 159)

Clearly, new technologies (e.g., molded plastic NoBoard stomp pads; three-dimensional polyethylene hulled snow-skates, snow-kite specific snowboards, light-weight backpack-shoots for B.A.S.E jumping) and entrepreneurial activity among participants seeking new commercial opportunities, account for many of the developments in snowboarding. In the highly competitive snowboarding industry, producers and marketers not only cope with rapidly and continually changing styles of participation, they capitalize upon them no matter how short term or limited their influence.

new markets: snowboarding comes to china

With the North American snowboarding market having reached "saturation point" (Robinson, 2006, para. 5), and the Japanese market steadily shrinking, many companies are looking for new consumer groups necessary for ongoing economic growth. According to Burton Snowboards representative William Avedon, China has been identified by many within the industry as "the next step" (cited in Robinson, 2006, para. 5). Indeed, snow-sports are increasingly gaining appeal among the rapidly growing Chinese middle class (Thorpe, 2007a). Prior to the mid-1990s, there were only an estimated 500 skiers in China, many of who were professional athletes. However, with more than 200 ski resorts opening since the introduction of the five-day work week in 1995, the ski industry in China is currently "booming" (Chinese Go, 2005). According to the China Ski Association, there were more than 5 million skiers in China in 2010, up from just 500,000 in 2000; the same report predicted that there will be more than 20 million skiers and snowboarders by 2014 (Irvine, 2010). Unlike other countries, skiing and snowboarding were introduced to China simultaneously and, while skiing remains the preferred activity, snowboarding is gaining popularity among Chinese middle class youth. A strong advocate for snowboarding in China, Steve Zdarsky identifies some of unique cultural considerations involved in developing the sport: "Snowboarding is growing a lot in the bigger city centres, especially Beijing. Here, the people have income and can afford to buy gear and go snowboarding . . . [but due to China's one-child policy] all the riders are twenty-plus, [there are] no young kids. You finish university first and then you start to snowboard" (cited in Air China, 2008, para, 8). The *Shanghai Star* comments that many Chinese youth are "under heavy pressure to study" and some consider extreme sports, such as snowboarding, "a waste of time" (Yu, 2002, para. 18). Drawing upon two studies on Chinese youth culture, U.S.-based research firm Label Networks notes that few parents want their only child to participate in dangerous sports such as snowboarding, and that they still prefer basketball, table tennis, and martial arts (China X, 2007, para. 6). Interestingly, while the "extreme" image of snowboarding has attracted many participants in Western countries, it seems to be hindering participation rates in China (Thorpe, 2008b).

Many North American snowboard companies are employing an array of innovative marketing strategies to further raise the profile of the sport and their companies among Chinese youth. Burton Snowboards was one of the first to identify the potential of the Chinese market, and in 2005, signed a three-year deal to sponsor the National Snowboard Team of China, which consisted of six boys and six girls, selected solely on their athletic (rather than snowboarding) abilities. According to Bryan Johnston, vice president of global marketing for Burton Snowboards, "snowboarding's expansion into China presents a huge opportunity in the sport's overall growth . . . and we're extremely pleased to have the chance to work with the National Snowboard Team of China" (cited in Burton Sponsors 2005, para. 4). Interestingly, two of the young women on this team competed in the 2006 Winter Olympics in Turin, Italy with less than 18 months snowboarding experience. More recently, the Chinese athletes were serious medal contenders at the 2010 Winter Olympics in Vancouver, Canada, and are expected to perform well in Sochi, Russia, in 2014.

Further attempting to promote the development of snowboarding in China, Burton Snowboards became the title sponsor of "The Burton Quiabo Mellow Park" in Beijing—China's first indoor year-round terrain facility which opened in 2008. Many other U.S.-based companies are also investing heavily in major events and competitions (e.g., Red Bull Nanshan Open) to raise the profile of snowboarding and their companies among Chinese youth. For example, Oakley partnered with champion snowboarder and skateboarder Shaun White to co-present the 2010 "Air + Style" event in Beijing. Oakley CEO Colin Baden was frank about the company's motives for investing in this event: "China has one of the largest and fastest growing middle class demographics in the world, and Chinese youth are currently experiencing a cultural revolution. All accounts point to these young people moving toward urban culture, music and action sports, and Air + Style delivers on all fronts. We'll bring the excitement of snowboarding to a new frontier, and the industry will likely follow our lead" (cited in Oakley and Shaun White present Air and Style 2010, 2010, para. 2). White was equally enthusiastic, describing the event as "an amazing honor" and "a

Burton-sponsored snowboarder Liu Jiaya of China started training in 2003 and placed fourth in the women's half-pipe event at the 2010 Winter Olympics in Vancouver. (AP Photo/Mark J. Terrill.)

huge opportunity" to "share our ever-progressing sport with Beijing and Chinese society as a whole" (cited in Ibid, para. 4).

climate change, snowboarding, and environmental activism

For many snow-sport industry members, changing seasonal patterns and snowfall is a serious concern. Despite difficulties attributing local seasonal patterns (e.g., a "good" season or a "bad" season) to broader shifts in the global climate, numerous studies are forecasting dire consequences for the future of downhill skiing and snowboarding. A study conducted by the United Nations Environment Program research team shows levels of snow falling in lower lying mountain areas becoming increasingly unpredictable and unreliable over the coming decades. According to Rolf Burki, the lead researcher on this project:

Climate change will have the effect of pushing more and more winter sports higher and higher up mountains, concentrating impacts in ever-decreasing high altitude areas. As ski resorts in lower altitudes face bankruptcy, so the pressure in highly environmentally sensitive upper-altitude areas rises, along with the pressures to build new ski lifts and other infrastructure. The extent to which countries, regions and communities can adapt will depend on how the costs and technology of snow making equipment develops, how the economics of building extra, higher altitude infrastructure such as cable cars develops, and the location of existing resorts. However, it appears clear that many resorts particularly in the traditional, lower altitude resorts of Europe will be either unable to operate as a result of lack of snow or will face additional costs, including artificial snow making, that may render them uneconomic. (cited in Many ski resorts heading downhill as a result of global warming, 2003, para. 7)

Summarizing the regional-specific findings from this study, Radford and Wilson (2003) warn: "Up to half of all Switzerland's ski resorts could face economic hardship or bankruptcy because of global warming . . . and low-altitude resorts in Italy, Germany and Austria may have to move uphill . . . Others may have to rely on snow-making machines. U.S. ski resorts face similar challenges, while Australia could have no skiing at all by 2070" (para. 2). Another report conducted by the Rocky Mountain/Great Basin regional Assessment Team for the U.S. Global Change Research Program concluded that "most analyses project a decline, if not total demise, of downhill skiing by the mid or latter part of the 21st century," with some climatologists projecting the "disappearance of snowpacks by approximately 2070 in the northern Rockies" (cited in Thorne, no date, para. 12).

Atmospheric scientist Katharine Hayhoe offers similar predictions: "[I]f we continue our addiction to fossil fuels, 70 to 90 percent of the actual snow on the ground in the California Sierras could be gone by the end of this century" (cited in Thorne, no date, para. 15). Glaciologists also present evidence showing that half of the glacier ice in the Alps has disappeared over the past century (Zwingle, 2006). A recent report conducted by the European Environment Agency predicts 75 percent of the glaciers in the Swiss Alps to disappear by 2050, and the U.S. Geological Survey expects glaciers in Montana's Glacier National Park could disappear in 25 years if temperatures continue to increase at the present rate.

Perhaps not surprisingly, such studies have evoked concern among those whose livelihood is contingent upon regular snowfall. Increasingly, snow-sport enthusiasts and environmental activists are campaigning local and regional ski resorts to adopt more environmentally sensitive approaches to their day-to-day management and long-term investments. For Sergio

Savoir, Director of the WWF European Alpine Program in Switzerland: "Ski resort operators have a responsibility to reduce carbon dioxide and other emissions linked with global warming. . . . they're slowly waking up to the fact that global warming has serious local consequences, not only in environmental terms but also in cold hard cash. In the future, the ski industry could become a de facto ally in the struggle to fight climate change globally and in adapting to its consequences locally" (cited in Thorne, no date, para. 28). Increasingly, many ski-resort operators and mountain resort destinations are attempting to lower carbon emissions and reduce their impact on the local environment (e.g., recycling, minimal use of snowmobiles, fuel efficient lift systems, more eco-friendly snow management and production). Some professional snowboarders, industry members, and enthusiasts, are joining environmental social-movement campaigns such as "Keep Winter Cool," an initiative of the U.S. National Ski Areas Association, and "Protect Our Winters," the brain-child of culturally-renowned big mountain snowboarder, Jeremy Jones.

"protect our winters"

Established in 2007, "Protect Our Winters" (POW) is a nonprofit organization dedicated to educating and activating snow-sport participants on issues relating to global warming. Jones describes his initial motivation as stemming from his personal observations of the effects of global warming on mountains around the world, and the recognition that he had access to potentially useful resources (i.e., social, cultural, and financial) that could be fruitfully utilized to raise the awareness of snow-sport enthusiasts:

> Through snowboarding I started to see more and more the mountains were changing. Something needed to be done; I had built some great relationships in the snowboard and ski industry; and, I felt like our culture needed to come together and slow down climate change. I went back and forth on the idea for a while, because I had a lot of thoughts of, "Who am I to start this foundation? I'm not an environmental saint." But it was something that just wouldn't go away. So I went full on into it, because I felt our industry really needed it . . . .(cited in McDermott, 2009, para. 2)

With the support of various corporations (i.e., The North Face, Burton, Rossignol, Volcom, O'Neill, Dakine, Vans, Clif), media agents (i.e., *Onboard European Snowboard Magazine*, and *Backcountry Magazine*,

Transworld Snowboarding, Cruxco.tv), resorts (i.e., Grand Targhee Resort), and professional snow-sport athletes, POW aims to "unite and mobilize the winter sports community to have a direct and positive impact on climate change" (About POW, no date, para. 6). As the following comments illustrate, POW marketing fosters an imagined sense of community, and notions of individual and group responsibility, among snow-sport enthusiasts:

> As a community, *our* snowboarding and skiing culture has a lot of power to affect change and to get things going in a positive direction again. I've learned that making small changes in each of *our* daily habits can make a huge difference to fight the global warming battle—it's time to get this information out there and get *our* collective efforts reversing the damage (Jeremy Jones, 2007, para. 4; emphasis added).

> It's time for *us* to step up and take responsibility to save the lifestyle that *we* all value so much. POW was founded on the idea that if *we* harness *our* collective energy and put forth a focused effort, the winter sports community can have a direct influence on reversing the damage that's been done and ensure that winters are here for generations behind *us*. (www.protectourwinters.org; emphasis added)

The official POW Web site identifies four key areas of action: (1) "inspiring our members to become involved locally," (2) "educating the next generation of environmental leaders," (3) "supporting innovative, alternative energy projects," and (4) "establishing corporate and resort partners as leaders in the fight against global climate change" (About POW, no date, para. 8). Understanding the individualistic, and often short-range, perspectives of many young snow-sport enthusiasts, POW's marketing and educational documents and products (e.g., films, Web sites) emphasize the immediate consequences of global warming for participants (e.g., shorter winters, resorts closing) and offer simple, everyday strategies that can be employed to help "save the winters" for current, as well as future, generations (e.g., carpooling to resorts; supporting "green" ski resorts; campaigning local resorts to be more environmentally conscious). While some respond by supporting POW initiatives via donations, others are moved to action within their local, regional, national, and global communities. Many of the latter pitch their ideas on various POW-related social networking sites (e.g., Facebook) and gain feedback, advice, and support from other environmentally conscious and politically engaged POW "members" from around the world.

Having starred in more than 45 snowboarding films during his career, Jones is very aware of the power of this medium to communicate with young snow sport enthusiasts. Thus, the organization regularly posts short educational video clips on their Web site and YouTube. Directly targeting young snow-sport enthusiasts, many of these clips feature professional skiers and snowboarders proffering key information about the threat of global warming and other POW-related information (e.g., simple strategies for reducing personal energy consumption), carefully interspersed with evocative footage of the athletes skiing and snowboarding in deep powder, juxtaposed with images of snowless mountain-scapes. In 2009, POW released *My Own Two Feet*, the first "sustainable snowboarding film." The film covers Jones (and others) predominantly human-powered backcountry expeditions (e.g., using a snow-plane and then hiking, climbing, and camping to access terrain, in comparison to helicopter or snowmobile accessed travel) during the previous winter. In so doing, the film offers big mountain and backcountry snow-sport enthusiasts a visually stimulating and thought-provoking "greener" alternative to participation and performance. As well as demonstrating Jones' exceptional big mountain snowboarding abilities in exotic locations, the film also provided space for him to discuss and illustrate some of the joys (and challenges) of pursuing personal and professional snowboard travel with a "different mindset," that is, with the aim of minimizing his carbon footprint rather than "run, after run, after run" provided by heavily polluting helicopters and snowmobiles. Describing the sensual and affective pleasures offered from such an approach, Jones writes:

> Since I can remember the dream was always about getting paid enough snowboarding so I could spend the spring in Alaska flying in helicopters and making snowboard movies . . . Now the dream is about taking a plane deep into unridden mountains, setting up a base camp and hiking and riding first descents on foot. It is a much more intimate experience with the mountains because I am not retreating back to our hotel rooms when nightfall comes or a storm blows in. I see every layer in the snowpack form as it falls. We watch our projected lines day and night for weeks on end and get to learn their moods . . . .(Jones, 2009, para. 1)

In 2010, Jones released *Deeper*, another environmentally conscious film that documents his latest efforts to snowboard new terrain without the

On set of his second environmentally-conscious snowboarding film, *Deeper* (2010), Jeremy Jones prepares his splitboard next to his campsite in the Alaskan backcountry. (Credit: O'Neill/ Greg von Doersten.)

use of helicopters, including a number of extreme camping experiences. As the recipient of eight "big mountain rider of the year" awards, Jones' cultural status lends much credibility to his initiatives. He is critically aware of the value of his position within the culture for encouraging support for his campaign: "leading with your actions will inspire others to do the same, and ultimately make a difference in global warming" (cited in The POW perspective: Jeremy Jones' Protect Our Winters campaign, 2008, para. 2).

Partnering with outdoor sport conglomerate The North Face and snowsports film company Teton-Gravity Research, POW also coproduced a 17-minute film titled *Generations: A Skiers' and Snowboarders' Perspective on Climate Change*. According to a press release offered by Teton Gravity Research, the film:

> discusses climate change through the perspectives of those for whom snowy winters have a deeper personal significance. Going beyond charts and numbers, *Generations* humanizes the debate on climate change by exploring the delicateness of winter and the intrinsic value of snow to people across generations and cultures. (TGR Releases, 2009, para. 1)

The North Face director of corporate sustainability and strategic marketing, Letitia Webster, also emphasizes the desire to personalize the global warming debate: "We wanted to produce something that went beyond the traditional climate change speech. *Generations* takes the conversation a step further by relating global warming to real consequences and personal affection" (cited in Download TGR's new movie *Generations*, 2009, para. 3). After its release, the film won a number of awards, including "Best Environmental Film" at the Rossland Mountain Film Festival and "Best Environmental Message" from the Backcountry Film Festival. Perhaps more significantly, however, the film was screened as part of a January 2010 U.S. Congressional conference on climate change. According to Congressman Jared Polis:

> The perspective provided by *Generations* ... provided a valuable and often overlooked component of the climate change debate in Washington. ... These athletes are on the front lines of this crisis, watching snow, ice and communities disappear all over the world. In sharing their story with Congress ... these individuals show us how we all stand to be personally affected by this global problem. (cited in Jeremy Jones, 2010, para. 5)

As these comments suggest, the pioneering efforts of some environmentally conscious snowboarders, such as Jeremy Jones, are helping to mobilize the snow-sport industry to initiate social change at the individual, local, national, and global level, and may help prolong the joys of snowboarding for future generations.

new terrain: from snow-domes to mount everest

With the cost of international travel rising, and snowfall becoming less predictable, climate controlled, indoor snow-slopes created with snow manufactured from snow canons, may continue to gain popularity. In 2005, Ski Dubai, a 22,500-square meter (73, 819 square feet) indoor ski area, opened as part of the Mall of Emirates (one of the world's largest malls). The facility features an 85-meter (279 feet) high indoor mountain with five slopes of varying steepness and difficulty, including a 400-meter (1312 feet) long "black" level run, and a 90-meter (295 feet) long half-pipe designed primarily for snowboarders. Similar facilities are available in countries around the world: Japan and the Netherlands each have seven indoor ski resorts, and there are six such facilities in the United Kingdom, five in Germany, three in China, at least one in Australia, France, New Zealand, South Korea, and Spain, and many more under construction in destinations ranging from Bahrain to Las Vegas.

Artificial or "dry ski slopes" are also gaining popularity in places where natural snow-covered slopes are unavailable yet there is a demand for snow-sliding facilities, particularly in the UK and the Netherlands. Dry ski slopes typically consist of purposefully constructed terrain covered in synthetic materials (e.g., Snowflex, Dendix, Permasnow, Atroride, Neveplast) which mimic (to varying degrees of success) the attributes of snow. Dry slopes are constructed both indoors and outdoors, and are typically lubricated using a mist or jet system to increase speed and prevent damage to equipment from friction heat buildup. Dry slopes have provided those living in locations without immediate access to snow-covered slopes, accessible opportunities to learn or practice the basic snowboarding skills (often before or after a trip to a ski resort). However, as technologies develop, snowboarders are increasingly practicing and performing skills on jumps and rails on dry slopes. Interestingly, many UK-based snowboarding Web sites feature forums dedicated to dry slope snowboarding with enthusiasts debating preferred synthetic slope materials, sharing tips for board preparation (e.g., using hardest grade ski wax), and discussing injury prevention (e.g., wearing additional padding). In some countries, particularly the UK, dry slope snowboard competitions are also gaining popularity. For example, the 2010 British Dryslope Snowboard Championships held at the Norfolk Snowsports Center, hosted more than 60 competitors who participated in big air, slopestyle, and snowboard-cross events. Despite the surface being considerably harder than natural snow, the competitors proceeded to perform an array of highly technical maneuvers, including 720 degree spins in the big air. As more indoor skiing facilities are built in cities around the world, skiing and snowboarding are becoming more accessible to those less able or willing to visit remote, expensive, and often elitist, alpine resort destinations. It is important to note, however, that for many passionate snowboarders, indoor and dry slopes do not replace the experience of snowboarding on a snow-covered mountain, but rather offer a novel or accessible substitute when natural resources are unavailable.

In radical contrast to artificial indoor ski slopes where patrons can literally step off the street (or out of the mall) and onto the snow, some highly committed snowboarders spend many weeks and months planning, hiking, climbing, and ultimately, descending some of the world's most

A snowboarder enjoys the half-pipe facilities offered at an indoor "snow fun-park" in Germany. (AP Photo/Frank Hormann.)

remote mountains. In 2001, for example, the separate quests of two European snowboarders coincided as they simultaneously sought to make the first snowboard descent of Mount Everest. On May 22, 2001, Austrian snowboarder and mountaineer Stefan Gatt became the first snowboarder to reach the 29,035-foot summit of Mount Everest; he did so without using oxygen and carrying all of his own equipment. He then proceeded to snowboard from a height 28,317 feet, but when the snow became "too hard and not very fun to ride," he un-strapped his board and climbed down a difficult part of the ascent route (Mount Everest snowboard controversy solved, 2008). When conditions improved, he returned to his board and rode from 24,934 feet to 21,151 feet.

Just one day after Gatt's impressive feat, 22-year-old French snowboarder and mountaineer Marco Siffredi reached the summit. Unlike Gatt, Siffredi's ascent was assisted with oxygen and by Sherpas who carried his snowboarding equipment. As with Gatt, Siffredi began his descent down the Norton Coloir North Face, but just 656 feet below the summit (and near the same altitude that Gatt removed his board and began climbing), his binding broke due to the extreme cold (−31 degrees Fahrenheit). Luckily, one of his Sherpa was able to fix the binding with a tool kit, enabling Siffredi to proceed with his descent. Snowboarding from 29,029 feet to 20,997 feet, Siffredi rode slopes of 40 to 45 degrees without the use of ropes or rappels. Taking a short break to rest part the way down, Siffredi reached Advanced Base Camp less than four hours after leaving the summit. Upon Siffredi's arrival back at Base Camp, his team was "already on the satellite phone and it was only a matter of minutes before the amazing news spread to every corner of the snowboarding universe" (Cook, 2006). As the following comments from *Transworld Snowboarding* journalist, Trey Cook (2006) reveal, making claim to the Mount Everest snowboard record was highly political: "Although Gatt had summited less than 24 hours ahead of Marco, he had taken his board off and down-climbed past 100 meters of the steepest terrain. Because he rode all the way from the summit back to Advanced Base Camp, Marco's historic descent was recorded as the first continuous snowboard descent of the world's highest mountain" (para. 12).

In 2002, Siffredi made a second ascent of Mount Everest with the aim of becoming the first person to snowboard down the highly technical 9,842-foot Hornbein Couloir. But conditions were considerably more challenging the second time around:

Sunday, September, 2002: . . . at 2:10PM, after twelve-and-a-half hours in the Death Zone, the team [Siffredi and two Sherpa] reaches 8,848 meters (29,028), the highest point on earth. . . . the ascent has taken three times longer than Marco's first Everest ascent. "Tired. Tired, Too much snow. Too much climbing" says Marco. . . . [But] at 3:00PM, Marco replaces the empty bottle of oxygen in his pack with a fresh one and straps in . . . Marco drops in to shred the world's highest freshies, makes a few turns, and waits on the ridge for the Sherpa to catch up. He's breathing hard, shattered by the effort of making turns with a pack at 8,800 meters after more than twelve thigh-burning hours of some of the most exhausting climbing on the planet. He lets them pass in front . . . and then makes his way left toward the Hornbein Couloir. The clouds billow up around him, and at 3:15PM, his Sherpa friends watch as Marco morphs into the soft mountain light of imagination and memory. (Cook, 2006, para. 28, 30)

Siffredi did not return to base camp: "His body has never been recovered, and no trace of him has ever been found beyond his initial tracks descending from the summit" (Cook, 2006, para. 33). Coming from a family familiar with the risks of mountaineering—his father was a mountain guide, and the family had previously lost another son to an avalanche in Chamonix—they were realistic about his fate: "We should not delude ourselves. He is dead," his mother, Michele, told reporters (cited in Smith, 2002, para. 7).

In 2003, Stephen Kock attempted to become the first person to snowboard the highest peaks on all seven continents, with Mount Everest as the grand finale. But, his goal of ascending and descending Mount Everest without oxygen and carrying all of his own equipment, ultimately eluded him. As *Mount Everest News* reports:

Stephen Koch recently returned from the North side of Mount Everest and his bold alpine style attempt on the Japanese Couloir and Hornbein Couloir. [His] . . . first summit attempt on August 29 ended when unstable conditions resulted in a harrowing serac fall that collapsed too close for comfort. They turned around and waited another week before heading up for a second and final attempt on September 9. The team climbed through the night and reached 6900m, quite short of the 7800m goal they'd planned. After evaluating the climbing conditions, the lateness of the hour, and the chance of success in continuing on with no fixed ropes, high camps or bottled oxygen, at the pace they were moving, they made the difficult decision to turn around and end the expedition. ("Mount Everest," 2003, para. 2)

According to Kock, his past experiences with mountain accidents and tragedy helped him "make the difficult decision to turn around" ("Mount Everest," 2003). He was at the Mount Everest base camp during the 1996 climbing tragedy that claimed eight lives, and in 1998, sustained multiple injuries when an avalanche in the Tetons dragged his body over half a mile in less than 30 seconds; after spending the night on the mountain alone, he was rescued the following day. Following ten months of intense rehabilitation, Kock returned to successfully climb and then snowboard down the same route. He believes such experiences helped him develop an intimate understanding of risk, consequence, individual strengths and weaknesses, and personal responsibility. In his own words, Koch described the Mount Everest experience as "a revelation": "It was about the journey. . . . I have to say that I honestly feel like I've learned so much more by not obtaining the ultimate goal. I've learned more about myself, about life, about dealing with people. It was a good ego check," before concluding, the "best thing about the trip" was that "everyone returned safely" ("Mount Everest," 2003, para. 12). When asked his advice to others interested in approaching such high-risk challenges, Koch replied: "Go light. Go fast. Take chances. Listen to your instincts.

Trust your heart. Not your ego. Your ego can get you into trouble. It has for me in the past. The mountain is beautiful. Risk is dangerous, but we make it dangerous" (cited in "Mount Everest," 2003, para. 16).

While some mountaineers cast those who snowboard high altitude peaks as "reckless," others celebrate their courageous pursuits. For example, Chris Warner, an experienced mountain guide who was on Everest in 2001 with Siffredi, finds the efforts of mountaineering snowboarders, such as Gatt, Siffredi, and Kock, "inspiring": "It is all about testing individual limits and understanding ourselves. We need people who are out there on the edge to impress upon us that our own limits are farther than we imagine" (cited in Smith, 2002, para. 11).

In sum, contemporary snowboarding culture is highly fragmented with participants demonstrating varying levels of commitment and physical prowess. Today, snowboarders engage in a plethora of styles (e.g., NoBoarding, snow-kiting, snow-skating, snowboard B.A.S.E jumping, backcountry, freestyle and jibbing, and alpine racing) in locations ranging from snow-domes in Dubai to freestyle terrain parks in New Zealand. While many contemporary forms of snowboarding are relatively safe, some styles of participation and destinations are certainly high risk. Arguably, it is in relation to riding big mountains in remote destinations, such as Alaska or Mount Everest, which exposes the individual to the raw power of the natural environment, including gale-force winds, subzero temperatures, 60-degree slopes, ice, rocks, slides, avalanches, cliffs and crevasses, that the term "extreme" has most relevance to snowboarding.

glossary

this glossary is intended to explain terms used in the text and illustrate the diversity of the language used within snowboarding culture to describe techniques, conditions, and performances. However, it does not attempt to define all of the snowboarding-specific jargon used in the culture. For an extensive and evolving list of such terms see http://www.abc-of-snowboarding-com/ snowboardingdictionary.asp or http://snowboarding.transworld.net/ 1000022565/how-to/the-sol-lexicon-a-dictionary-of-snowboard-terms/

backside. Performing a rotational maneuver in the direction the toes are facing when strapped into the board.

bail. To fall while riding or performing a maneuver; sometimes refers to withdrawing from the maneuver part the way through.

beat. A term used to describe something that is not in good condition. For example, "The landing on that jump is beat."

betty. A colloquial term for a female snowboarder; sometimes used to refer to a woman who is more interested in the snowboarding styles and fashion than active participation.

bluebird. A clear, sunny day, often after a fresh snowfall.

board-slide. Performing a slide on a rail in which the board is perpendicular to the coping or rail.

bombing. To ride fast down a slope, often "straight-lining it"—not using turns to control speed.

boost. To launch off a jump.

booter, table-top, hip, spine, cheese-wedge. All terms used to describe types of jumps either in the terrain park or backcountry.

corduroy.   A term used to describe the appearance of snow after it has been freshly groomed.

cork or corked.   A term used to describe freestyle maneuvers performed off-axis on jumps in the terrain parks, half-pipes, or backcountry.

cornice.   A sudden drop off, often in the backcountry.

dropping-in.   To take ones turn in the lineup to ride a slope or jump.

fakie.   A term used to refer to riding backwards.

fall-line.   The direction of least resistance down a slope in which gravity would pull you. If a snowball was released at the top of a slope, it would naturally follow the fall line.

first descent.   The first time a slope has been ridden by a snowboarder or skier.

freestyle.   A popular form of snowboarding in which individuals perform creative and technical maneuvers on jumps and other obstacles (e.g., rails) in found- and purposely created-spaces (e.g., terrain parks, half-pipes).

frontside.   Performing a rotational maneuver in the direction the front heel faces when strapped into the board.

50/50.   Performing a slide on a rail in which the board is parallel to the rail.

gap jump.   A type of jump with an empty space or "gap" between the take off and landing.

gnarly.   A term used to describe something (e.g., weather, terrain, a jump) that is difficult or challenging. For example, "It's so windy and snowing hard, it's pretty gnarly on the slopes today."

goofy.   Individual rides predominantly with their right foot forward on the board.

grommet.   A young snowboarder, often very passionate about snowboarding.

half-pipe.   A snow structure built specifically for freestyle snowboarding. A half-pipe consists of two opposing radial transition walls of the same height and size. Snowboarders use the half-pipe to "catch air" off the top of the walls, and perform tricks by traveling back and forth from wall to wall while moving down the fall line.

heel edge and toe edge. Snowboards have two edges. The heel edge refers to the edge along which the heels rest; the toe edge is the edge closest to the toes.

jibbing. A playful substyle of freestyle snowboarding that involves performing various skateboarding-inspired maneuvers on obstacles including trees, stumps, and rails, both on and off the ski resorts.

line. The path or route chosen by the snowboarder either down a slope in the backcountry or through a terrain park. For example, "She took the most technical line down that face. She dropped into the chute on the left, then went wide to hit a 20-foot rock drop, then spun a three off a cornice."

lingo. Snowboarding specific terminology used to describe techniques, equipment, or snow conditions.

lip. The top of the jump, often on a steep angle to help the rider get enough "pop" or "air" to perform their maneuver off the jump; also used to refer to the top edge of both walls of the half-pipe.

moguls. The bumps on a mountain slope that are created from snow being pushed down the mountain (often by skiers making tight turns).

noboarding. A modern form of snowboarding on a board without bindings and with a bungee; often performed in the backcountry.

nose. The front tip of the snowboard.

nuckle. The edge on the top of the jump landing. If a rider performs a jump without enough speed to cover the distance between the takeoff and the landing, they may "hit the knuckle," which can make for an uncomfortable landing and may "bounce" the rider down the landing area.

ollie. A jump performed by pulling the front foot and back foot up in quick succession.

out-of-bounds. Outside of ski resort boundaries.

pipe. Common abbreviation for half-pipe.

piste. Managed slopes within ski resort boundaries.

poach.   To ride a closed area such as a half-pipe or terrain park under construction or maintenance, terrain outside of a ski resorts boundaries, or a ski resort closed to snowboarders.

pow.   Common abbreviation for powder (or fresh snow).

quarter-pipe.   A half-pipe with only one wall used as a jump to perform a single maneuver.

regular.   Individual rides predominantly with their left foot forward on the board.

ripping.   A term used to refer to riding well.

rolling-down-the-windows.   A term used to describe when someone loses control while performing a jump such that they rotate their arms wildly in the air to try to regain balance.

scorpion.   When a snowboarder traveling at speed accidentally digs their toe edge into the snow causing them to fall face forward with such velocity that their legs extend, their back arches, and the board hits (or nearly hits) them in the head (like a scorpions tail).

shred.   Snowboarding with vigor and skill. For example, "Dude, you were shredding out there today."

sick.   An expression used to describe something that is exceptionally good. For example, "They shaped the pipe last night and it's sick."

snake.   Cutting in front of others in a line either for a chairlift or a terrain park or half-pipe.

snow-skating.   A playful form of snowboarding performed on a board the size of a skateboard and without bindings.

snowsurfing.   A term used to describe early forms of snowboarding practiced on rudimentary technologies often without bindings (e.g., Snurfers), before the term "snowboarding" was adopted.

snurfer.   An early snowboard-like device developed by Sherman Poppen in 1964, and later sold in supermarkets and sports stores across North America for between $10–30.

spray.   Snow that flies up when a board falls or lands a jump, or when a snowboarder comes to an abrupt halt by putting excessive force on one edge of their board.

steeze.   A colloquial term used to refer to demonstrating style with ease.

stomp.   A term used to refer to performing a good landing from a jump. For example, "He stomped his five-forty off the 60-footer, but then bailed when he hit the knuckle on the next jump."

superpipe.   A large half-pipe with 22-foot walls.

tail.   The back tip of the snowboard.

three, five, seven, nine, or ten.   Colloquial terms used to refer to the degrees of rotation in a maneuver. For example, a three is a 360 degree rotation; a five is a 520 degree rotation (one and half turns in one direction), a seven is a 720 degree rotation (two full turns in one direction), a nine is a 900 degree rotation (two and half turns in one direction), and a ten is a 1080 degree rotation (three full turns in one direction).

tricks.   Technical maneuvers often performed on jumps or rails in terrain parks or in the half-pipe, but also on jumps in the backcountry, or rails in urban environments.

tweak.   Emphasis of style in a trick, often involved twisting and extending movements and/or grabbing the board; sometimes the term "boned out" is also used to refer to a maneuver that has been successfully "tweaked" via sustained extension of a limb or board. For example, "He really boned out that method by grabbing the nose of his board and pulling it across his body while simultaneously extending out his back leg."

wack.   Something that is not good. For example, "That guys outfit is so wack."

yard sale.   A term used to refer to a snowboarder or skier that falls with such momentum that they are stripped of their beanie, gloves, goggles, backpack, etc.

bibliography

About POW. (no date). Retrieved March 8, 2010, from http://protect ourwinters.org/about/

"Action sports: The action sports market." (2007). Retrieved November 20, 2010, from http://activemarketinggroup.com/ Assets/AMG+2009/Action+Sports.pdf

Adler, J. (no date). Chad's Gap: The gap no one can shut up about. Retrieved August 12, 2010, from http://www.powdermag.com/ features/onlineexclusive/chads-gap/

Air China. (February 10, 2008). *Transworld Snowboarding.* Retrieved December 10, 2010, from http://snowboarding.transworld.net/ 1000026579/photos/air-china/

Ammann, W. J. (1999). A new Swiss test-site for avalanches in the Vallée de la Sionne/Valais. *Cold Regions Science and Technology,* 30(1–3), 3–11.

Anderson, K. (1999). Snowboarding: The construction of gender in an emerging sport. *Journal of Sport and Social Issues* 23(1), 55–79.

Anderson, P. (2008). NoBoarding: Staking their claim. *Transworld Snowboarding*, October, pp. 154–161.

Andrews, E. (March 28, 2009). Xavier de la Rue interview. *huck.* Retrieved August 3, 2010, from http://www.huckmagazine.com/ features/xavier-rue-interview/print/

Anna, T., Jan, B., & Aleksander, T. (2007). Goals in sports career and motivation as the measure of professionalism in snowboarding. *Medicina Sportiva, 11*, 27–31.

Anonymous. (June 19, 2007). Snowboard base cliff strike. Retrieved October 26, 2010, from http://snowboarding.transworld.net/

1000026830/uncategorized/craig-kelly-the-gatekeeper-april-1-1966-january-20-2003/

Araton, H. (February 19, 2006) "Davis is Right to Let Dream Trump Team," *The New York Times*. Retrieved February 14, 2008, from http://select.nytimes.com/2006/02/19/sports/olympics/19araton.html?_r=1&oref=slogin

Athlete bios (no date). *EXPN.com*. Retrieved from http://expn.go.com/athletes/bios/DAKIDES_TARA.html

Atkins, D. (2010). White Book, Avalanche awareness provided by Recco. Booklet produced by Recco.

Avalanche fatalities. (no date). Ultimate Ski. Retrieved October 9, 2010, from http://www.ultimate-ski.com/Off-Piste/Avalanches_and_Mountain_Safety/Avalanche_fatalities/index.html

Avalanches. (no date). *National Geographic*. Retrieved October 27, 2010, from http://environment.nationalgeographic.com/environment/natural-disasters/avalanche-profile/?source=A-to-Z

Baccigaluppi, J., Mayugba, S., & Carnel, C. (2001). *Declaration of independents: Snowboarding, skateboarding and music: An intersection of cultures*. San Francisco: Chronicle Books.

Bailey, R. (February 1998). Jake Burton: King of the hill. *Ski*, 62(6), pp. 60–66.

Baldwin, S. (2006a). Riding high? Skiing, snowboarding and drugs. *Snowsphere.com*. Retrieved March 12, 2010, from http://www.snowsphere.com/special-features/riding-high-skiing-snowboarding-and-drugs

Baldwin, S. (January 2006b). Snowboarding vs skiing: The dying feud. *SnowSphere.com*. Retrieved March 12, 2009, from http://www.snowsphere.com/special-features/snowboarding-vs-skiing-the-dying-feud

Bale, J. & Krogh-Christensen, M. (Eds.) (2004). *Post-Olympism? Questioning sport in the twenty-first century*. Oxford: Berg Publishers.

Bang, K., Brooks, G., Alberto Delaroca, J., Jiménez, M. (2010). The Multiculturals in Action Sports Report: 2010 Hispanic Snow Summary. Retrieved from http://www.masreport.com/wp-content/uploads/2010/11/2010_MAS-Report_HispanicSnow-FULL.pdf

Banked slalom. (February 10, 2008). *Transworld Snowboarding.* Retrieved from http://snowboarding.transworld.net/1000026811/photos/banked-slalom/

Barr, M., Moran, C., and Wallace, E. (2006) *Snowboarding the world.* Bath, UK: Footprint.

Basich, T., with Gasperini, K. (2003). *Pretty Good for a Girl: The Autobiography of a Snowboarding Pioneer.* New York: HarperCollins.

Beal, B., and Weidman, L. (2003). Authenticity in the skateboarding world. In *To the extreme: Alternative sports, inside and out,* edited by Robert Rinehart and Synthia Sydnor (pp. 337–352). New York: State University Press.

Becker, K. (March 6, 2009). Snowboarder Twitters for Rescue. Retrieved October 4, 2010, from http://www.gadling.com/2009/03/06/snowboarder-twitters-for-rescue

Benedek, D. (October 24, 2009). David Benedek interviews Jeremy Jones. *Snowboarder.* Retrieved from http://fresh.snowboarder mag.com/feature/david-benedek-interviews-jeremy-jones/

Bengal (December 20, 2008). Against the Grain: Tara Dakides interview. *Transworld Snowboarding.* Retrieved March 2, 2010, from http://snowboarding.transworld.net/1000082738/uncategorized/against-the-grain-tara-dakides-interview/

Best big mountain snowboarder of 2009: #1 Jeremy Jones. (2009). *Snowboarder.* Retrieved August 3, 2010, from http://www.snowboardermag.com/exclusives/best-big-mountain-snowboarder-of-2009-1-jeremy-jones/

Blehm, E. (September 3, 2003). Craig Kelly: The gatekeeper. *Transworld Snowboarding.* Retrieved August 10, 2010, from http://snowboarding.transworld.net/1000026830/uncategorized/craig-kelly-the-gatekeeper-april-1-1966-january-20-2003/

Blevins, J. (April 17, 2007). Terrain-park safety becomes top priority after lawsuit. *The Denver Post.* Retrieved March 18, 2010, from http://www.denverpost.com/skiing/ci_5682314

Blount, R. (February 3, 2010). Winter Olympics: Halfpipe takes a dangerous turn. Startribune.com. Retrieved November 12, 2010, from http://www.startribune.com/sports/83060467.html

Blumberg, A. (January 2002). "Launch." *Transworld Snowboarding*, p. 16.

Bogle, L., Boyd, J., & McLaughlin, K. (2010). Triaging multiple victims in an avalanche setting. *Wilderness and Environmental Medicine, 11*, 102–108.

Booth, D., & Thorpe, H. (2007). The meaning of extreme. In Booth & Thorpe (Eds.), *Berkshire encyclopedia of extreme sport* (pp. 181–197). Great Barrington, MA: Berkshire Publishing.

Bourdieu, P. (1984) *Distinction: A social critique of the judgement of taste*. London: Routledge.

Boyd, M., & Kim, M. (2007). Goal orientation and sensation seeking in relation to optimal mood states among skateboarders. *Journal of Sport Behavior, 30*, 21–35.

Bradley, S. (January 28, 2010). Campaign targets boozy Brits on the piste. *Swissinfo.ch*. Retrieved March 12, 2010, from http://www.swissinfo .ch/eng/culture/Campaign_targets_boozy_Brits_on_the_piste.html ?cid=8178712

Branch, J. (February 17, 2010). Never too cool for a hard workout. *The New York Times*. Retrieved October 8, 2010, from http:// www.nytimes.com/2010/02/18/fashion/18fitness.html

Breivik, G. (1996). Personality, sensation seeking and risk-taking among Everest climbers. *International Journal of Sport Psychology, 27*, 308–320.

Breivik, G. (1999). Personality, sensation seeking and risk-taking among top level climbers, parachute jumpers and white water kayakers. In Breivik (Ed.), *Personality, sensation seeking and arousal in high risk sports* (pp. 8–26). Oslo: The Norwegian University of Sport and Physical Education.

Bridges, P. (November 2004). Romain DeMarchi. *Snowboarder*, 94–105.

Bridges, P. (2005a). Blood Leines: The Erik and Bjorn interview. *Snowboarder*. Retrieved from http://snowboardermag.com/magazine/ features/leines/#http://snowboardermag.com/magazine/features/ leines-110105-01.jpg

Bridges, P. (August 2005b). The next Shaun White. *Snowboarder*, pp. 82–93.

Brisick, J. (2004). *Have Board Will Travel: The Definitive History of Surf, Skate, and Snow*. New York: HarperCollins.

Britain tells alpine enthusiasts don't drink and ski. (December 9, 2009). Retrieved from http://www.reuters.com/article/idUSTRE5B84D0 20091209

Brodit, B. (2009). What causes avalanches? *ABC of Snowboarding.* Retrieved from http://www.abc-of-snowboarding.com/info/avalanche -causes.asp

Brooks, R. (2010). Success stories: Jake Burton charts a new course in snowboarding. *Success.* Retrieved January 7, 2010, from http:// www.successmagazine.com

Brugger, H. & Falk, M. (2002). Analysis of avalanche safety equipment for backcountry skiers. Retrieved December 2, 2010, from http://www .avalanche-research.com/files/documents/1/brugger_falk_report.pdf

Bryson, L. (1990). Challenges to male hegemony in sport. In M. Messner & D. Sabo (Eds.), *Sport, men and the gender order: Critical feminist perspectives* (pp. 173–184). Champaign: Human Kinetics.

Bull, J. (April 1, 2009). Fluid snowboarding. Retrieved December 20, 2009, from personal blog, http://www.jamesbull.ca/blog/tag/ snowboarding/

Burton and NSAA introduce terrain park safety program. (February 10, 2010). *Transworld Snowboarding.* Retrieved from http://snow boarding.transworld.net/1000027775/other/burton-and-nsaa-introduce -terrain-park-safety-program/

Burton Carpenter, J. & Dumaine, B. (October 2002). My half-pipe dream come true. *Fortune Small Business*, 12(8), p. 64.

Burton history. (2005). Retrieved July 15, 2006, from http://www.burton .com/Company/Companyresearch.aspx

Burton sponsors national Snowboard Team of China. (October 14, 2005). Retrieved from http://www.twsbiz.com/twbiz/print/0,21538,11 19465,00.html

Burton, J. (2003). Snowboarding: The essence is fun. In R. Rinehart & S. Sydnor (Eds.), *To the extreme: Alternative sports, inside and out* (pp. 401–406). New York: State University Press.

Butt, D. (2006). The 2006 NZ Snowboarder Magazine rider poll. *New Zealand Snowboarder*, July/August, pp. 52–60.

Butt, D. (2005, July/August). Pro's and con's. *New Zealand Snowboarder*, pp. 88–92.

Buyers Guide (2003, May/June). *New Zealand Snowboarder*, pp. 84–104.

Celsi, R. (1992). Transcendent benefits of high-risk sports. *Advances in Consumer Research, 19*, 636–641.

Celsi, R., Rose, R., & Leigh, T. (1993). An exploration of high-risk leisure consumption through skydiving. *Journal of Consumer Research, 20*, 1–23.

Chinese go mad for the snow. (March 9, 2005). Retrieved October 27, 2010, from http://www.natives.co.uk/news/2005/03/09chin.htm

Chow, T. K., Corbett, S. W., Farstad, D. J. (1996). Spectrum of injuries from snowboarding. *Journal of Trauma, 41*, 321–325.

Coleman, A. G. (2004). *Ski Style: Sport and Culture in the Rockies*. University Press of Kansas: Kansas.

Costios, D. (2005). Aussies behaving badly. *Australian, New Zealand Snowboarding*, p. 15.

Cook, T. (February, 2006). The disappearance of Marco Siffredi. *Transworld Snowboarding, 19*. Retrieved from http://snowboarding .transworld.net/1000027305/uncategorized/the-disappearance-of-marco -siffredi/

Coyle, C. (2002). The siege at summit. *Transworld Snowboarding*, September, pp. 128–135.

Comprehensive study of sports injuries in the U.S. (2003). *American Sports Data*. Retrieved December 9, 2009, from www.american sportsdata.com/sports_injury1.asp

Crane, L. (1996). Snowboard history timeline part 2 (1980s). Retrieved March 22, 2004, from http://www.transworldsnowboarding.com/ snow/features/article/0,26719,246573,00.html

Cronin, C. (1991). Sensation seeking among mountain climbers. *Personality and Individual Differences, 12*, 653–654.

Csiksentmihalyi, M. (1990). *Flow: The psychology of optimal experience*. New York: Harper and Row.

Curtes, J. Eberhardt, J. and Kotch, E. (2001). *Blower: Snowboarding inside out*. Booth-Clibborn Editions Ltd, London.

Davies, C. (September 6, 2009). White death. *Geographical*. Retrieved from http://www.geographical.co.uk/Magazine/Avalanches _-_September_06.html?print=pa

DC Snowboarding. (January 31, 2011). DC's Torstein Horgmo makes X Games history and takes home gold. Retrieved February 23, 2011, from http://snow.dcshoes.com/news

Deemer, S. (January 24, 2000). Snow business is booming in sunny Orange County. *Los Angeles Business Journal.* Retrieved from http://www.findarticles.com/cf_dIs/m5072/4_22/59634968/p

Diehm, R., & Armatas, C. (2004). Surfing: An avenue for socially acceptable risk-taking, satisfying needs for sensation seeking and experience seeking. *Personality and Individual Differences, 36,* 663–677.

Download TGR's new movie *Generations.* (December 4, 2009). *Free Skier.* Retrieved March 9, 2010, from http://www.freeskier.com/article/artide.php?article_id=4449

Dresser, C. (January 2005). Getting deep: The DCP interview. *Transworld Snowboarding,* pp. 132–149.

Dunn, K. (2001). What are the health hazards of snowboarding? *Western Journal of Medicine, 174*(2), 128–130.

Ebner, D. (February 11, 2009). U.S snowboarder at top of fame mountain. *Globe and Mail.* Retrieved January 5, 2010, from http://license.icopyright.net/user/viewfreeuse.act?fuid=NjM5MTQ1MQ%3D%BD

Edwards, G. (March 9, 2006). Attack of the flying tomato. *Rolling Stone,* 995, pp. 43–45.

Elliot, J. (January 21, 2001). "The it girl," *Sports Illustrated.* Retrieved from http://sportsillustrated.cnn.com/features/siadventure/11/it_girl/

Engrebretsen, L., Steffen. K., Alonso, J. M., AUbry, M., Dvorak, J., Judge, A., Meeuwisse, W., Mountjoy, M., Renström, P., & Wilkinson, M. (2010). Sports injuries and illnesses during the Winter Olympic Games 2010. *British Journal of Sports Medicine, 44,* 772–780.

Everest's Stephen Koch: "I learned so much more by not obtaining the ultimate goal," (November 20, 2003). *Mount Everest.net.* Retrieved October 24, 2010, from http://www.mounteverest.net/story/EverestsStephenKochIlearnedsomuchmorebynotobtainingtheultimategoalNov202003.shtml

Fact sheet: Burton Snowboards (2003). Retrieved from www.burton.com

Fact Sheet: State of the Snowboard Industry in 2004. Retrieved July 17, 2004, from http://www.burton.com/company/default.asp

Facts about skiing/snowboarding safety. (2009). *National Ski Areas Association.* Retrieved from http://www.nsaa.org/nsaa/press/facts-ski-snbd-safety.asp

Fast, A. (2005). *Transworld Snowboarding Resort Guide*, p. 24.

Fastest Growing Sports. Retrieved March 14, 2005, from http://www.extrememediagroup.com/xchannel/xcha_main.html#4

Falk, M., Brugger, H., & Adler-Kastner, L. (1994). Avalanche survival changes. *Nature, 368*, 21.

Farley, F. (1986). The big T in personality: Thrill-seeking often produces the best achievers but it can also create the worst criminals. *Psychology Today, 20*, 44–48.

Farley, F. (1993). The type T personality. In L. Lipsitt & L. Mitmick (Eds.), *Self-regulatory behavior and risk-taking* (pp. 371–382). New Jersey: Ablex.

Fastest growing sports (no date). Retrieved March 14, 2005, from http://www.extrememediagroup.com/xchannel/xcha_main.html#4

Fave, A. D., Bassi, M., & Massimini, F. (2003). Quality of experience and risk perception in high-altitude rock climbing. *Journal of Applied Sport Psychology, 15*, 82–98.

Ferrera, P., McKenna, D., & Gilman, E. (1999). Injury patterns with snowboarding. *American Journal of Emergency Medicine, 17*, 575–577.

Ford, N., & Brown, D. (2006). *Surfing and social theory.* London: Routledge.

Frohlick, S. (2003). Negotiating the "global" within the global playscapes of Mount Everest. *The Canadian Review of Sociology and Anthropology, 40*(5), 525–542.

Frohlick, S. (2005). "That playfulness of white masculinity": Mediating masculinities and adventure at Mountain Film Festivals. *Tourist Studies, 5*, 175–193.

Fry, J. (January 2005). The arrogance of risk. *Ski.* Retrieved from http:www.skimag.com/skimag/travel/article/0,12795,847444,00.html

Gagnon, O. (February 2008). Snowblind. *Snowboarder*. Retrieved March 10, 2010, from http://www.snowboardermag.com/features/news/february-08-on-sale-now/

Galbraith, J. and A. Marcopoulos, A. (2004). Terje Haakonsen. *Frequency: The Snowboarder's Journal, 3*(3), 62–83.

Griffith, J., Hart, C., Goodling, M., Kessler, J., & Whitmire, A. (2006). Responses to the sports inventory for pain among BASE jumpers. *Journal of Sport Behavior, 29*, 242–254.

Goma, J. (1991). Personality profile of subjects engaged in high physical risk sports. *Personality and Individual Differences, 12*, 1087–1093.

Goodman, D. (January/February 2003). Chairman of the board. *Yankee*, 67(1), 64.

Graves, W. (February 16, 2010). "Ski Jeans Turning Heads at Cypress Mountain," *ABC News*. Retrieved March 10, 2010, from http://abcnews.go.com/Entertainment/wireStory?id=9848152

Hagerman, E. (November 2002). The cool sellout. *Outside*. Retrieved March 27, 2008, from http://outside.away.com/outside/features/200211/200211/cool_sellout_2.html

Hammond, J. (October 20, 2000). "Hot seat with Tara Dakides," *Transworld Snowboarding*. Retrieved from http://www.transworldsnowboarding.com/snow/snowboard_life/article

Hansom, D. & Sutherland, A. (2010). Injury prevention strategies in skiers and snowboarders. *Current Sports Medicine Reports, 9(3)*, 169175.

Hard numbers. *Transworld Snowboarding*, October, 2005, p. 56.

Heino, R. (2000). What is so punk about snowboarding? *Journal of Sport and Social Issues, 24*, 176191.

Helmich, P. (August 8, 2000). Chairman of the board. Retrieved from http://www.vermontguides.com/2000/8-aug/aug1.html

Holt, R. (2005). *Australian and New Zealand Snowboarding*, p. 91.

Horovitz, B. (February 7, 2010). Jake Burton puts his stamp on Burton Snowboards. *USA Today*. Retrieved from http://www.usatoday.com/money/companies/management/entre/2010-02-07-jake-burt

How are the best pipes built? (April 20, 2000). Boardtheworld.com. Retrieved October 25, 2010, from http://www.boardtheworld.com/Home/Magazine/Features/Features?&riID=44

How do you stay diesel for snowboarding? (April 2003). *Transworld Snowboarding*, p. 16.

Howe, S. (1998). *(SICK) A Cultural History of Snowboarding*. New York: St. Martins Griffin.

Huberman, J. (1968). *A psychological study of participants in high risk sports*. Unpublished doctoral dissertation, University of British Columbia.

Huffman, J. (December 25, 2009). A snowboard does a split and becomes a pair of skis. *The New York Times*. Retrieved October 2, 2010, from http://travel.nytimes.com/2009/12/25/travel/escapes/25split.html ?pagewanted=print

Huffman, J. (February 15, 2008). For NoBoarders in British Columbia, it's no bindings, no problem. *The New York Times*. Retrieved November 12, 2010, from http://travel.nytimes.com/2008/02/15/ travel/escapes/15noboard.html?pagewanted=print

Hughes, K. (1988). Surfboarding shifts to the ski slopes and cultures clash. *The Wall Street Journal*. March, 1988. http://global.factiva .com/en/arch/display.asp (accessed March 10, 2003).

Humphreys, D. (1996). Snowboarders: Bodies out of control and in conflict. *Sporting Traditions*, 13(1), 323.

Humphreys, D. (1997). Shredheads go mainstream? Snowboarding an alternative youth. *International Review for the Sociology of Sport*, *32*, 147–160.

Humphreys, D. (2003). Selling out snowboarding. In R. Rinehart & S. Sydnor (Eds.), *To the Extreme: Alternative Sports, Inside and Out* (pp. 407–428). New York: State University Press.

Hymbaugh, K., & Garrett, J. (1974). Sensation seeking among skydivers. *Perceptual and Motor Skills, 38*, 118.

In your head (2005, February). *Transworld Snowboarding*, p. 54.

Is snowboarding a religion? (July 2002). Retrieved June 7, 2004, from http://www.boardtheworld.com/magazine/editorial.php?month =2002-07-01

Insider the action: Snowboard halfpipe. (2010). *The New York Times*. Retrieved from http://www.nytimes.com/interactive/sports/olympics/ olympics-interactives.html#tab0

Irvine, D. (February 10, 2010). China's ski boom faces uphill challenges. *CNN.com*. Retrieved October 27, 2010, from http://edition.cnn.com/2010/BUSINESS/02/08/china.ski.industry/index.html

Jake Burton Carpenter interview. (February 10, 2008). *Transworld Snowboarding*. Retrieved from http://snowboarding.transworld.net/1000030391/photos/backcountry/jake-burton-carpenter-interview/

Jamieson, B., & Geldsetzer, T. (1996). Trends and patterns in avalanche accidents in Canada 1984–1996. *Canadian Avalanche Association*, Revelstoke, BC: Canada, pp. 7–20.

Jealouse, V. (July 31, 2005). Interview. Powderroom.net. Retrieved August 5, 2010, from http://www.powderroom.net/profiles/victoria-jealouse

Jenkins, L. (February 18, 2006). "With a Final, Risky Flourish, Gold Turns to Silver," *The New York Times*. Retrieved February 14, 2008, from http://www.nytimes.com/2006/02/18/sports/olympics/18cross.html

Jenkins, S. (February 18, 2006). Biff, crash, bang: Jacobellis loses chance to show off a gold medal. *The Washington Post*. Retrieved August 18, 2006, from http://www.washingtonpost.com/wp-dyn/content/article/2006/02/17/AR2006021701471_pf.html

Jeremy Jones establishes Protect Our Winters (POW) in fight against global warming crisis. (March 28, 2007). Retrieved March 10, 2010, from http://www.snowboard-mag.com/node/19938

Jeremy Jones, POW and TGR meet with Congress. (January 29, 2010). *Powder*. Retrieved March 12, from http://blogs.powdermag.com/industry-news-and-events/jeremy-jones-pow-tgr-go-to-washington

Jones, J. (December 14, 2009). Backcountry basics, part two. "Just say no." Retrieved October 24, 2010, from http://blog.jonessnowboards.com/2009/12/backcountry-basics-part-two-just-say-no/

Karan, P. (2005). *Japan in the 21st Century: Environment, Economy and Society*. Kentucky Press: Kentucky.

Karleen Jeffery interview. (October 2, 2008). *Transworld Snowboarding*. Retrieved August 6, 2010, from http://snowboarding.transworld.net/1000027012/other/the-karleen-jeffery-interview/

Kay, J. & Laberge, S. (2003) "Oh say can you ski?" Imperialistic construction of freedom in Warren Miller's *Freeriders*. In R. Rinehart & S. Sydnor (Eds.) *To the extreme: Alternative sports, inside and out*. New York: State University of New York.

Kelly, C. (2008). John Buffery interview. *Transworld Snowboarding*. Retrieved September 8, 2010, from http://snowboarding.transworld .net/1000030559/photos/backcountry/john-buffery-interview/

Keoki. (no date). Lord of the boards: Mike Hatchett. *Snow Quest*. Retrieved March 12, 2010, from http://snowquest.com/edge/hatchet1.html

Kinkade, S. (January 13, 2010). Local man's halfpipe to be feature in US Snowboarding Grand Prix. *MtShastaNews.com*. Retrieved September 7, 2010, from http://www.mtshastanews.com/sports/ x1672008376/Local-man-s-halfpipe-to-be-featured

Krakauer, J. (1997). *Eiger Dreams: Ventures among Men and Mountains*. Anchor Books: New York.

Krüger, A. & Edelmann-Nusser, J. (2009). Biomechanical analysis in freestyle snowboarding: Application of a full-body inertial measurement system and a bilateral insole measurement system. *Sports Technology, 2* (1–2), 17–23.

Kurland, A. (no date). Victorian Jealouse: Defying time. *huck, 7*. Retrieved from http://www.huckmagazine.com/features/victoria-jealouse

Larsen, M. (January 28, 2011). Horgmo lands first triple in competition. *ESPN.com*. Retrieved February 23, 2011, from http://sports.espn .go.com/espn/print?id=6070285&type=story

Leap of faith: Annie Boulanger. (February 10, 2008). *Transworld Snowboarding*. Retrieved from http://snowboarding.transworld.net/ 1000026581/photos/leap-of-faith-annie-boulanger/

LeFebvre, E. (August 29, 2005). Shut the f – k up. *Transworld Snowboarding*. Retrieved April 1, 2006 from http://www.trans worldsnowboarding.com/snow/features/article/0,13009,1099403,00 .html

Lewis, M. (November 6, 2008). Snowboarding tops outdoor sports injury list. *Transworld Business*. Retrieved December 10, 2010, from http://business.transworld.net/6984/news/snowboarding-tops -outdoor-sports-injury-list/

Lewis, M. (October 14, 2010a). Finding opportunities in an aging action sports demographic. *Transworld Business*. Retrieved November 23, 2010, from http://business.transworld.net/49555/features/finding -opportunities-in-an-aging-action-sports-demographic/

Lewis, M. (November 17, 2010b). How to grow your business in the Hispanic community. *Transworld Business*. Retrieved November 23, 2010, from http://business.transworld.net/51577/features/ how-to-grow-your-business-in-the-hispanic-community/

Lidz, F. (December 1997). Lord of the board. *Sports Illustrated*, 87, pp. 114–119.

Lipton N. (February 26, 2010). High fives with Todd Richards: Olympic drag. *Yo Beat*. Retrieved March 2, 2010, from http://www.yobeat .com/2010/02/26/high-fives-with-todd-richards%E2%80%94olympic -drag/

Many ski resorts heading downhill as a result of global warming. (December 2, 2003). *United Nations Environment Programme*. Retrieved December 8, 2010, from http://www.unep.org/sport _env/pressrelease/skiresort3.asp

McClung, D. & Schaerer, P. (2006). *The Avalanche Handbook*, 3rd edition. Seattle: The Mountaineers Books.

McDermott, M. (November 24, 2009). Interview with Jeremy Jones: Founder of Protect Our Winters. *Tree Hugger*. Retrieved April 5, 2010, from http://www.treehugger.com/files/2009/11/the-th -interview-jeremy-jones-protect-our-winters.php

McNab, N. (2008). Change your attitude. *Chamonix Guiding*. Retrieved September 4, 2010, from http://www.chamonixguiding.com/ index.php/eng/Features/Change-your-Attitude

Media Man Australian Extreme Directory (no date). Retrieved November 19, 2009, from www.mediaman.com.au_profiles_snowboard.pdf

Mellegran, D. (January 7, 1998). AP reports Terje boycotting Nagano? *SOL Snowboarding Online*, www.solsnowboarding.com/compete/terje.html

Messner, M. (2002). *Taking the Field: Women, Men and Sports*. London: Minnesota Press.

Meyers, C. (1996). On the edge: New riders on the Olympic stage. *Ski Magazine, 25*, p. 35.

Mickle, T. (May 31, 2010). White-out. *Sports Business Journal.* Retrieved December 9, 2010, from http://www.sportsbusinessjournal.com/article/65843

Moore, T. P. (2000). Snowboarding injuries. *British Journal of Sports Medicine, 34,* 79.

Moran, C. & Gibson, O. (February 5, 2010). Snowboarder's double cork flip becomes hot issue for Olympics. *The Guardian.* Retrieved from http://www.guardian.co.uk/sport/2010/feb/05/shaun-white-double-cork-olympics-ban

Morris, J. (June 2008). Research on the slopes: Being your own customer can be essential to success. *Change Agent: The Global Market Research Business Magazine.* Retrieved January 1, 2010, from http://synovate.com/changeagent.index.php

Mount Everest snowboard controversy solved. (2008). *Transworld Snowboarding.* Retrieved http://snowboarding.transworld.net/1000022968/uncategorized/mount-everest-snowboard-controversy-solved/

Mueller, S. & Peters, M. (2008). The personality of freestyle snowboarders: Implications for product development. *Tourism, 56*(4), 339–354.

Murphy, C. (January 22, 2006). Sloping off to Mont Blanc. *The Post IE.* Retrieved December 2, 2009, from http://archives.tcm.ie/business post/2006/01/22/story11123.asp

Muzzey, J. (April 2003). Interview: Romain De Marchi. *Transworld Snowboarding,* pp. 126–139.

Nelson, J. (January 26, 1989). Snowboarding: Riding the bank sideways. *The New York Times.* Retrieved March 12, 2004, from http://proquest.umi.com/pdfweb?did+157078261&sid=2&Fmt=3&client

Newitz, A., Cox, A. M., Johnson, F., & Sandell, J. (1997). Masculinity without men: Women reconciling feminism and male identification. In L. Heywood & J. Drake (Eds.), *Third-wave agenda: Being feminist, doing feminism* (pp. 178–205). Minneapolis: University of Minnesota Press.

NGSA: Skiers/snowboarder profile continues to change. (November 12, 2001) *NGSA Newsletter,* 3(21).

NGSA: Women's participation ranked by percent change 2003. *National Sporting Goods Association: Research and Statistics.* Retrieved

January 12, 2005, from http://www.nsga.org/public/pages/index.cfm?pageid=155

Norcross, D. (February 23, 2006). The flipside: "He is not human." *The San Diego Union Tribute*. Retrieved January 17, 2011, from http://www.signonsandiego.com/uniontrib/20060223/news_lz1s23shwhite.html

Oakley and Shaun White present Air and Style 2010: Global snowboarding challenge to take place in Beijing, China. (October 21, 2010). Retrieved November 14, 2010, from http://www.oakley.com/sports/air-style-china/posts/2555

Oakley Arctic Challenge: Quarterpipe under construction. (2007). Snowrev.com. Retrieved October 10, 2010, from http://www.snowrev.com/News/All/Oakley-Arctic-Challenge-Quarterpipe-Under-Con

Ober, L. (January 5, 2010). Should big air snowboarding be "reined in"? Retrieved August 8, 2010, from http://7d.blogs.com/blurt/2010/01/should-big-air-snowboarding-be-reigned-in.html

Olympic gold: Your complete guide to the Vancouver Games. (March 2010). *Transworld Snowboarding*, pp.67–83.

O'Neill, D. F., and McGlone, M. R. (1999). Injury risk in first-time snowboarders versus first-time skiers. *The American Journal of Sports Medicine, 27*, 94–97.

On the wave of death. (May 2004). Retrieved June 2, 2004, from http://www.methodmag.com/index.php?id=121

O'Shea, M. (2004). Snowboard jumping, Newton's second law and the force of landing. *Physics Education, 39*(4), 335–341.

Ouse, L. (March 1, 2005). Jump building bickering. Boardtheworld.com. Retrieved August 10, 2010, from http://www.boardtheworld.com/Home/Magazine/Editorial/Editorial?&riID=761

Peltzman, S. (1975). The effects of automobile safety regulation. *Journal of Political Economy, 83*(4), 677–725.

Pennington, B. (March 26, 2010). Playgrounds for skiers and snowboarders in New Hampshire. *The New York Times*. Retrieved April 4, 2010, from http://www.nytimes.com/2010/03/26/travel/escapes/26loon.html?pagewanted=print

Poll results: How many times have you snowboarded in a foreign country? Online posting. Retrieved February 1, 2006, from:http://snowboard

.colonies.com/Polls/PollResults.aspx?pollID=36&shouldShowPoll
Results=True

Press release (October 17, 2004). Burton teams with Mandalay
Entertainment. Retrieved November 12, 2006, from http://www
.transworldsnowboarding.com/snow/snowbiz/article/0,13009,7109
87,00.html

Press release. (November 8, 2007). Resorts of the Canadian Rockies
focuses on terrain park safety with an industry leading initiative.
Snowboard. Retrieved March 20, 2010, from http://www.snow-
board-mag.com/node/28059

Pries, L. (ed.) (2001). *New transnational social spaces: International
migration and transnational companies in the early twenty-first
century.* London: Routledge.

Pro file: Chris "Gunny" Gunnarson of SPT. (February 4, 2010). *Shredstix.com.*
Retrieved October 26, 2010, from http://shredstix.com/blogs/
detail/Pro-File-Chris-Gunny-Gunnarson-of-SPT/5471.html

Question and answer. (January 19, 2006). *Transworld Snowboarding.*
Retrieved from http://www.transworldsnowboarding.com/article
_print.jsp?ID=1000027333

Randall, L. (March 27, 1995). The culture that Jake built. *Forbes*, 155(7),
pp. 45–46.

Radford, T., & Wilson, J. (December 3, 2003). On the rocks: the grim forecast for winter sports as global warming increases. *The Guardian.*
Retrieved October 27, 2010, from http://www.guardian.co.uk/world/
2003/dec/03/research.sciencenews

Rebagliati, R. (2009). *Off the chain: An insider's history of snowboarding.*
Vancouver: Greystone Books.

Reed, R. (2005). *The Way of the Snowboarder.* New York: Harry N. Abrams.

Reff, M. (January 12, 2009). The North Face Masters Rob Kingwill interview. *Snowboard*. Retrieved July 12, 2010, from http://www.snow-
board-mag.com/node/33989

Richards, T. with Blehm, E. (2003). *P3: Pipes, parks, and powder.* New
York: Harper Collins.

Rinehart, R. (2000). Emerging/arriving sport: Alternatives to formal
sports. In J. Coakley & E. Dunning (Eds.), *Handbook of sports studies* (pp. 504–519). London: Sage.

Risky maneuver lands snowboarder in a coma. (January 5, 2010). *ABC News*. Retrieved March 12, 2010, from http://abcnews.go.com/video/playerindex?id=9479741

Roberts, S. (February 7, 2002). Some winter stars prefer green to gold. *The New York Times*, p. A.1.

Robinson, D. W. (1985). Stress seeking: Selected behavioral characteristics of elite rock climbers. *Journal of Sport Psychology, 7*, 400–404.

Robinson, O. (December 7, 2006). Moving mountain: Bringing out the best in Beijing's boarders. Retrieved from http://www.thatsbj.com/blog/index.php/2006/12/07/sport_moving_mountains

Roenigk, A. (February 23, 2004). Tara Dakides talks. *EXPN.com*. Retrieved from http://expn.go.com/expn/story?pageName=040220_tara_talks_2

Rossi, P. (December 2002). Nothing snows him down: Marc Montoya: Professional Snowboarder. *Latino Leaders: The National Magazine of the Successful American Latino*. Retrieved January 12, 2010, from http://findarticles.com/p/articles/mi_m0PCH/is_6_3/ai_113053352/

Schneider, T., Butryn, T., Furst, D. & Masucci, A. (2007). A qualitative examination of risk among elite adventure racers. *Journal of Sport Behavior, 30*, 330–357.

Science of snowboarding in the Olympics. (February 15, 2010). *National Science Foundation*. Retrieved from http://www.nsf.gov/news/special_reports/olympics/

Seelenbrandt, G. (February 2, 2001). Jamie MacLeod stands tall in women's Slope Style, *EXPN.com*. Retrieved from http://expn.go.com/xgames/wxg/2001/s/women_slope.html

Self, D. and Findley, C. (2007). Psychology of risk. In D. Booth and H. Thorpe (Eds.), *Berkshire Encyclopedia of Extreme Sport* (pp. 246–254). Berkshire, Great Barrington.

Self, D., Henry, E., Findley, C., & Reilly, E. (2007). Thrill seeking: The type T personality and extreme sport. *International Journal of Sport management and Marketing, 2*, 175–190.

Settimi, C. (February 9, 2010). Top earning athletes of the 2010 Winter Olympics. *Forbes.com*. Retrieved March 1, 2010, from http://www.forbes.com/2010/02/09/top-earning-winter-olympic-athletes-business-sports-top-olympians.html

Sherker, S., Finch, C., Kehoe, E. J., & Doverty, M. (2006). Drunk, drowsy, doped: Skiers' and snowboarders' injury risk perceptions regarding alcohol, fatigue and recreational drug use. *International Journal of Injury Control and Safety Promotion, 13*(3), 151–157.

Sherowski, J. (November 2003). Q and A. *Transworld Snowboarding*, p. 48.

Sherowski, J. (January 2005). What it means to be a snowboarder. *Transworld Snowboarding*, pp. 160–169.

Singer, B. (no date). Information centre: Snowboarding heaven. *New Outlooks in Science and Engineering.* Retrieved from http:// www.noisemakers.org.uk/modules/articles/show-press.cfm?id=15

Skaters and Snowboarders Most Buzzed about Athletes at Olympics (February 17, 2010). Retrieved March 16, 2010, from http://blog .nielsen.com/nielsenwire/online_mobile/skaters-and-snowboarders -most-buzzed-about-athletes-at-olympics/

Smith, S. (September 27, 2002). Everest snowboarder vanishes on second try. *National Geographic News.* Retrieved December 7, 2010, from http://news.nationalgeographic.com/news/pf/82988738.html

Snowboard base cliff strike. (June 19, 2007). BASEjumper.com. Retrieved August 3, 2010, from http://www.basejumper.com/articles/ stories/snowboard_base_cliff_strike_784.html

Snowboard culture shares blame with Lindsey. (February 18, 2006). Retrieved February 19, 2006, from http://www.nbcolympics.com/ snowboarding/5116870/detail.html

Snowboard shocker! Burton announces big layoffs. (April 12, 2002). Retrieved July 12, 2006, from http://www.skipressworld.com/us/ en/daily_news/2002/04/snowboard_shocker_burton_announces _big_layoffs.html?cat

Snowboarding and the Olympics. Retrieved July 17, 2004, from http:// www.burton.com/company/default.asp

Soldiers perish in avalanche as World War 1 rages: December 13, 1916. (no date). Retrieved October 11, 2010, from http://www.history.com/ this-day-in-history/soldiers-perish-in-avalanche-as-world-war-i-rages

Sport and the environment: Many ski resorts heading downhill as a result of global warming (November 2003). *United Nations Environment Program.* Retrieved October 27, from http://www.unep.org/sport _env/pressrelease/skiresort3.asp

Stassen, L. (June 10, 2005). Donna Burton Carpenter clears a path. *Transworld Business*. Retrieved from http://www.twsbiz.com/twbiz/profiles/article/0,21214,1114933,00.html

Stepanek, C. (no date). When did snowboarding become cool? *YoBeat*. Retrieved January 15, 2010, from http://www.yobeat.com/features/snowboardcool.htm

Straub. W. (1982). Sensation seeking among high and low-risk male athletes. *Journal of Sport Psychology, 4*, 246–253.

Sullivan, J. (2010). Pro file: Chris "Gunny" Gunnarson of Snow Park Technologies. Shredstix.com. Retrieved August 6, 2010, from http://shredstix.com/blogs/detail/Pro-File-Chris-Gunny-Gunnarson-of-SPT/5471.html

Tara-bly dangerous (December 19, 2000). *EXPN.com*. Retrieved March 10, 2004, from http://expn.go.com/xgames/wxg/2001

Tarazi, F., Dvorak, M. F., & Wing, P. C. (1999). Spinal injuries and snowboarders. *American Journal of Sports Medicine, 27*, 177–180.

Taylor, D. (no date). Victoria Jealouse interview. *Powder*. Retrieved from http://www.powdermag.com/onlineexclusives/victoria090704/index.html

Terje breaks world record air. (February 10, 2008). *Transworld Snowboarding*. Retrieved from http://snowboarding.transworld.net/1000024378/news/terje-breaks-world-record-air/

Teton releases new climate change film *Generations* (November 2009). Retrieved March 18, 2010, from http://www.tetongravity.com/blogs/T-G-Rreleasesnewclimatechangefilm-Generations-1546892.htm

TGR releases new climate change film *Generations* (2009). Retrieved March 9, 2010, from http://live.tetongravity.com/_TGR-releases-new-climate-change-film-Generations/BLOG/1546892/75233.html

The interview: Karleen Jeffery and Craig Kelly. (February 10, 2008). *Transworld Snowboarding*. Retrieved from http://snowboarding.transworld.net/1000030576/photos/backcountry/karleen-jeffery-and-craig-kelly-interview/

The mainstream media still don't get it. (January 5, 2010). *The Angry Snowboarder (blog)*. Retrieved January 10, 2010 from http://www.angrysnowboarder.com/?p=5497

The POW perspective: Jeremy Jones' Protect Our Winters campaign (2008, January). *Future Snowboarding*. Retrieved March 10, 2010, from http://protectourwinters.org/wp-content/uploads/2009/02/futurejanuary.pdf

The principles of snowboarding (August 2002). Retrieved July 2008, from from www.boardtheworld.com

Thomas, P. (January 29, 2011). Torstein Horgmo makes X Games history with big-air triple cork. Retrieved February 23, 2011, from http://www.grindtv.com/snow/blog/23980/torstein%20horgmo%20makes%20x%20games%20history%20with%20big-air%20triple%20cork/

Thorne, P. (no date). How environmental change affects winter sports and how winter sports affect the environment: Experts comment. *Snow Japan*. Retrieved October 27, 2010, from http://www.snowjapan.com/e/features/green-snow-factoids.html

Thorpe, H. (2004). Embodied boarders: Snowboarding, status and style. *Waikato Journal of Education*, 10, 181–202.

Thorpe, H. (2005). Jibbing the gender order: Females in the snowboarding culture. *Sport in Society, 8*(1), 76–100.

Thorpe, H. (2006). Beyond "decorative sociology": Contextualizing female surf, skate and snow boarding. *Sociology of Sport Journal, 23*(3), 205–228.

Thorpe, H. (2007a). Snowboarding. In Booth & Thorpe (Eds.), *Berkshire encyclopedia of extreme sport* (pp. 286–294). Great Barrington, MA: Berkshire Publishing.

Thorpe, H. (2007b). Extreme media. In Booth & Thorpe (Eds.), *Berkshire encyclopedia of extreme sport* (pp. 90–94). Great Barrington, MA: Berkshire Publishing.

Thorpe, H. (2008a). Foucault, technologies of self, and the media: Discourses of femininity in snowboarding culture. *Journal of Sport and Social Issues, 32*(2), 199–229.

Thorpe, H. (2008b). Extreme sports in China. In F. Hong (ed.) with D. Mackay and K. Christensen, *China Gold: China's Quest for Global Power and Olympic Glory*. Berkshire, Great Barrington.

Thorpe, H. (2009). "Understanding Alternative Sport Experiences: A Contextual Approach for Sport Psychology." *International Journal of Sport and Exercise Psychology (special Issue: De-colonizing methodologies: Approaches to sport and exercise psychology from the margins*), 7(3), 359–379.

Thorpe, H. (2010a). Have board, will travel: Global physical youth cultures and transnational mobility. In J. Maguire & M. Falcous (Eds.), *Sport and Migration: Borders, Boundaries and Crossings* (pp. 112–126). London: Routledge.

Thorpe, H. (August 2010b). Snowboarding at the Olympics: A cultural history, *Curl*, http://www.curl.co.nz/category/featured/

Thorpe, H. (2011a). *Snowboarding Bodies in Theory and Practice.* Hampshire: Palgrave Macmillan.

Thorpe, H. (2011b). "Sex, drugs and snowboarding": (il)legitimate definitions of taste and lifestyle in a physical youth culture. *Leisure Studies*, DOI: 10.1080/02614367.2011.596556

Thorpe, H. & Rinehart, R. (2010). Alternative sport and affect: Non-representational theory examined. *Sport in Society*, special issue: Consumption and representation of lifestyle sport, *13*(7/8), 1268–1291.

Thorpe, H. & Wheaton, B. (2011). The Olympic movement, action sports, and the search for generation Y. In J. Sugden & A. Tomlinson (Eds.), *Watching the Olympics: Politics, power and representation* (pp. 182–200). London: Routledge.

Transworld Media Kit. (2007). Retrieved from December 9, 2010, from http://www.transworldmediakit.com/2007GenMediaKitLR.pdf

Trice: An interview with Travis Rice. (February 10, 2008). *Transworld Snowboarding*. Retrieved August 12, 2010, from http://snowboarding.transworld.net/1000026787/featuresobf/trice-an-interview-with-travis-rice/ Troetal, S. (February 6, 2004). Snowboarder out of hospital after Letterman stunt. *CNN New York*. Retrieved from http://www.cnn.com/2004/SHOWBIZ/TV/02/06/letterman.accident/

Ulmer, K. & Straus, A. (2002). Action figures: the girls of extreme sports. Retrieved May 10, 2004, from http://www.maximonline.com/sports/girls_of_extreme_sports/dakides.html

Van Tilbury, C. (2000). In-area and backcountry snowboarding: Medial and safety aspects. *Wilderness and Environmental Medicine, 11*, 102–108.

Voskinarian, L. (July 31, 2005). Victoria Jealouse. *Powderroom.net.* Retrieved from http://powderroom.net/profiles/victoria-jealouse

Wagner, A., & Houlihan, D. (1994). Sensation-seeking and trait anxiety in hang-gliding pilots and golfers. *Personality and Individual Differences, 16*, 975–977.

W.A.S. Launched. (March 31, 2011). Retrieved September 8, 2011, from http://www.snowboardermag.com/industry-news/was-launch-we-are-snowboarding/

Wark, P. (March 19, 2009). Skiing: Fun on the slopes or a risky business? *The Times.* Retrieved August 10, 2010, from http://women.times online.co.uk/tol/life_and_style/women/the_way_we_live/article5934 246.ece

Watson, C. (February 4, 2001). "Sweet repeat," *EXPN.com.* Retrieved from http://expn.go.com/xgames/winter/s/women_bigair.html

Weir, E. (2001). Snowboarding injuries: Hitting the slopes. *Canadian Medical Association Journal, 164*(1), 88.

What causes avalanches. (April 29, 2000). *Snowboarding the World.* Retrieved August 6, 2010, from http://www.boardtheworld.com/Home/Magazine/Features?&riID=48

What makes a good kicker? (April 29, 2000). Boardtheworld.com. Retrieved October 22, 2010, from http://www.boardtheworld.com/Home/Magazine/Features/Features?&riID=45

Wheaton, B. (2000). "New lads?" Masculinities and the "new sport" participant. *Men and Masculinities, 2*, 436–458.

White defends men's halfpipe title. (February 18, 2010). *ESPN.com.* Retrieved March 12, 2010, from http://sports.espn.go.com/olympics/winter/2010/snowboarding/news/story?id=4923369

Williams, P. W., Dossa, K. B., and Fulton, A. (1994). Tension on the slopes: Managing conflict between skiers and snowboarders. *Journal of Applied Recreation Research*, 19(3), 191–213.

Winter X Games 13. (January 26, 2009). Street and Smiths *Sports Business Daily.* Retrieved August 12, 2010, from http://www .sportsbusinessdaily.com/index.cfm?fuseaction=archive

Winter X Games celebrates multimedia growth and record attendance. (February 9, 2011). Retrieved February 22, 2010, from http://www

.espnmediazone3.com/us/2011/02/09/winter-x-games-15-celebrates -multimedia-growth-and-record-attendance/

World record: Mads Jonsson 187 feet to landing! (May 9, 2005). *Snowboarder*. Retrieved September 7, 2010, from http://www .snowboardermag.com/news/world_record/

Wulf, S. (January 1996). Triumph of hated snowboarders. *Time, 147*, 69.

Yamakawa, H., Murase, S., Sakai, H., Iwama, T., Katada, M., Niikawa, S., Sumi, Y., Nishimura, Y., & Sakai, N. (2001). Spinal injuries in snowboarders: Risk of jumping as an integral part of snowboarding. *Journal of Trauma, Injury, Infection, and Critical Case, 50*, 1101–1105.

Yant, N. (2001). Marc Frank Montoya interview. Retrieved May 10, 2004, from http://www.transworldsnowboarding.com/snow/ magazine/article/0,14304,242627,00.html

Yeadon, M. R. (2000). Aerial movement. In V. Zatsiorsky (ed), *Biomechanics in Sport: Performance Enhancement and Injury Prevention* (pp. 273–282). Oxford: Blackwell Science.

Yellow snow. (September 2002). *Transworld Snowboarding*, pp. 204–206.

Young, K., White, P., & McTeer, W. (1994). Body talk: Male athletes reflect on sport, injury, and pain. *Sociology of Sport Journal, 11*, 175–194.

Zwingle, E. (2006). Meltdown: The Alps under pressure. *National Geographic*. Retrieved October 27, 2010, from http://environment .nationalgeographic.com/environment/global-warming/alps-meltdown .html#page=6

index

About the Author

HOLLY THORPE is senior lecturer in the Department of Sport and Leisure Studies at the University of Waikato, New Zealand, where she teaches courses on the sociology of sport and physical culture. Her published works include the *Berkshire Encyclopedia of Extreme Sports* (with Douglas Booth) and *Snowboarding Bodies in Theory and Practice.* She has won academic awards and been published in journals including *Journal of Sport and Social Issues*, *International Journal of Sport and Exercise Psychology*, and *Sociology of Sport Journal.* Thorpe was an active participant in snowboarding competitions, and continues to pursue fresh snow around the world.